Roxan
D0724660

Inside Separate Worlds

Inside Separate Worlds

Life Stories of Young Blacks, Jews, and Latinos

Edited by David Schoem

Ann Arbor

THE UNIVERSITY OF MICHIGAN PRESS

Copyright © by the University of Michigan 1991
All rights reserved
Published in the United States of America by
The University of Michigan Press
Manufactured in the United States of America

1994   1993   1992   1991   4   3   2   1

Distributed in the United Kingdom and Europe by
Manchester University Press, Oxford Road,
Manchester M13 9PL, UK

Library of Congress Cataloging-in-Publication Data

Inside separate worlds : life stories of young Blacks, Jews, and
    Latinos / edited by David Schoem.
        p.   cm.
      ISBN 0-472-09452-1 (cloth : alk. apper). — ISBN 0-472-06452-5
(paper : alk. paper)
      1. Minorities—United States—Biography. 2. United States—Race
relations. 3. United States—Ethnic relations. 4. Afro-American
college students—Biography. 5. College students, Jewish—United
States—Biography. 6. Hispanic American college students—
Biography.   I. Schoem, David Louis.
E184.A1I47   1991
973'.04—dc20   91-9689
                                                                            CIP

British Library Cataloguing in Publication Data
Inside separate worlds : life stories of young blacks, Jews
    and Latinos.
      1. United States. Ethnic groups. Social interactions
      I. Schoem, David
305.80073

ISBN 0-472-09452-1
        0-472-06452-5 pbk

To Karyn

Acknowledgments

I wish to thank the Project on Intergroup Relations and Conflict, which is part of the Pilot Program / College Community Program of the University of Michigan, for its support and encouragement of my courses, of this project, and of the participating students. In particular, I wish to express thanks to my colleagues Mark Chesler, Pat Gurin, Dick Meisler, Andrea Monroe-Fowler, Luis Sfeir-Younis, and Ximena Zúñiga. Mark Chesler and Ximena Zúñiga also provided useful feedback for my introduction to the book and were of great assistance at many points throughout the project. A portion of the proceeds from sales of this book will go to supporting ongoing activities of this project.

I also wish to thank colleagues of the Program on Conflict Management Alternatives at the University of Michigan for their commitment to the exploration of ideas such as those expressed in this book as part of their ongoing work on social justice. Special thanks go to Alex Aleinikoff, Percy Bates, Barry Checkoway, Mark Chesler, Jim Crowfoot, Elizabeth Douvan, Barbara Israel, Edith Lewis, and Helen Weingarten as well as Amy Schultz and, in fond memory, Susan Gold.

Thanks, too, to my colleague Marshall Stevenson for the time spent together researching and thinking about teaching intergroup relations in the classroom and, in particular, issues around Black-Jewish relations.

Mary Erwin provided valuable assistance to me and the authors as the U of M Press editor for this book. Colin Day and the Executive Board of the U of M Press, especially Beth Reed, who provided useful feedback on my introductory chapter, have been supportive throughout.

Of course, credit for this book goes foremost to the authors, my former students, of whom I write extensively in the introduction to this book. I have learned an enormous amount from them and have treasured the excuse of this book to remain regularly in touch with them since the finish of my class. Those relationships and the students' essays have truly served as an inspiration to me. Josephine

Hobson, with whom I have worked for over a decade, and Maribel Cruz were both outstanding graduate student teaching assistants for the course from which this book emerges. Elsa Barboza, Rachel Berlin, David Boris, Falesa Ivory, Billy Manns, Jr., Frank Matthews, Erica Rosenthal, Rachel Steckelman, and Gina Terry all contributed to the writing project. I know, too, how very much the students who have participated in face-to-face dialogue on intergroup relations and conflict in years prior to this class have helped me and the current generation of students to reach this point.

Finally, I must thank my children, Adina and Shana, who have happily grown up knowing many of my students and also put up with me at my desk in my study, asking questions, entertaining with song and dance, drawing pictures, teaching me at every instant about life and meaning from their most important perspective, and making sure I had my priorities in order—that they come first! And thanks most of all to my wife, Karyn, for everything, always.

Contents

Part 1: Introduction

Inside Separate Worlds

David Schoem

The effort it takes for us to know so little about one another across racial and ethnic groups is truly remarkable. That we can live so closely together, that our lives can be so intertwined socially, economically, and politically, and that we can spend so many years of study in grade school and even in higher education and yet still manage to be ignorant of one another is clear testimony to the deep-seated roots of this human and national tragedy. What we do learn along the way is to place heavy reliance on stereotypes, gossip, rumor, and fear to shape our lack of knowledge.

What has been most striking to me over the past ten years in my work as a college teacher and dean is that my students know so little, personally and academically, about other racial and ethnic groups, or even about their own. Students take the same classes but sit grouped by race, ethnicity, and religion. Students play sports together but don't get past talk of jump shots and rebounds. Students live together in the same residence halls but merely share a polite "hello" or nod if they are sufficiently daring to attempt to break down barriers. Students placed together as roommates for their first year of college discover ingenious ways to sidestep substantive conversations about their lives in terms of race and ethnicity. We live in separate worlds.

This book represents a direct challenge to this conspiracy of separateness, misinformation, and ignorance. It provides an opening, a glimpse, into worlds heretofore unknown to most. The authors invite us to look into their racial and ethnic lives. For those from other groups who will read the stories, they've been secret worlds, and much about them is often unspoken even within one's own group. They are too dangerous, they are too delicate, they are too challenging, and they are too honest to be shared easily. Now these young authors call to us in a single voice, saying, "Come see who I really am. This is my life. This is how I have lived. This is what I have faced in this country in the first quarter of my life. I am proud of who I am. I have struggled. I continue to struggle—with you, the reader, and the world you control, with my own people and the barriers we put in front of one another, with my family and my own self, growing up, becoming an adult. Come meet me in the flesh, not in your frightened imaginings, not in your nightmares, not in your destructive stereotypes, not in your communities and institutions that have real and invisible walls to keep me apart from you. Come inside to listen to my story."

The unspoken. We don't talk about racism when Blacks and whites are present, face-to-face. We need not confront our own anti-Semitism if we keep apart from Jews. We don't even speak with Latinos because we assume they can't speak English, acting on our unconscious bias that they are all first-generation U.S. citizens. We just don't realize how much our histories have in common or that we are not monoliths as groups even though we may present ourselves as such to the outside. We don't recognize our individual differences and commonalities, that one can make close friends with members of other groups and not be comfortable with others. We run from difference, we fear it, we label it as being bad, and we try to control it and oppress it.

We have systematically limited our visions of the world. We have narrowed our personal life experiences in our society, and we have limited our intellectual horizons by placing boundaries on what our schools and universities allow us to know. We allow ourselves to see and understand social and historical events from just one point of view. By building friendships with one group of people and isolating ourselves from others, we have severely diminished the potential immediately available to us to enrich our lives and the lives of those around us. Our schools don't teach us about different groups and how they see the world; we learn but one truth, one vision of our past and future. First our parents and teachers, then our friends, and then even we ourselves restrict whom we should play with, live in neighborhoods apart from others, go to schools where we won't meet those "others," read certain books so we won't want to learn about others, divide resources and opportunities so we aren't likely to cross paths at work, school, or play, and then make up stories that confirm our doubts and make sense of our isolation and ignorance. We live as aliens within the same classroom, the same college, and the same city, and on the same planet.

The young authors in this volume take a risk by publishing their stories. Will readers honor the trust that is bestowed by the authors by their open sharing of personal and group "secrets"? Or will readers intentionally misinterpret or abuse such honesty or merely incorporate these stories into the pool of stereotypical misinformation that we all carry with us? Will readers try to relate this information to their own ethnic group experiences or their own lives, using themselves as the norm for comparison? Or might readers attempt to understand the authors on their own terms, in their own worlds as they describe them, as difficult an undertaking as that may be?

The publication of these refreshingly honest autobiographies is illustrative of the life histories and experiences of the authors because, for many of them, the very essence of their lives has been risk taking. It represents their readiness to enter a new era in our nation's history. These are the educated voices of a multicultural nation, a country that will look very different from what we know now. These are the eyes and minds that see the world through very different perspectives than those our history has previously taught us. Their horizons are broader than ours; they have listened to one another and have pictured realities that few of us, young or old, have yet considered.

Simply put, these authors are ready for a society in the making that celebrates their different backgrounds, accepts them for who they are—for their differences as well as their similarities—and does not push them to be who they are not, encourages them to learn from one another, and expects and allows for equal opportunity and success from one another. As much as they are prepared for change, they recognize that it might not come easily. They are ready to have the power, to be the power, and to share the power. They are our future leaders.

Nevertheless, for these authors the path ahead is an uncertain one. They have struggled until now just to find a common language to address the issues that confront them and to reconcile the anger associated with others' denial of their visions of the future. They are determined to create a new reality, but even they are not sure that they're prepared or yet know how to work together across groups to bring it about. That is the challenge. This discourse is their start.

The Program on Intergroup Relations and Conflict

This book arises out of a particular course, "Ethnic Identity and Intergroup Relations," taught at the University of Michigan (U of M) during the winter term, 1989. The course evolved from the Program on Intergroup Relations and Conflict, an effort to bring different groups of students together to learn about what had previously been the "mysteries" of their separate worlds and to explore relations between and among different groups.

The Program on Intergroup Relations and Conflict was funded by an Undergraduate Initiatives Grant from Harold Shapiro and James Duderstadt, then president and provost, respectively, of the University of Michigan. It was allocated to a coordinating partnership of the Pilot Program, an academic-residential program with considerable history in these kinds of student projects, and the Program on Conflict Management Alternatives, an interdisciplinary faculty research and development project.

This program represents perhaps the only systematic, institutional attempt at the University of Michigan to offer students curricular and nonformal academic opportunities, through courses, workshops, and dialogue groups, to study theory and discuss issues of intergroup relations and related conflicts face-to-face with members of various ethnic and racial groups. Three core courses were offered, including an initial course, "Introduction to Intergroup Relations and Conflict," followed by two seminars, "Intergroup Conflict and Change" and the course from which the essays for this book originated, "Ethnic Identity and Intergroup Relations."

In addition to courses, a new form of student discussion was offered, called "dialogue groups," which involved members of two or more groups meeting face-to-face to explore commonalities and differences. Despite an atmosphere on campus of considerable intergroup distrust, numerous dialogue groups were organized involving students from various backgrounds, such as white students and students of color; men and women; Blacks and Jews; straight, bisexual, and lesbian females; and Asian Americans and Blacks. In addition, intragroup dialogues were initiated that included, for example, the various groups comprising the Asian-American population and also those under the Latino umbrella. Workshops, a film series, and residence hall discussion groups were also held.

Significantly, these courses and dialogue groups represented the first opportunity many students had had to engage peers from other groups about the pressing issues and concerns of their ethnic and racial groups. It was as if the program lifted a lifelong taboo on these discussions, giving permission for all the pent-up feelings, questions, and fears to come forward. For many students the results have been transforming, as is evident in the authors' essays.

The Course: Ethnic Identity and Intergroup Relations

Organization

The course was organized into three components: the intergroup dialogue, the intragroup dialogue, and the ethnic autobiography writing groups. The intergroup dialogue was the central focus of the course for the twenty-three Black, Jewish, and Latino students in attendance, with class meetings held for two hours each week. This section of the course emphasized academic content based on extensive readings and served as the basis for extensive discussion among students from the different racial/ethnic groups.

Students met in smaller subgroups for the intragroup dialogue, which met for one hour per week under my own direction and the direction of Josephine Hobson and Maribel Cruz, graduate student teaching assistants for the course. The idea for the intragroup dialogue was for students to use one class hour for further reading and discussion to reflect on the intergroup dialogue, examining issues such as intragroup divisions and gender and class and pondering their own ethnic identities. They provided students something of a safe haven from the intensity of the intergroup discussions yet, on their own, generated lively and heated debate for internal group issues. Often the issues raised in these groups, including the intragroup differences, found their way back to the intergroup discussion so that an unusually stimulating circle of ideas and perspectives was constantly inserting itself into the learning process.

Students were assigned randomly to the writing groups, which provided the source and structure of the inspirational essays that comprise this book. These class sessions included individual and peer critiques of writing as well as oral presentations and discussion of the ideas and issues of the essays. These critiques and discussions allowed for the development of trust and the examination of commonalities and differences of student life experiences across groups.

Topics

While the themes of ethnic identity and intergroup relations are tightly interwoven and, throughout the semester, were addressed together, I attempted to give distinct focus to each theme in the different sections of the course. Students explored their own and one another's ethnic and racial group experiences as well as their personal experiences as members of one or more ethnic and racial groups through a variety of approaches. Numerous topics were discussed, including issues of power, marginality, and definitions of "minority" and "difference." There was considerable attention given to the intersections of ethnicity/race, gender, and class in all of these issues.

As we examined minority-majority group relations, we explored the problems of survival and maintenance of ethnic identity in a pluralistic society as well as the lasting and penetrating pain of oppression, racism, and anti-Semitism. Students discussed ethnic/racial group pride and also the ambivalence, tensions, and constant consciousness involved in being a member of a minority group. There was discussion of mixed ethnic, racial, and religious backgrounds and their implications for individuals, groups, and society as a whole.

Students talked about their experiences growing up through childhood and adolescence as ethnic/racial group members, family and peer influences, and their first awareness and lessons in being "different." There was considerable interest in the topic of self-esteem as it affects members of different groups. The introduction of gender issues and male-female relations within each group raised the level of complexity yet again.

We took the ideas arising from these discussions and applied them to case studies of Latinos, Blacks, and Jews and each group's relations to others. Thus, we looked individually at Latinos, then Blacks, and then Jews in terms of minority-majority relations and minority-minority relations. We followed these discussions with a look at conflicts and alliances between and among Blacks, Jews, and Latinos on a regional and national level as well as on the U of M campus.

Clearly the issues discussed are not easy ones to examine, understand, or, by any means, resolve. The issues themselves are exceedingly complex, and they hold incalculable emotional value and weight for every individual ethnic group member. The additional step of placing the members of each group together face-to-face to study and confront these issues becomes extraordinarily difficult, provocative, and stimulating. The opportunity for making leaps in understanding and insight as well as misunderstanding and tension is tremendous, and it provides for the most exciting and challenging teaching and learning situation imaginable.

Intergroup Dialogue

The intergroup dialogue gives students permission to express the intense emotions that come with being a racial/ethnic minority—pride, anger, inner strength, hurt, and ambivalence. It helps to break down the barriers between individuals and groups, even in those few cases in which at the end students decide to put coalition building aside to pursue strategies that recommend separate group approaches to addressing problems. The intergroup dialogue provides an opportunity for students to discover and develop an interest (which is usually there but has been repressed over the years) in ethnic and racial groups other than their own.

Most students have reported to me in the course of the semester and after that the intergroup dialogue has made them painfully aware of how little they know about both their own group and other groups. They have subsequently pursued additional reading and other courses beyond this experience. The deeper interest in their own group comes partly as a result of unfamiliar, often probing questions from members of another group—either the most basic ones, for which answers are assumed so the questions are not asked, or the more difficult ones that are politically taboo within a group so members never have to confront the problems they raise—as well as from the public embarrassment of appearing so ignorant about one's group in front of one's own and other group members.

The intergroup dialogue provides students with insights into the sociopolitical concerns of racial/ethnic groups. The presence of actual group representatives in this learning context forces students to acknowledge and make a commitment to address the interconnected issues of ethnicity/race, class, and gender. It is too easy, intellectually and personally, to avoid issues and topics when certain categories of people are absent; the intergroup dialogue avoids that visual and intellectual invisibility. And when the issues are addressed and connections are made, students are forced to think and rethink many of their assumptions and political and social understandings, and in that process they begin to see the world more clearly, even in its much greater complexity.

Further, the intergroup dialogue forces students to address real problems among the minority groups, within individual minority groups, and between minority groups and majority groups. The face-to-face encounter, grounded in scholarly readings and research, prevents the obfuscation of information, the glossing over of innuendo, the reliance on normative assumptions, and the overlooking of loaded subtleties. Little passes by unchallenged. All of the easy rules are open game. Everyone is forced to think and to listen carefully, and real learning takes place.

Finally, what is the social and intellectual significance of the intergroup dialogue? As I have indicated above, for me it has been the most stimulating teaching/learning experience I have had, without comparison. That is not to say it is easy or that all goes well or smoothly. But there is an electricity of intellectual excitement attached to these classes that is very unusual. Students know they are about to embark on a journey of new understanding that is so central to their own existence and the state of our nation. They know they are going to talk about real issues, uncovering the layers of silence about racism and racial/ethnic issues that our educational system has maintained for so long.

The Writing Project

Eighteen- to twenty-two-year-old college students want to read about the life experience of their contemporaries. In the course of teaching classes on intergroup relations for many years, my experience has led me to incorporate some novels, essays, and autobiographies into my otherwise traditional social science reading list. While I found that these works helped students understand the empirical studies in a deeper, more personal way, there was always a level of dissatisfaction that these books and articles were not the voices of their contemporaries, and that they were dated. That fact did not lessen the value of authors such as Alice Walker and Ntozake Shange, or Anne Roiphe and Paul Cowan, or Piri Thomas and Sandra Cisneros, but it did leave students still wanting books of their generation, about themselves, not about the 1950s or the 1960s, or about adults in the 1970s or 1980s, or about any generation but their own.

My experience led me to think that students might be able to fill this gap with their own writing and with their own and their peers' life stories. Certainly this is an age group that is deeply involved in examining its own personal identity and issues of independence. As a result, the motivation for introspection and self-exploration among this group is ready to explode with the slightest prodding.

I decided that the writing of ethnic autobiographies as the primary writing assignment for this course just might provide a special entry point for students to immerse themselves in the study of ethnic identity and intergroup relations. This was an opportunity for students to discover for themselves the impact of these themes on their own lives and to recognize (at least for most) the degree of isolation and separation from others with whom they had lived their lives. It seemed worth a try.

Frankly, when the class first met, most students were not thrilled with the idea of writing a thirty-to-fifty-page paper. But together we compiled a list of possible topics to write and think about, and we developed a very strict writing schedule for getting our work done. The topics were less important for their substance than they were as cushions that allowed students to make the writing project more manageable in their own minds. Once students started writing, they no longer needed to refer to the list. The writing schedule required students to turn in five pages of writing each week for the first half of the semester. While not everyone followed this pattern, it, too, comforted and supported students to get their initial ideas down on paper without much regard for mechanics and style. It allowed them to think in manageable five-page units instead of an overwhelming fifty-page block, and it reassured them that a full half of the semester would be available for rewriting, rethinking, and revising.

The weekly writing period provided a structure for three small writing support groups. Organized across ethnic and gender lines, students had a collaborative task to work on. One hour each week students came together to generate ideas and to critique each other's work. We first practiced together as a group how to give feedback that was honest, critical, practical, and sensitively presented so that the author could hear and accept the feedback. Working in these mixed groups, students were required to become familiar with individual and group communication styles in order to participate effectively in the groups. Feedback on writing was given orally and in writing by both the students and the instructors. Clearly, one of the benefits of giving feedback was that students had the opportunity to read all the other essays and discover important ideas and strategies for their own autobiographies.

The critique of writing was directly linked to a critique and discussion of the substance of the writing. These discussions, in the small writing groups or in pairs reading each other's papers, provided invaluable insight into the issues of ethnic identity and intergroup relations. Students became increasingly proficient at asking gentle yet challenging and probing questions. Of course, the material we were working with was exceptionally open, honest, and provocative—life experiences laid out before peers—and students trusted that they would be addressed with great care and respect. Students were engaged in the constant comparison of intergroup and intragroup experiences and were deeply moved by what they read, discussed, and learned and also by what they had to throw away from old assumptions, misinformation, and stereotyping.

The student autobiographies are striking in their depth, richness, and passion. Their writing represents a greater thoughtfulness and new visions of themselves as members of racial/ethnic groups. The writing project helped students achieve a greater awareness of their personal identities of themselves as minority group members in relation to the majority. It allowed them to see more clearly the individual differences within ethnic groups, the commonalities of individuals across groups and of the groups themselves, and to see other groups without the screen of stereotyping. Finally, the writing project and support group brought home to students the complexities of intergroup relations. It helped students synthesize the first part of their racial/ethnic life and provide a clearer basis upon which to proceed in their racial/ethnic lives and their relations with other groups and members of other groups.

This Book

> The barrio taught me to survive in a world where you don't know what is going to happen. It prepared me for the struggles of daily life and the unexpected. It taught me to be strong when there was crisis. It also taught me to believe in myself. In the barrio you do not plan your goals; you just take them as they come. It is a constant struggle with life because you do not know what is going to happen the next day. It was a prep school for life, and the experiences were your grades. Nobody pays for this school but you.

Amelia Valdez's penetrating essay, "Surviving in the Barrio," opens part 2. Like the other authors in this section, Amelia knows now very clearly "who I am and where I come from." She and the others have struggled with racism, anti-Semitism, and the marginality imposed upon them, and they have come out on top, in control of their lives, now taking their turns as the central players, the in-group.

Matt Wexley describes his own journey first from ridicule and later from marginalization to find solid ground as a strong, identified Jew. He sarcastically relates: "When I was a freshman in high school, this other kid used to throw pennies at me. He thought I would crawl on the floor groveling after them because 'everyone knows how cheap and money hungry we are.'" But Matt also struggles to overcome pressures from the outside that are much more subtle and insidious so that he starts his essay's journey by stating: "I have, for my entire existence as a Jew, felt as though I never quite fit in in many aspects of my life."

When Carlos Manjarréz's family moved to a white neighborhood, he recognized that he "represented what the people there most feared—the infiltration of their community by minorities.... Our color, our language, our food—everything about us was extraordinary." Carlos's use of language in that line is precise because his story and he himself are, indeed, extraordinary. Carlos describes his courageous voyage from being made an outcast and discarding his sense of identity to then rediscovering himself and his heritage and the power and strength that journey holds. Against great odds, he has become one of our leaders, from initially being "left on my own to deal with what it meant to be Chicano in the United States, while continually having the image of Dick, Jane, their two parents ... and their white picket fence forced upon me."

Max Gordon writes with power and intensity. "I am damn tired of apologizing for being angry, and I am tired of looking for a definition of myself in other people.... I am tired of being afraid of groups of white men who act as if the world is their playground, or toilet, or video game."

In part 3 the authors talk about issues we ordinarily don't hear about outside each community. Lauren Shapiro's letters allow us to see a Jewish community that is not monolithic, when she writes, "I don't feel like I really fit in anywhere in the Jewish community except with other Jews who, like myself, feel completely lost with their cultural, religious baggage.... I mean, honestly, Bean, Jews are just as much a minority as anyone else, and yet we choose to ignore this fact and disassociate ourselves from everyone. I can't believe how many Jews I know that are racist against Blacks and all other people of color . . . not to mention the inherent sexism of our patriarchal religion." But she also lets us see her more positive attachment as well. "I guess I feel this way a lot when I'm with a group of Jews and I feel comfortable. There's such strength in knowing that we share this kind of bond." Lauren sensitively and clearly shares with us her "struggle to understand" these and other issues. Like many of the other authors, she looks at relationships, writing to her sister: "Why do we both have this aversion toward Jewish men? I think we would both eventually like to marry a 'nice Jewish boy,' or NJBs, as my friend Romy calls them—but, hey, we sure can't seem to date any."

Sherri Campbell continues on this same theme of cross-group dating, writing: "My identity as a Black has been questioned many times because of my assimilated behavior, such as my ability to hang out with and date people outside of my race . . . I mean by Blacks who have in their minds how a Black should behave." Sherri reviews her attitudes over time in much the same way that Lauren has struggled with the "JAP" issue, writing: "I was a racist toward my own kind, stereotyping them based on past experiences." Yet Sherri's strongest message to us is her desire but great difficulty in building a new, multicultural life for herself and those around her, stating with some despair: "I want to connect the two worlds without feeling marginal, yet at times it seems that I have to be one way or the other."

Leslie Fair describes the disturbing societal assumptions she encounters as she moves to college from her Black community in Chicago. "I loved my Black world because everyone there was judged on their abilities without question, and I also liked that I was in a comfortable, accepting majority." But Leslie is also able to function successfully in the wider environment because she has watched carefully the insipid socialization of racism while growing up, from Barbie dolls (white or Black) to noticing that "all of the girls invited to the parties were the ones who were light-skinned with 'long hair.'" She writes, "The white Community has an invisible hand working for them in the Black communities; this hand is echoing a message that is poisoning the minds of young Black children. It conveys the message that 'lighter is better.'"

"This older man in my Black Family class keeps using the phrase 'real bruthahs,'" writes Nicole Hall. "In his eyes, we college Black kids aren't 'real bruthahs.' . . . I told him to shut that shit up and stop alienating middle-class Blacks on the basis of economics." Nicole, whose honesty and directness make one sit up and listen, poignantly follows up on Leslie Fair's comments on skin color, saying, "This is a vicious cycle, a cycle I know is totally wrong but that I can't break out of, and it makes me sick, really. Skin shade stratification in Black America is a nightmare. I hope we can wake ourselves up in time."

Finally, Andre Reynolds speaks frankly about his experience with assimilation, growing up with friends from many different backgrounds and being challenged from both African Americans and from his white, Jewish, and Asian-American friends. He writes passionately: "I have two sets of beliefs that clash only because this society isn't mature enough to handle them. I am proud to be African-American, and I strongly agree with most pro-African-American platforms, but I have developed a character for over twenty years now, and I'm not going to and couldn't change it overnight. Thus, I am living with a dilemma. However, my dilemma is a dilemma only to this society, and the more I think about it the more I come to understand that I'm not in the wrong."

Part 4 lets us see the routine, the commonplace—which is to say, the anger, the humor, the pride, the love, and the readiness to fight back. It reveals new issues, discusses family, peers, and religion, and continues the search for identity.

John Diamond tells how he learned early on that "I was welcomed as long as I knew my place. . . . The whites in this area made a habit of thinking of Blacks who didn't fit stereotypes as exceptions. They were not racist against the 'good niggers,' only the bad ones." John comes to feel that Blacks "are trapped in a place where we don't necessarily want to be, and we are hated for being here." But John learns from observing the strength of his family and by drawing upon his own internal fortitude to hold onto his self-esteem and overcome the obstacles that have been put in his way. "I realize now that nothing is more powerful than inner strength—the inner strength that overcomes adversity, that quietly demonstrates pride."

"People used to tell me I was weird because I generally liked going to Hebrew school," writes Steve Blonder. He continues his story with his experience as a young adult, telling of the seeming irony of finding himself marginalized by other Jews precisely because of his strong commitment as a Jew:

I felt they were making me out to be some kind of "Super Jew." These people were making me an example, setting me apart because of my strong faith. It really pissed me off. A Jew is a Jew! One group of Jews isn't better than another group of Jews because of the amount of devotion they have, or the number of mitzvot they fulfill. Why couldn't other Jews accept me for my choices about religion?

In her humorous yet very serious writing style, Anne Martínez provides glimpses into different personal experiences that tell us much about her life and perspective as a proud Chicana. Of her travels to Spain, which she had approached with a high degree of trepidation, she writes, "Of course, I didn't expect to walk the streets of Madrid and be singled out as a Chicana, imprisoned, and tortured—but then nobody expects the Spanish Inquisition." Of her reknown as a forceful student leader, she says, "Sometimes I think I've been unofficially declared the goddess of uplifting *La Raza* and have become everybody's pawn in some crazy game of chess."

Sabrina Austin talks from personal experience about faith and family. She writes, "I think that so many people have been suckered into believing that all single-family households are detrimental to Black youths." She also writes about economic class differences and "struggling with my Black identity." "I really wanted to be like other Blacks and then I really didn't. . . . To them I was part of the bourgeoisie, the upper crust. . . . And I feel strong ties to the Black community; like most other Blacks, there is nothing that I would not do to help other Blacks in need. But somehow similarities were not always noticed by my peers."

In the final essay of the book, Joey Goldman takes us along for the captivating ups and downs of his search for self and Jewish identity. He begins his essay by writing: "At one time Thanksgiving was my favorite holiday. It used to be so nice to be with my family and not have to say prayers or go through the formal ceremonies of Passover in order to eat." Later, he writes, "I still couldn't forgive the foolish religious school instructors I had at the Temple for telling me what I knew were lies. . . . But I actually began to light candles on Friday nights and cook Jewish foods. I started to tell other people I was Jewish without feeling the uneasiness I always had because I had felt like there was something bad about being Jewish and because I never liked other Jews."

These autobiographies and the ideas and ideals they hold are time bound, as a number of the authors have urged me to say here. They represent the thoughts of these so very talented, aware, and remarkably open authors only at this point in their lives—that is to say, at the time they took this course and during the subsequent year, which, on their own time, they devoted to rewriting and revising.

While we hope that these essays will be read for some time into the future, they have been written by people who will not stand still but will change, reflect, rethink, grow, agitate, question, and critique. We can only await with anticipation for what they will have to tell us over the next ten, twenty, or fifty years.

Part 2: From the Margins to Center Stage

Surviving in the Barrio

Amelia Valdez

I dedicate this paper to my family. To my madre, Maria Valdez, for her strong commitment to the family and the love she gave us. To my padre, Joe Valdez, for educating us but leaving it up to us. To my sister Mary Ann, whose strong support kept me from giving up. To my brothers, Bayboy and Georgie, who at some times made it rough for me but it only made me stronger. To the baby of the family, Natalia, who also supported me and gives me advice.

For the third generation, my nieces and nephews, I leave this paper. Joe Blanco, 18; Georgia Ann Valdez, 9; John Jr. Valdez, 8; Llianna Valdez, 7; George Jr. Valdez, 5; Valerio Valdez, 4; Amamda Valdez, 2; April Valdez, 1; Vinceint, 8 months; Daniel, 7 months; Rudy, 3 months.

The Barrio

In this paper I present the true facts, the way I lived and experienced my life as a Chicana. I don't like to write in theory because I would like my audience to read my paper and know where I am coming from.

Growing up in the barrio was a protected life. It protected me from the dangers of the outside world. The outside world did not exist, but the oppression of it did. The barrio was a family within a family. Everyone around me was either an aunt or uncle or some distant cousin. The rest of the barrio was just there. We never spoke to each other except to say hello.

There were always boundaries that I could not cross within the barrio. We were all from the same race, but there was a constant struggle for possession. There was a territory called the "ghost town," an area that everyone was afraid of. It had nothing to do with ghosts, but the people that lived there were seen as ghosts. There was a gang in the ghost town made up of Chicanos, and these people did not fear death. Every weekend someone would be shot or killed because someone overstepped the boundaries. The whole barrio did not have time to get scared because the violence was happening so fast. It was a place that felt like time was passing it by, and the fighting was a constant struggle for survival. It reminded me of a place that had no ending, like falling into a black hole.

We live on the side of the "Casianos" because this is the name of the park that we live in front of. The ghost town Chicanos did not mix with the Casianos Chicanos. The Casianos also had a gang, and these two groups did not mix or talk to each other. My brothers and cousins were in the Casianos gang. There is a creek with a bridge that separated the two areas, and there was always trouble between these two groups. There was one incident that I will never forget. My mother and I were taking a shortcut through the ghost town. We crossed the bridge over to our side, and the Casianos Chicanos on our side were watching us cross. My house was about a half mile from the bridge, and in order to get to my house you needed to cross the park. As we were walking along, the ghost town Chicanos (the gang) started shooting at us, but my mother kept saying, "Run and don't stop until you reach the house." I kept hearing the bullets hitting the ground next to me. My heart kept beating faster as we approached the house, and my mother kept dragging me until we got to the house. I felt my mother sweat as she held my hand. But she held on and did not show any signs of fear. The guys on our side were returning fire, which led to some injuries on the other side. My mother called the police, but they never arrived, which was typical of them. The only way fights got resolved was by revenge. The next strike would be ours. These kinds of incidents always happened, and we lived in fear day by day. I never knew why these gangs were always fighting, but the fights were carried on from past generations. The gangs were at their strongest while I was growing up, and the only way to survive was to be in one. My brothers were always being pressured into joining. It was a sign of being "macho." The gang members were always angry, and their faces were so tight from the anger. I remembered my brother being shot once and nearly dying. There were always fights and gangs seeking revenge. The fights were endless, and I lost cousins and uncles, killed by other gangs. It is sad to know that even within the same race problems still existed. The identity of the group was in conflict because of who we were and what we stood for. Why could we not get along? Every time a Mexican from

Mexico would pass by the barrio, they would either threaten him or shoot him.

I mentioned Mexicans earlier, but I was not quite sure if we called ourselves Mexicans. We were not born in Mexico. We were not Americans, even though we were born in the United States. The identity was not really defined. We spoke Spanish, but the schools taught some other form of Spanish. To them, our Spanish seemed to be right, but it lacked some preferred form of pronunciation.

I guess one word that we did use among ourselves was *Chicano*. My grandparents did not like the word *Chicano* because to them it was a radical word.

My grandparents were Mexicans from Mexico. They celebrated some holidays, but the most important one was Independence Day (September 16, 1917). This day meant independence from Mexico, a country that did not treat them well. The people in the barrio treated my grandparents with respect. My family protected us from the violence, but sometimes it was hard to keep track of us when there was violence. I was not afraid to live in the barrio because I felt safe from outside intruders. The world saw us as bandits because we were isolated from the outside world. I was afraid to try new things because of the fear of rejection. We were fighting in our own little world in order to get a decent education for a decent job. These were the pressures that the educational system did not get you prepared for. The schools in my area did not care if a student got a decent education. The kids in the barrio were dropping out of school because of the lack of motivation from the teachers. The barrio is poor and hard working. Sometimes the families need an extra income so the kids had to drop out of school in order to help out. My family was sort of middle-class because my father had a good civil service job. We were always helping out other relatives. My mother was always helping with donations for other families. I guess you could say that we were one of the lucky ones. The peer pressure was the hardest part to deal with. My brothers were always forced to fight and join gangs. My sisters and I were always bullied around by the same kids in the barrio. You had to be tough, and crying was out of the question. Both my parents were working and did not have the time to watch us. I understood that my parents had to work. They knew that we could take care of ourselves.

The barrio taught me to survive in a world where you don't know what is going to happen. It prepared me for the struggles of daily life and the unexpected. It taught me to be strong when there was crisis.

It also taught me to believe in myself. In the barrio you do not plan your goals; you just take them as they come. It is a constant struggle with life because you do not know what is going to happen the next day. It was a prep school for life, and the experiences were your grades. Nobody pays for this school but you.

As I grew older I had choices to make, or, rather, my family did. The family had to struggle with alcohol—my father's alcohol problems. The whole barrio had this problem, but it was hidden away and to confront anyone was out of the question. I think it was the pressures of society in general. In a broader view the job market was not booming. The pressure fell harder on the people in the barrio. The failure to get a job and low education levels were discouraging. It was hard to live in an area where the fighting never stopped. If you were not fighting for your life, you were fighting to survive.

I always seemed angry and frustrated because I was trapped in an area that was exploding with anger. The gangs and the fighting among the same race made me realize that things do not change because you want it to change. It just is the way things are, and the only way to change is to help yourself and try to live with the horror of it. But sometimes I feel for my people, and I want them to get the same opportunity I have. I don't want to leave them behind, but life goes on for me, and I can only help the ones that want to be helped.

The Anger

The barrio always made me feel safe, but sometimes I felt the anger of being trapped. Even though I survived this seclusion, I did not know how the rest of the world lived. As a child, I felt the frustration of the barrio. Jobs were very limited, and the people did not have very many skills. There were always constant fights within the families due to lack of income. There were some alcohol problems, which made things worse. It helped the people forget the problems and the frustrations.

I remember running away for one day because of the pressures from home and the barrio. I ran away to my best friend's house, which was not very far. I kept telling myself, "I am not going back to the barrio." My best friend's house was a safe place to hide because her family did not have many problems. In this family, there was a tradition of every generation attending college. They planned summer trips together and all the other fun things middle-class families did together. I think I wanted this for my family and other families in the barrio. Why can't the people of the barrio forget their problems and get it together? Sometimes I don't believe the things I say. It bothered me that nobody wanted to better themselves and stop killing each other. When does it stop? How does it stop? When do people start listening to one another? The barrio could not answer these questions, and I could only wonder about them.

Sometimes I felt ashamed of the barrio, but I know it's a terrible thing to say. I think I understand some of the problems. I never heard of improvements for the community or some type of program to help pinpoint the problems. The power to do this was in someone else's hands. But who was it? My memory only recalls the struggle of this community, which was reflected in the families in the barrio. I don't think running away would solve the problems. Maybe it can. I can only speak for myself and try to soften the anger that I might have for my barrio. I can only understand the things that affected the problems, which were violence and frustrations.

At one point I wanted to forget where I was from, but it only made matters worse. My family used to visit relatives out of state when I was young. I remembered the scenery and how beautiful the huge stretches of land were. My aunt's family spoke English and did not know how to speak Spanish. It was funny that this family was also Mexican and did not know one word of Spanish. My aunt and uncle spoke Spanish but spoke English to my cousins. I remembered my aunt saying to me, "Speak Spanish to them so they can learn." I would say to myself, "I can't believe this"; back home we spoke the language all the time. After returning home, I would start speaking English to my friends, and they would hate me. To them it was "gringo" talk, and if you spoke it, you were thought of as being conceited and would be alienated from the rest of your peers. Living in the barrio was a no-win situation because when someone tried to improve themselves or learn something different they would be hated. This was part of growing up in the barrio; you either learn to deal with it or get out. I hated that fact that people would actually get beaten up for trying to improve themselves. If you were caught reading or showing any interest in school, you were considered a "sissy." I can't believe the things I had to put up with living in the barrio. Some days I would love it, and some days I would hate it. In junior high school I remember being chased after school by a girl who hated my guts.

She actually waited to beat me up and chase me around this fenced-in swimming pool. Around and around I went like a fool trying to escape from this madwoman. And, of course, no one was around to save me. Finally, I would get away on my own, but I did not look forward to the next day because of the fear of being beaten again. I don't know how I survived, but it was not easy.

I was always angry at myself for not running away farther. How could I escape from an angry barrio that protected itself from invasion by others? The barrio protected what was theirs and then some. So sometimes people took what was not theirs, but there were reasons why: Did we get a raw deal because we were different? Did we deserve to be isolated from others? I think the barrio had the right to be angry ever since the land got divided and was given to someone else. I am talking about the history of oppression of past generations. The land was taken away from my ancestors by the dividing of Mexico and Texas. The fighting continues on a sublevel; we make it better for future generations to survive without struggle.

I wrote a poem about the struggle of the Chicano and what we accomplish for the sake of others. This poem is for my own use. It gave me a sense of how far we have come from the oppression of the white society.

Walking Tall

Walking tall no matter who you are.
Walking tall no matter where you are.
It's the Chicano that got left behind.
I came to get what is mine.
I know because I learn through my eyes.
Walking tall no matter who you are.
Walking tall no matter where you are.
We are in a place where nobody knows us.
I learn and gain knowledge just like you did.
When is it my turn to be who I am.
Walking tall no matter who you are.
Walking tall no matter where you are.

I wrote this poem one day when I was very angry at the university for not listening to Chicano issues and the problems of racism toward Chicanos and other minorities on campus. I cannot believe that this goes on, not only in society but also at the university level, which is an institution of learning.

I believe in myself and my people, who are rising very rapidly. My family had a lot to do with my beliefs and about how much we should join together to help one another. *La Raza* (the people) can accomplish and succeed what they set out to accomplish. The way to do this is to believe in yourself and forget the past because the future is already here. My family has supported me, and I have learned more about who I am. It gave me strength to survive in an unpredictable world.

Sometimes I feel confused as to who I am and how I have come this far and survived. Before I came to the university I would not identify myself as Chicana. I seemed to want to assimilate into the white society, but only until I learned that being Mexican was not bad. It seemed that in the barrio there was always trouble, and Mexicans were always looked upon as lazy. This was a label that other people gave us. For some Chicanos it is safe to remain in the barrio. For me I feel that getting away and learning about why we were labeled is frustrating, and understanding it is all I can do. There are certain questions I feel could never be answered. Why are Chicanos concentrated in one area? Why is there so much segregation? How far can we go before we, as Chicanos, catch up? After I learned that it was not bad to be a Chicana, I felt stronger. The anger was making me aware and helping me to understand. The more I learn about myself, the more I identify myself as Chicana. The only way I could do this was to understand the barrio. Being raised in the barrio was more a positive than a negative experience. I think the times are right to learn about being a Latino. It is important to me that I can always go back to the barrio and share my learning experience with the rest of the barrio.

The Family

There we were, my family and I, in the middle of an angry barrio. The only way of surviving was to get lost in it. My family has always been aware of what went on in the barrio. We were a working-class family in the middle of an angered barrio. Both my parents worked hard for the things we needed and even for those extra things we did not need. I always felt that my family came through when I needed them. My father always said, "A job is important because of the benefits and longtime security." This was instilled in my mind. He also said that an education is important. My brothers and sisters and I would get tired of listening to his lectures, but we nodded our heads to say yes to make sure he knew we were listening. My oldest sister was always making sure we paid attention.

I remember her as being very quiet and also looking in the mirror making sure that her makeup was on right. I think she looked beautiful without any, but to her it was the "in" thing for teenagers. She was always laughing with her friends, and she always looked happy. Until one day she stopped laughing, but I was too young to understand. I kept hearing adult voices and massive confusion among them. I'd rather not talk about it because it hurt too much to remember her pain and laughter disappear. I love my sister very much because she survived the hardship. She went through a lot and still gave me the support that I needed. I vaguely remember growing up with my two older brothers, but I remember them always getting into trouble. My younger sister was my best friend, and we always got into trouble together. We played together and made up pretend stories. We laughed together and cried together when we got spanked by my mother, who truly believed in discipline. She always managed to grab something to hit us with. She was good at throwing shoes and hitting her target. I think it was from years of practice with us being the targets.

My mother is a very important person in my life. She supported me through my separation from my lover of five years. She told me that in any relationship breakup you learn to survive for the next one. My mother is a strong woman, and she has been through rough times with my father's alcohol problem. He put her through a lot, and I don't think he realized the pressures he gave her, especially when he was drowning his problems in liquid. He had a serious problem, but, being Mexican, it was a little hard for him to admit it. This was a sign of being "macho." To this day I don't really understand why.

My father came from a generation of alcoholics, and he had to support my aunts and uncles, a family of fifteen. He was thirty-five when he married my mother, and she was twenty-two. He served in World War II before he married my mother. The war was a nightmare for him, and he wished that he had not gone, but he had no choice. He was drafted, and, according to him, he had to serve his country. My mother tried hard to keep the family together, but with my father's problems this task was not easy. The barrio sort of covered up these problems by not dealing with the problems.

It was a tradition to drink after funerals and talk about the person who died. I never liked the way some of the men made their own traditions. The people in the barrio were always following traditions; some of them were good, but some were made up. My family followed the good traditions, but the made-up ones were also somewhat followed because of the pressures. I think that the American Dream my father had was part of the problem. The barrio had similar identity problems: Who are we? What do we do? The media had a lot to do with the American Dream because only they knew what this dream was. The dream was the Dick and Jane story—a house with a white fence, two kids, and a dog named Spot. Not until now can I understand my father's drinking problem and how much pressure he was under. But to confront this would only break the habit of not living in the real world. You learn to live between worlds depending on which one is accepted. My family lived in the pressured world that was accepted but would rather have lived with traditions. The anger lies in the confusion between worlds. I feel frustrated because my family and other families are *La Raza* who got pushed aside and forgotten.

My mother is a strong woman and always did what was best for the family. She kept the family together, and I admired her for putting up with my father for as long as she did. She protected the family from the problems with my father. She kept him happy and always kept dinner on the table. She kept things from the family, but sometimes it did not work. We always heard them arguing, but they argued where we could not hear them well. The arguments got worse as I was growing up and school was getting impossible to attend. Sometimes we would wait for him all night, wondering what he was going to do. Who do you blame? Where do I go for answers? This society makes it hard for them to live the American Dream. Can you imagine how some minorities have lived? The only way my father could live was not to live in reality because there was not any for him. His identity was suppressed by the war. How can someone live in a dream if the dream was not even his or hers? My family anger has always been based in the identity. Who are we? The barrio helps the anger go away—but for how long? Surviving in the barrio was the best way a family could maybe have an American Dream.

Tradition

The barrio was full with tradition when I was growing up. To define what kind of tradition we had was a different story. There were holidays that pertained to us, as Chicanos, and, last but not least, were the made-up ones. I think we made up some traditions because there was a sense of question of identity. We were either Mexicans, Mexican Americans, or Chicanos. We celebrated the major American holidays like Christmas, Thanksgiving and others but they had a mixture of the Mexican tradition. On Christmas we spent hours in the kitchen making tamales, *bunulos,* and other favorite plates. We must not forget putting up the tree and the opening of presents. I enjoyed celebrating Christmas because of the presents and the family gathering. We were together and happy, and the closeness of the family was always there.

Our traditions started to fade away once the family started to separate. Both my oldest and youngest sisters got married very young, and my brother ran away from home. My other brother was always in trouble, so he was never home. Traditions were not as important then because there were so many problems. I felt frustrated because the family was not together.

The traditions started to fade away, too, once I decided to have my own values. I kept my identity, and I am proud to be a Chicana, but for me the traditions are not as important anymore. The only way I want to preserve my identity is to learn more about my ancestors and how their struggles brought me to where I am now. I realize that the traditions are going to come up on occasions. I still feel close to the traditions, but not as strongly as I should.

In the 1980s the white society enjoys our tradition and, according to them it is okay to be Mexican because they say so. You either assimilate their way or come and be like us. I mean, non-Chicanos sing our songs, and they add sour cream to our tacos. It's the acceptance of the white society that only brings us one step ahead. Other Chicanos work hard to survive, and hatred from whites only makes us stronger and more determined to succeed.

Mi Madre (My Mother)

As far as I can remember my mother was strong and independent. She loved us so much that she protected us from the dangers of the barrio. She kept the family together as long as she could, and the traditions were a big part of her life. *Mi madre* is the pride and joy of my life, and she is not only my mother but my closest friend. She is a very pretty woman with strong Mexican Indian features: high cheekbones and a tired, clear face. She is short, heavyset, and has a physically tired body. She always wore a little makeup and red lipstick. She also wore her kinky, long hair in a bun. But she stopped paying attention to herself and had to deal with my father's alcohol problems.

We recently got even closer when my relationship of five years ended so abruptly a year ago. I had fallen in love for the first time with a person who meant so much to me. We were living with my mother at the time because we could not afford to live on our own. We both went to college, and my mother helped us out. My mother was there when I needed her and helped me realize that it was not the end of the world.

My mother had a rough life. She lost both her parents when she was very young and was raised by her grandfather and her oldest sister. She dropped out of school when she was very young because she needed money. Her grandfather was blind and very old, and she had to support him. Her sister ran away from home because she could not get along with her grandfather. My mother stayed to take care of him.

My mother would always go out of her way to keep our family happy. She worked hard because my father did not give her very much money. My father did not help her much and did not give her any credit for her work around the house. He spent a lot of time working and spending his money on liquid. She raised us on her own and worked hard. She always went out of her way to give us more than she could.

I remember, when I was twelve years old, my younger sister and I needed a bedroom set. My father gave my mother his credit card to purchase the bedroom set. He always believed in the cheaper the better. He kept reminding my mother to make sure to get the cheaper set. My mother reminded him that the reason we always had to go back to the store was because the bedroom sets did not last more than a month. My mother knew that if he was using his money to spend on liquid, that he could afford a decent bedroom set for us. I remember that day clearly. She put almost three hundred dollars on his charge card. She got a queen-size bed, matching dressers, lamps, sheets, and even a canopy that went over the bed. The mattress alone cost one hundred dollars. She even had the bedroom set delivered to our house. The next day the set got delivered and, boy, did shit hit the roof. For the next week my sister and I slept in comfort, but my mother took the punishment. My father insisted that she take everything back to the store. The delivery truck came back and took everything back to the store. We ended up getting a cheap bedroom set, and my father will never let my mother forget what she did.

Sometimes he would get so angry at her for the smallest thing, and my mother put up with his anger and his drinking. She protected us from him because his anger would sometimes get out of hand and he wanted to hit us. She pretended to be happy, but I saw her sadness. She kept a lot to herself. She put up with him for twenty-five years until she decided to leave him in 1978. I was seventeen, and my youngest sister was fifteen.

We left town, away from the danger of my father's drinking and the barrio's violence. We started a new life because of my mother. She kept us safe and pretended nothing happened. At least my father was temporarily gone and could not hurt us anymore. To *mi madre* I dedicate my success in college and my degree from the university. I love her for her strong commitment to the family and the love she gave us.

Yo (Me)

After surviving in the barrio and surviving all the anger, my family got stronger, and we have *mi madre* to thank for it. We have survived in a world of the unexpected.

In the barrio and in the outside world the next step is to open new doors. The struggle is all behind me, and the rest is up to me. Nothing can stop me from giving up the one thing that is important to me, and that is where I came from.

I am an alumna of the barrio, and I will go back to the barrio to help motivate other Latinos. I will teach them that they already know what I am learning, only the university teaches it a different way. The Chicano has experienced living in the real world, and that is the prerequisite.

My sister-in-law asks me, "What do they teach you at the university?" I told her theory, and she said, "Look around the barrio and see where we are, and I know that for a fact." In a way she is right— sometimes the university does not teach you facts, only theory. I knew for a fact that she was as capable of learning as I was, given the chance.

When I left the barrio, I was seventeen. My mother sent for my sister and me after she got some money. As my sister and I sat on the bus traveling to a faraway place where we had never been before, I kept thinking to myself, "What kind of place are we going to? Are we almost there? What do I do next?" I was afraid I would do something wrong or get lost. My younger sister depended on me, but I had no idea where I was going. I knew that we were going to a different state, but how far was it? Finally, the bus driver said, "We are in Battle

Creek, Michigan." I said to myself, "I heard 'Michigan.'" I immediately got up but the bus driver checked our tickets and said, "You cannot get off here. You are going to Ann Arbor, Michigan."

The hardest thing that I went through was identifying who I was. I decided to work for a while, but I feared the outside world. The barrio was no longer there to protect me. I was lost in a white society trying to assimilate. I was so happy because I was leaving the barrio, and the problems were gone. The violence was no longer a threat to me, but I was no longer safe because the barrio was no longer there. Protection from the outside world vanished.

I attended a community college for two terms, and I felt so out of place. I met a very nice person when I joined the college basketball team. I was good in sports, and in this way I released a lot of anxiety. My new friend helped me feel more comfortable and treated me very nicely.

It was not until I attended the university that I started to identify myself as a Chicana. I went to the university for a year and joined a Chicano organization. I had new experiences there and finally knew who I was. I attended a lot of functions and met a lot of Chicanos. I learned not to be ashamed of who I was, and I also felt comfortable with them. This organization was my new family, which I was proud to be a part of. By this time I had gotten so involved in this organization that my grades started going down.

My experience at this university was a learning experience. It taught me a lot about Mexicans and Mexican Americans. It made sense to me why some Mexicans were always having rallies on behalf of their people and why there was so much anger and violence between the United States and Mexico.

The Anglo society manifested itself through a large area of the United States, breaking some of our cultures and stripping us of our land. Even the Treaty of Guadalupe Hidalgo in 1848, which gave rights to our land, did not mean anything.

I learned so many things about myself at the University of Michigan. My opinions are my own, and I believe in myself. I know who I am and where I come from. The identity is very strong and I don't hesitate to say I am Mexican American.

I Never Quite Fit In

Matthew H. Wexley

> I hope the story of my search will help other orphans in
> history find their way home.
> —Paul Cowan, *An Orphan In History*

For my parents who taught me always to question myself,
and Hadass Tesher, my special friend

I have, for my entire existence as a Jew, felt as though I never quite
fit in in many aspects of my life. I feel as though I am an outsider as
a Jew. I was raised in a town where there are so few of us I never had
the opportunity to know any others. I never had the experience of
being around many Jews in school. Sometimes I feel like I am becoming an outsider as a member of my own family. As I strive to try to
find my own niche in Judaism, my family is, in a sense, walking away
from me. They feel fed up with the cold, apathetic aspects of an
organized religion. I feel like an outsider in a religion in which I
never took the time to explore as much as other students my age, who
are able to read Hebrew and were raised in an area with other Jews.
I feel apart because, on the one hand, I am taught that my people
were murdered by bigots, as were Afro-Americans. Yet, when I see
the injustice done to Black Americans now and try to reach my hand
out to them to help, it is slapped away because I do not understand
their situation due to the color of my complexion. Finally, I am an
outsider to myself. I am struggling to become more "Jewish," yet I do
not know if it is a genuine yearning to explore my religion and heritage
or a sense of guilt for not carrying on the traditions of my people.
This autobiography/essay is a way of examining my feelings about
Judaism and the people and places I have experienced. It is a way of
examining my life as a person who never quite felt like he fit in.

When I was in high school I used to joke with my brother that he and I made up the majority of Jews in our school. In retrospect, this was probably not true; however, I really never had the opportunity to be friends with any of the other Jews in the school because we never went around advertising our identities. Due to the fact that not many Jews live in the city where I grew up, it was extremely difficult for my family and me to establish a true "ethnic identity." There are a lot of people in town who are half Jewish, and they celebrated Christmas along with the other 99 percent of the city. This always led to confusion when I tried to explain that my family did not celebrate Christmas, nor did we have a Christmas tree, even though other families who were half Jewish in town did.

Around Christmas is when I found myself to be most apart from the rest of the town. Around the holidays my hometown looks like a winter wonderland. Every house is lit with lights, nativity scenes, and Santas until you come to my house. From the outside it looks like the Grinch lives there. Although it really does not bother me now, it epitomizes how distant my family is from others in the town.

My brother David has often expressed the desire to set up a Christmas tree. His best friend is Christian, and he always goes over to his friend's house to help decorate the tree. There are many Jews who own Christmas trees because of the pagan value associated now with the tradition. I have a difficult time with this subject. I have always been adamant that I would not feel comfortable with the idea of having a Christmas tree glowing in front of my house. I think Christmas trees are beautiful, but nothing would add to the confusion over my ethnic identity more than having a tree. I feel marginalized as it is in my community. I would feel as though something like a "Hanukkah bush" or "Hanukkah lights" would be a tremendous pull from the few Jewish roots I have left within my family. It would pull me into the larger Christian society into which I do not feel I fit.

People always say, "You don't look Jewish." I think that is why the people of my town do not perceive me as Jewish either, yet, if I had a tree for Hanukkah illuminating from my house, people would naturally assume that I am like the other 99 percent of the town who celebrate Christmas. Well, I am not like the other people in town, and the tree, or lack of one, symbolizes this fact to me. I am different at a time of the year when the rest of the community feels close, yet I do not feel that warmth or closeness because I do not believe in their God. I have always felt that I am different due to my religion and its beliefs. I have had experiences that I would consider to be examples of ignorance on the part of others.

The administration of my high school scheduled the homecoming dance on the night of Yom Kippur, the highest Jewish holiday. Although my family is not very observant of Jewish traditions, my parents called to complain how insensitive it was to disregard the fact that some members of their community could not go to the game or the dance because of a religious holiday. This incident is particularly strong in my mind as one that fuels the idea of how truly distant I felt at times in high school. Even though I am not religious in the traditional sense, I find the total lack of respect and the ignorance of scheduling events like a homecoming dance and a game terrible. It reinforced my feelings of being an outsider in the community. At a time in our country when the importance of promoting racial and religious harmony is expounded, nothing is as ignorant as the sponsoring of an event on the eve of the holiest Jewish holiday. It never would have happened had I lived in an area with a significant amount of Jews. The school administration could have thought about the significance and tradition of the holiday and moved the event back a day, but they would have caused hundreds of angry students and parents to complain before the board because of the consideration of a holiday misunderstood by most and celebrated by so few in the community.

The possibility of dating Jewish women in high school was basically out of the question. I never really knew too many in high school, and until I came to the university I never had the opportunity to do so. My parents do not feel that I have to marry someone who is Jewish; however, they like to point out that I would probably be happier going out with, and eventually marrying, someone who is Jewish. I have a special bond with other Jews, and this carries over to Jewish women. Although Judaism is a religion, there are cultural ties between families, which gives us something to talk and joke about. Since on the average Jews tend to be more liberal than other groups, I find that many Jewish women tend to therefore share my own political views. I also like Jewish women because the ones I have dated are in tune with their own feminist rights and those of other oppressed groups, such as Afro-Americans, which I admire.

I know that I place a large significance on the idea of marrying a Jewish woman. The plain and simple truth is that I feel more comfortable with a woman who is Jewish and who can relate to my family and our experiences, as I to hers. Jewish families are very similar to one another, and I see this as a positive thing. They often are warm, intelligent people who are sensitive to others (although this is a generalization, and these are qualities of non-Jewish families as well). When I date someone who is Jewish I feel a sense of security because I am not afraid to get serious with her as I would feel if I dated a non-Jew.

I want my children to be Jewish and to have a clear sense of their ethnicity, something for which I am still striving. I hope my future wife is able to speak Hebrew and that she grew up with an appreciation of the religion so she can teach my children and me the meaning of Judaism. This is important to me both in the security of keeping my religion going and, more importantly, in relating to my wife and children as Jews. The importance of marrying a woman who is Jewish is one idea that has been growing along with my increasing sense of my Judaism. I feel powerful and warm when I am around someone Jewish because I know my views are safe. Although I often feel awkward around very religious Jews, because I cannot read or speak Hebrew, I know that I could always make the effort to learn.

In the past I dated women who were not Jewish. One, in particular, showed me how much I really want to date someone who is Jewish. My senior year of high school I went out with a woman who came from a strict Christian family. Her father was excited when he heard my name and saw the color of my hair and eyes but was, to say the least, angry about my religious preference. Since there are relatively few Jews in town, I do not think the family was ever exposed to the religion. "Lisa's" parents obviously never thought their oldest daughter would date a person who did not believe in Jesus, and I think this is why they had so much difficulty with me. There was a time at the beginning of our relationship when she was unsure if it would be all right for her to go with me. I asked what her parents were doing to decide, and she replied that they were praying to Jesus to ask his opinion. I guess it was all right with him because we were allowed to go out, and, for the following ten months I realized that the more we went out the more I wanted a relationship with someone Jewish. During the time we were going out I always got the impression it was her mother who convinced her father that it was all right for Lisa to go out with me. Her mother was always very nice to me, but her father was too nice. Once he asked me if I had read a certain passage from the New Testament. When I replied that I had not because I was Jewish and we did not believe in the New Testament, he chuckled and walked away.

Another time when I was over at their house her grandmother was there. Before I met her, Lisa pulled me aside to warn me against making any reference that I was Jewish because her grandmother disliked Jews. I was insulted, but I did not know what to do. I should have walked out in disgust, but instead I swallowed my pride and met her grandmother, "passing" as a Christian.

I sometimes feel as though I did not stand up to Lisa or her family when I felt they were anti-Semitic. I was not bold in my attempts to assert my own sense of ethnic identity to her because I really did not have a strong sense of my religion and what I wanted. In retrospect, I doubt I would have gone out with her for the amount of time I did because I was often hurt by some of the vibes I got from her family. I broke up with her a month into my freshman year at the University of Michigan. I broke off the relationship with Lisa when I saw the tremendous differences in people, both non-Jewish and Jewish, here at the university.

Since I came to the University of Michigan, I have, in a sense, divorced myself from my hometown. I have changed physically, mentally, and emotionally since I came to college. I suppressed myself in high school because I always had the sense that I never totally fit in, and this caused me to feel uncomfortable sometimes. When I go back home and visit my friends, many of whom go to Michigan State University, they are amazed at how much I have changed. Now I wear glasses, have longer hair, and wear an earring. I derive so much pleasure from my outwardly different appearance. It represents the changes I have undergone internally in terms of my ideas about politics, my religion, and my goals in life. I want people to know that I dramatically changed from a clean-cut, Midwestern, marginalized Jew to Matt Wexley, a Jew trying to learn about his ethnicity and his values. I view my different appearance as a representation of the social and ethnic changes I have undergone since I came to school.

I am a different person now, no longer willing to sit back and allow people to make racist or anti-Semitic comments, as I once did with my old girlfriend's parents. There are times when I think about telling her father off about his beliefs about me or any other person who questions my history. I think what disturbs me the most about the way I handled myself in high school with her parents was that I usually defend myself against people who are anti-Semitic.

When I was a freshman in high school this other kid used to throw pennies at me. He thought I would crawl on the floor groveling after them because "everyone knows how cheap and money hungry we are." I handled it first by ignoring him, but he continued to throw them. There was nothing I could do but confront him. I made it clear to him one day that I would love the opportunity to meet him after school to kick the shit out of him if it would shut him up. He never showed up, and after that he stopped being such an asshole. I realized after that experience that there will always be people who will not like me because I am Jewish and that I will have to defend myself verbally and physically if the need arises. The most important thing I have is my dignity, and being Jewish is something of which I am proud.

My parents are both Jewish, although neither one of them is particularly religious. I never grew up in what one would call a religious house because neither of my parents particularly likes organized religion. I did, however, grow up in a culturally Jewish home. My parents always stressed the importance of keeping in contact with and having respect for the cultural aspects of Judaism. Several years ago when my family went to Israel, each member of my family felt a special bond with the people, the history, the food, and the places that we visited. Israel, however, sparked a curiosity in me to explore more in depth the religious traditions of Judaism and an interest in learning Hebrew as a language. Although I have never followed through on my desire to become more knowledgeable about the religious aspect of Judaism or my desire to someday go to Israel and learn Hebrew, I still keep these ideas in the back of my mind in the hope of someday fulfilling them.

My father's great uncle was Maurice Schwartz. He was the founder of the Yiddish Art Theater in New York City in the earlier part of this century. He was one of the greatest Jewish actors of all time and one of the most integral people in bringing theater to American Jews. My father is especially proud of his uncle and has always tried to instill in my brother David and me an appreciation for the Yiddish Art Theater and the effect it had on Jews in the United States. In Israel I visited a museum in Tel Aviv where I viewed a movie about Maurice Schwartz with my father. I felt a tremendous sense of pride in my family and their accomplishments. At the same time, visiting the museum gave me a sense of belonging with the other Jews from around the world.

When I visit New York City, I find the most exciting and rewarding part of the trips to be the visits to the old Jewish neighborhoods where the Yiddish Art Theater once stood or to Brighton Beach (Brooklyn) where my great-grandparents once strolled the streets. I look at the people, the apartments, and the stores and feel a sense of my history when I walk along the streets. I imagine myself sixty years ago as a young man walking through the area in New York

City. This is what I mean when I say that I am a cultural Jew. I appreciate the history, struggles, and lifestyle of my great-grandparents and yearn to really explore and learn what life was like for them.

Even though I am not a religious person (I do not go to synagogue, nor do I keep kosher), I feel that I am missing a part of my culture because I do not read Hebrew or take part in the religious services at a synagogue. In my opinion, being a cultural Jew in an area in Michigan without a large Jewish population symbolizes assimilation, and I never want to assimilate to the point where I lose my ethnic identity. Without other Jews around, it is difficult to have a Jewish culture. Without religion, it is often difficult to be a Jew.

The fact that I never had a formal synagogue bar mitzvah still bothers me. I moved when I was twelve years old to an area with a Conservative synagogue. They wanted me to relearn the prayers I already knew and learn more Hebrew by going back a few grades in Hebrew school because, up until that time, I had been educated in a Reform temple. I do not regret my decision not to have a formal bar mitzvah as much because I realize how little Hebrew school or my bar mitzvah meant to me at thirteen. I do, however, wish that my parents would have forced me to continue my Hebrew education so that I could have had my bar mitzvah because I would appreciate it now. I miss not carrying on a tradition that, although no longer thought of in the same manner as it once was, is still an important step in becoming a Jewish man or woman. When I go to temple I feel out of place because I do not know the songs of prayers anymore. I know I could walk into the temple close by and learn. Sometimes, however, I feel as though I let so many of the important years slip away that I would never take the time to learn the service and feel totally comfortable in temple. In many respects, I am a Jew trying to find myself while at the same time trying to gain some form of acceptance from other Jews who have had religious training. I am not as much a Jew, nor am I looked upon as complete without having had my formal bar mitzvah.

I had a small ceremony in English in Israel at the Wailing Wall, and if I were truly committed to the idea of having a formal bar mitzvah, I could always go back to Hebrew school to relearn the language and have the bar mitzvah now, but this is not what I want. Unfortunately, my ego is too big to go back to Hebrew school. I would like to learn to speak, read, and write Hebrew, then go and live in Israel to gain a feeling that I have not assimilated so much into the mainstream society that I cannot appreciate or be knowledgeable about my history, religion, and culture. I have not always felt this way. In many respects, I felt that the key to being a "good Jew," or Christian, Muslim, Hindu, Buddhist, etc., was to be tolerant, loving, and charitable to everyone, and I still feel this way. However, what has transformed in me is a sense that, in order for me to feel that I am a genuine Jew and a part of my heritage, I need to try and learn Hebrew and live for some time in Israel. After I graduate from the University of Michigan, I want to live in Israel for a year to find myself before I go on to graduate school. Even if I never become religious in the conventional sense, I want to feel a part of the same people of whom my grandparents and great-grandparents were a part.

Several of my friends who are Jewish never had a bar mitzvah. They did, however, grow up in a setting with Jewish friends and organizations that I would have enjoyed if I would have taken the opportunity to experience these things. Even though they never had a bar mitzvah, they still feel a sense of belonging due to their involvement in Jewish things. I, on the other hand, feel as though I have assimilated into the non-Jewish mainstream of society so much because I never grew up doing things among other Jewish people. The feeling that I have assimilated is strongest when I go back home. The feeling has weakened considerably since I came to the University of Michigan, where I am with other Jews.

When a thirteen-year-old boy or girl has a bar mitzvah, they are accepted into the synagogue as a religiously trained member of that congregation, regardless of whether the ceremony means anything to the individual. Now I appreciate Hebrew and its relation to Israel, but at thirteen I did not. I think this is the case for many Jews when they think about their Hebrew training (due to the way in which the language is taught today). Now they appreciate the fact that they went through all the trouble to learn Hebrew and carry on a tradition.

The ideas of heritage and tradition are important in Judaism. We have been persecuted in virtually every country we have inhabited, with the exception, in most cases, of this one. In many respects, this lack of direct persecution against us in the United States has caused a significant amount of assimilation of our traditions into the dominant Christian society. We have had to assimilate into this society in order to be the successful group we are in this country. We are the quintessential autonomous minority with its defining factor the cloud of persecution hanging over our heads. The first instance of persecution against the Jews in this country would bring us closer together, and we would see a reemergence of the religion because of the violence against us.

When I see hate politicians such as David Duke, the ex-grand dragon of the Ku Klux Klan, win a seat in the Louisiana State legislature, I think to myself that, no matter how much I think I have assimilated or we, as Jews, feel that we may stop looking over our shoulders, the same instant men like Duke will come down on our heads.

You might wonder why I think growing up with other Jews, or the knowledge of what it means to be a Jew, is important. Since I did not have this until I came to the University of Michigan, I have come to the realization of how much I need to be with other people, especially Jews who can share my experiences. If I would have been around other Jews while I was in middle and high school, I might not have this feeling of not fitting in either a Jewish or Christian society. I had the unfortunate experience of dealing with anti-Semitism at a much younger age than my father because of where I grew up. Ironically, most Black students my age are not segregated to the same extent that their parents were. I, on the other hand, have had to deal with anti-Semitism more as a young child than my father did.

A lot of times when minorities are placed in an area with few other members of their group, they often gain strength from one another and actually begin to delve into their culture, race, etc. The Afro-American students at the University of Michigan who number so few are very close to one another and try to keep their identities, even though they are surrounded by a majority of white students, professors, and staff. Because I am "white" and am Jewish I can pass for the majority, unlike Afro-Americans, who are singled out due to the color of their skin. If Jews could not pass and there were open anti-Semitism, I think Jews would band together and become stronger in the upholding of traditions and customs. If I could always have been singled out for being Jewish, I am sure that I would have derived strength from the other Jewish people around me.

I would quickly like to digress and discuss that, although Jews in my town or any other area of the country are not often subjected to the direct racism toward Black Americans (or other minorities), there are forms of subtle anti-Semitism. I am especially referring to the idea of born-again Christians trying to save me from burning in hell by trying to convert me to Christianity. I realize that they are trying to help me by informing me of Jesus before I go to hell for my sins, but I take a personal offense to the idea of trying to convert people.

I think it shows a total lack of regard for my religion, beliefs, and traditions of my people. Jews do not go around trying to impose their beliefs on other religions, nor do the Muslims, Hindus, or Buddhists go around with the intent of gaining converts.

In my opinion, I think it is very important to live in a diverse neighborhood. For instance, I rushed the fraternity I am in because of the diversity of the house and the various qualities each person in it has to offer. I have Black fraternity brothers who are often seen as outsiders by the other Afro-Americans because they are in a house that is predominantly white. I have a real problem with attitudes such as this. The members of my house who are Afro-American have a special quality about them. Besides living with the stigma of being one of only two thousand Blacks on an often oppressive campus they often are made to feel as though they have betrayed their Black "brothers and sisters" by rushing a predominantly white house. I did not rush a Jewish house because I felt that I could accomplish more by experiencing things with people who are different from me and who could teach me the meanings of various things from their perspectives. Although there are times I wished I had rushed a Jewish house to experience living just with other Jews, I feel in the long run I have benefited from such a diverse house. For instance, I have a fraternity brother John who is Black but is interested in studying Judaism and is always asking questions about Jewish holidays or even whether or not I think a word such as *JAP* is anti-Semitic. When one of my fraternity brothers was wearing a shirt that said, "JAP buster," John was one of the first members of my house to complain and tell the individual that it was offensive. Another time one of the house members complained that the cable TV had been turned off in his room. As the individual came down the stairs, he shouted out that "he had been niggered." To his surprise he came face-to-face with one of his fraternity brothers who is Black. The two talked about the word and what its meaning meant, with or without malice, and how much hurt and anger the word elicited from Afro-Americans and other people.

Instances like these show me why it is important to live with people who are both similar to you ethnically and can support you in certain instances but also at the same time with other people who are dissimilar, who can add a new meaning of diversity to their surroundings. If Blacks, Jews, and other minorities never rushed other houses besides their own, there would never be the explanations and experiences that go toward furthering the idea of race relations. There is nothing wrong with being with others who are similar to yourself. Most of my good friends outside of my fraternity are Jewish. It's fun because we joke about our similar experiences or families, which I would never do with someone who was not Jewish because they probably would not find the conversations very interesting or funny. I know the same can be said of Afro-American students or other minorities who stay together here at the University. Nothing goes further in causing stereotypes and racism/anti-Semitism than being exclusively with people who are similar to oneself, which is why diversity is so important.

One of the biggest influences of my life was a year I spent in Berkeley, California. My father was a visiting professor at the University of California when I was starting school, and I spent kindergarten at a school outside of town. The University of California has always had a reputation as a liberal school with a very diverse student population. That year had the biggest impact on my life when it comes to being tolerant and interested in people who are dissimilar to me. During my year in Berkeley I had the opportunity to meet people who were Afro-American, African, Japanese, Indian, etc., which came at an important time in my life. As a five-year-old going to school for the first time, I was very impressionable, and nothing was as interesting as the many different faces I saw sitting in class with me every day. I became curious about the other children in my class. Many of my classmates were children of visiting professors and students who were at the university. Their parents were from the countries we were studying. Every week different parents would come in and give speeches about their countries and then make us food from their lands. At five years old I learned to eat with chopsticks and to gain an appreciation for curry, sushi, and other foods, all because these parents took the time to teach me to appreciate the cultures and religions of different people. One of the most exciting things we did was to experience the Chinese New Year in 1975, the Year of the Rabbit. We took a trip to Chinatown in San Francisco and watched the parade and fireworks.

It's funny, but I have never thought about my year of living in California in the context of my ethnic identity. In retrospect, when I look at things that have influenced my ideas about my own Jewish identity, my interest in other cultures, and my desire to help other minorities, most definitely it would have to stem from my year of living in a diverse and liberal place like Berkeley.

I think that one of the best ways to have racism and other forms of prejudices eradicated is to educate young children about different peoples. Learning about various cultures and experiencing their foods and holidays is an excellent way to stop a lot of the stereotypes that form about different people. There are still many parents who are racist/anti-Semitic and exert a lot of influence on their children, but, by combating that racism at home with open minds at school, the children might grow into more open-minded and LIBERAL people.

I am a Jewish male. I am an American Jew. I am a Jewish American. I am white. I do not feel white, and sometimes when I am sitting in synagogue there are times that I do not feel Jewish. I cannot read Hebrew anymore, not that I really could even read it so well to start. I do not keep kosher, and my family is very unreligious, so much so that my brother David is an atheist at heart. Although I do not keep holidays or go to temple every Sabbath, I have become aware of my religion and what it is beginning to mean to me since I arrived on the campus a year and a half ago. I want my children to grow up being Jewish and would like them to be able to read Hebrew. There are some parents who send their children to Hebrew school, giving "I had to go when I was your age" or "every nice Jewish child goes to Hebrew school at your age" excuses, but I want my children to get the kind of Hebrew education I would have liked. For one thing, it is always nice to learn a language and actually understand and conceptualize what is being read. Hebrew, unlike some of the ways it is taught, is not a dead language such as Latin. I think Hebrew school would be more fun if we would have been taught to speak and understand Hebrew, then read the language of our forefathers and foremothers.

I think for many Jewish children, a bar or bat mitzvah is not an important part of their lives anymore, as it once was. For many it is just the idea of memorizing one's part from the Torah and then having a party with plenty of relatives and gifts. This critique is harsh, but, when I was studying for my bar mitzvah, this is what I and many of my Hebrew school classmates thought.

As I get older and I try and find myself as a Jew, I am finding it increasingly more difficult to go back home. I am extremely close to my family, but I can see that I am separating in many respects from them with regard to my religious desires and intentions. I am trying to experience being Jewish, but, as I try to find my niche as a Jew, I am myself more confused and angry when I go home. It makes me angry that we do not take part in more Jewish activities or know more

Jewish people. Every time I am home I am pulled back into this feeling that my family and I have lost so much of our ethnic identities and, in turn, parts of our history and individuality.

On Sunday mornings my father goes to a multireligious Unitarian group, which tries to focus on discussing the various religions and attempts to tackle social issues facing humanity. For instance, they volunteer at homes for battered women and AIDS halfway houses. My mother and father have not, nor will they ever, convert to another religion because they are proud to be Jews. My father, however, does not feel the religion of Judaism applies to real-world issues, and, since he does not know what God is or what she or he wants, my father feels he is doing more good by joining a group that does some actual good.

What bothers me the most about my father is the fact that he is right, and he has the right and duty to join any group that makes him happy. I think I am most disappointed because there is still religion in the group. I wish there were some Jewish organizations my parents could find that would give my father the same satisfaction he feels with the Unitarian group. I consider myself to be liberal, yet I have to admit that I am very skeptical of groups outside of Judaism that profess to help humanity. I always feel that their way of helping humanity is through Christianity. This approach is wrong, and I am trying to learn and be less pessimistic about other religious groups, but I am just careful that they are not anti-Semitic.

A major source of despair for me when I go home is the fact that my family is so assimilated that, when they do join something that is a religious group, even one that is multireligious such as theirs, I feel that, by going, they are breaking one of the last few lines we have as Jews.

One of the most important aspects of my ethnic identity is my allegiance to Israel and its people; this, however, does not mean that I am immune to criticism of the country and its policies. I am a Zionist, and I have always thought of myself as one.

Many people are critical of Israeli policies, and I am one of them. There is nothing wrong with this because no one should blindly believe in his or her country, or anything else for that matter. Being critical of something is often a form of love for a country. I, for one, am critical of many American policies. Israel is not strictly a "holy" place like many American Jews hold it up to be. They see Israel in some supreme and glorious light and expect its actions to reflect this attitude, unwilling to see many of its faults. Israel is a beautiful country, which I love, but it is a country with problems like any other one. It has a poor economy, unemployment, and military policies with which I do not always agree. I, however, criticize the policies of Israel, and not its right to exist. Ever since its creation as a Jewish state, the dispute over whether the Jews belong in Israel or if the Palestinians are entitled to the land has become a burning question. The *Michigan Daily* here on campus begins its articles on this issue with the premise that Israel has no right to exist and then proceeds to criticize Israeli policy. When we criticize France, England, and the Soviet Union, we do not begin with the premise that those countries do not have the right to exist, so why should we do so for Israel? Almost every Jew believes in the right of Israel to exist, so I do not usually take offense when I argue over Israel with another Jew. I do, however, take offense when I am arguing with someone who is against the right of Israel to exist and who, at the same time, criticizes its policies.

In the summer of 1986 I went to Israel for the first time when my father gave a speech at an international psychology convention in Jerusalem. I remember flying into Israel from Paris on Northwest Orient. I had never been so sure that my plane would either (a) blow up or (b) be hijacked. It was a year after the TWA plane was hijacked to Beirut, and on top of that we were not flying El Al, the safest airline, which added to my discomfort. When we touched down, the recognition of how real some of my fears were came alive when I saw the armored personnel carriers and soldiers checking us as we got off the plane.

In spite of the apprehension of flying to Israel and the sight of soldiers greeting us as we got off the plane, I had the complete opposite experience in Israel. I felt for one of the few times in my life as though I were truly comfortable and at home with my identity as a Jew. Up until that point in my life, I had never felt as comfortable being Jewish as I did there. I looked around at the accomplishments of my fellow Jews of all different colors and cultures and immediately felt a sense of pride in the things I saw around me. I visited the museums erected in honor of the millions of Jews who died at the hands of the Nazis. I felt a bond with the victims of the Holocaust, their families, and the other visitors to the museum, who, unlike the non-Jews I knew at home, could relate to the pain I felt for those victims of the extermination. I visited Masada on top of a mountain by the Dead Sea where a population of Jews held off the powerful Roman army who wanted to take them as slaves. Instead of giving up after they stood off the Romans, they committed suicide rather than be enslaved. I visited a museum of Jewish culture in Tel Aviv. I felt the pride I always knew I had for a group of people I always wanted to explore and identify.

My trip to Israel was one of the biggest influences in my life as a Jew up until that point, especially because I lost so much of my ethnic identity when I left Ohio and moved to Michigan. I visited the Hasidic section of Jerusalem. I imagined what it would have been like for my ancestors in Eastern Europe, and I watched as a young boy studied the Talmud with his grandfather in preparation for his bar mitzvah, which I would have done one hundred years ago with my grandfather.

When American Jews go to Israel they experience a sense of pride and hospitality when they are there. They have a feeling of being with their own people. My experience was no different. One thing that I remember feeling was that we, as Jews, have a bond with many of the people of Israel because it is a Jewish state. In this country we identify ourselves as Jews, yet, when I went to Israel, my label turned to "American." I felt that in a sense they believed that in order to be a true Jew I should come to Israel and work for my homeland. When I was living in Israel with my parents, I became caught up in the idea of doing my part. A romanticized version of myself in the Israeli army creeped into my mind. (Of course, thoughts of getting shot or wounded never entered my mind.) Military service in Israel and the use of weapons is not a macho, heroic part of the army, but instead a very real part of everyday life in Israel. I remember I had a conversation with some Israelis, who asked me why I did not move to Israel, become a citizen, serve in the military, and work in Israel. I contemplated my own thoughts that I might one day move to Israel, or be forced to go there. If that ever happened, I would want to know that I had done my part in keeping it safe.

I am glad, though, that I had not gone to Israel when I was younger because it would have been for the wrong romantic ideas. I registered for the draft in this country when I was eighteen years old. It is hard for me to believe that I am the average age of a soldier in Vietnam or a soldier in Israel. If I would have become an Israeli citizen and served in the army in the West Bank, I am not sure how I would feel right now. If I were ever drafted into the United States military and killed another human being, I could rationalize it by the fact that I was drafted and had no choice. The same cannot be said for me about the Israeli army. I would be indirectly volunteering for the military service by voluntarily becoming an Israeli citizen. I am not sure how I would feel later about going into military service for Israel.

Lately, however, I feel as though I want to move to Israel for a year after I graduate from college and become a dual citizen of Israel and the United States. It is important to me that I find myself as a Jew while I am there, whether that means embracing the religion more, staying in Israel, or returning to the United States, finding that I am more secure with myself as a Jew. If I ever did become a citizen of Israel, I would have to go into the military, and this has made my decision more difficult for me.

I recently saw a lecture at Hillel by an American who became a citizen of Israel, married an Israeli woman, and served his duty in the army in the West Bank. He hated what he saw but felt it was an educational experience. He saw the occupied West Bank firsthand and he did not agree with the biased views of Western journalists, who look for sensationalized stories. Because he had served in the army there, I felt that the lecturer had the right and the duty to criticize Israeli policy in the West Bank. The lecturer felt that the more humanitarians serve in the Israeli army, and in the West Bank, the better off Israel would be in the long run. This statement had an important effect on me; for the next two years I am going to think about my decision to go and become an Israeli citizen.

My search as a Jewish man has only begun. I am constantly changing my ideas and goals for the future. One thing, however, will always remain with me—a sense of pride in being Jewish. My girlfriend is an Israeli, and, for one of the few times in my life as a Jew, I feel as though I have met a person with whom I feel totally at ease. Since I have been going out with her, the idea that I need someone who is Jewish has become very important to me. I have listened to her speaking Hebrew with her family, and I realize how much significance at least trying to learn Hebrew means to me. I decided to enroll in Hebrew 201, Introductory Hebrew, so that at the very least I will be able to read when I go to synagogue and feel comfortable about myself. It is often difficult to be unlike the rest of society, and for a long time I "fit in" in my hometown, even though I was not happy doing it. I do not blame my parents for living in an area where there were few Jews because, until they moved, I am not sure they realized how much they appreciated the security of being around other Jews.

Mis Palabras

Carlos Arturo Manjarréz

La Fuerza de Esta Mujer

It was 1968 when Carmen Manjarréz left for the suburbs of Detroit to be closer to her job and to provide a better life for her children (Arturo, 9; Rosa, 8; and myself, 1 year old). Southeast Rochester was a working-class area; almost everyone at the time worked on the line for the Big Three (Ford, G.M., and Chrysler). Though in that area the homes were separated by sizable grassy lots that kept neighbors at a distance, there was a great deal of pressure concerning exactly where we could and couldn't live. And though the housing market was relatively open at the time (and all handled by the same realtor), Mamá was given the single option of purchasing the smallest and least expensive home in the area or none at all. She opted for the choice that provided her children with a roof over their heads. The contract was drawn up and signed, but not before the clerk made one final attempt to discourage her from purchasing the home by asking if she could read the contract. Frustrated by the realtor's contempt and tired from her bus trip from Detroit, she shot back, in beautifully broken English: "Yes I can read, write, and speak in two languages. What about you?"

Mamá hadn't anticipated the problems she would face. Scenes of the city of Detroit being torn by the riots of 1966 and of the city burning in 1967 were still fresh in the minds of many of our neighbors. Somehow our family, as we were the first people of color moving into the area, represented what the people there most feared— the infiltration of their community by minorities. They thought we were the early signs of an inevitable change in the community. Our color, our language, our food—everything about us was extraordinary.

There were daily reminders of the disapproval of people in the community. Mamá described it best when she expressed the pain she had felt on one of our many trips to the supermarket at a time when she didn't have her driver's license. The entire family had to make the weekly pilgrimage to the grocery store approximately one-half of a mile away. On our return Rosa would carry one light bag, Art a heavier bag, and Mamá would pull my red wagon, and my job was to collect any of the items that might have fallen from any of the three. It seems that invariably on these excursions we would bump into a family that lived on our little side street. What hurt Mamá was the fact that these people, our neighbors, wouldn't acknowledge her salutations let alone offer her a lift back home on those days when the snow made our trips to and from the market cold and difficult. It took years before a mutual sense of trust could be built and we established a relationship where we could rely on others for help and friendship.

Around this time Mamá was working afternoons at the Ford plant in Utica so that she could see her two eldest children off to school and take care of me during the day. Once the older children returned home, she would prepare their dinner, and we would eat together as a family (though Mamá was regularly getting up to warm tortillas or get more milk). Soon she would be off to the corner store to wait for her ride, and Art was put in charge of my care—*cuidando al bebe* (caring for the baby).

In these after-school hours a few children from the community would congregate at our home to play. We played together with sole regard to fairness of play, not fairness of skin. We were all color-blind in our relationships and remained so until our parents assigned the colors that were supposed to have meaning and made them ugly. Some of my friends were lost by this "education"; others continue unaltered to this day. It was through these childhood relationships that ties were made with other families in the community. Through our friendships we were able to bring down a wall of ignorance and distrust that was, from a child's perspective, an artificial and arbitrary boundary that adults had raised. This was the *real* indoctrination of the Manjarréz family on the Melvin Street block.

Years passed and the time soon came for Mamá to enroll her youngest in elementary school. It was a tremendous step, as she had relied so heavily on the comfort and closeness of her *pollitos* (little chicks) in both good times and bad. Mamá had planned to take me to school my first day. It was something she had been looking forward to for weeks. I remember her saying, "mi viejito ya va entrar a la escuela" (my little old man is going to start school). She had waited so long to see the school in which Arturo and Rosa had spent so many hours of their days. It was a privilege she hadn't allowed herself. She never told me why—she didn't have to. I think it was because she thought her presence might jeopardize their admission (she assumed that her heavy accent would raise the suspicion that the children weren't legal U.S. citizens, which they weren't). Since I was born in the States and spoke English without an accent, she no longer saw a problem with her presence. But a problem did arise either because of my skin color, as I am much darker than my brother and sister, or because of Mamá's accent.

"Mrs. Menjery, is your son a LEGAL U.S. CITIZEN?" Not waiting for a reply, this sarcastic man asked, "Does he speak ENGLISH or does he at least understand everything that is said to him?"

Here too Mamá showed the strength that defines her so beautifully. She said,

"He can speak and understand so well that you can ask him something in English and he will translate it into Spanish for me. Then I'll give him the answer in Spanish, and he will translate it back into English for you."

He put me through the test. I passed, just as Mamá had predicted, and I was enrolled that day.

Mamá, They Don't Serve Tortillas in the Lunchroom

It was in this new environment that I was really struck by the fact that none of the other children were brown like me. Never before had I been exposed to so many Anglo children my own age at one time. I became acutely aware that I was different and suppressed the thought (only the beginning of a long and painful practice). I felt an overwhelming pressure to conform to a type that diminished my uniqueness rather than one that celebrated and appreciated its value. This Anglo-biased assumption of homogeneity directly contradicted the obvious differences between my friends and me. When I was beginning to see that I was different in color and cultural heritage and needed to further explore and understand these differences, the issue was dropped (actually, it was never raised). I was left on my own to deal with what it meant to be Chicano in the United States, while continually having the image of Dick, Jane, their two parents (Daddy worked, and Mommy stayed at home), and their white picket fence forced upon me. The cynical assumptions propagated by my teachers and their instructional materials didn't allow me to cut and paste my way into the U.S. picture. According to them, I didn't exist.

I've divided the first years of my elementary school days into separate boxes in my memory. The first is filled with memories that end somewhere in my fourth-grade classroom. Though I was still confused as to who I was, serious questioning was suppressed, and I turned to my studies and sports for acceptance. I would always fall short of raising the question, maybe because I was afraid of the answer . . .

"O.K. class we have time for a couple questions before we say the pledge of allegiance and go home—Carlos, what is your question?"

"Teacher, why isn't there anyone here who looks like me? Not even the pictures in our books look like me. Teacher, are you like me? Do you eat warm frijoles when you get home? Does your family welcome you into the home with a language so sweet that you would think it was made just for lovers? Teacher, I'm not sure who I am or whether or not I belong here."

"I'm sorry Carlos, we can't discuss your questions today."

One of the fondest memories I have of those days was when my third-grade teacher, Ms. Hopling, told my mother that someday her son would be a writer. Everything was a playful challenge, and all challenges were met head-on. The hours in the classroom meshed with the hours spent on the playground. Of course there were times of crisis, like the many fights I found myself in because the other kids had called me "nigger" (most of the children had never seen a "spic" before me, thus it seemed the closest applicable slur). But for the most part I felt that my peers accepted my presence from the start.

My reflections of home and family at that time are just as strong. After school my afternoons were tied to the family. Mamá switched to the day shift so that she could be with her *pollitos* in the afternoon and evening hours. Though she wasn't home to greet us when we got off the bus, she would arrive shortly thereafter, fix us our afternoon snack, and then retire to a much-needed nap. She worked so damn hard in those days, harder than I have or ever will in my life. She used to say, "Line hours [assembly line hours] are the longest of all." I believe her. When Mamá retired to nap, Arturo, Rosa, and I were free to do as we chose. I remember little about this time at home other than the fact that the family was closer then than it would ever be again. All of us played together and shared our beds, Rosa with Mamá and Art with me. On Sundays Mamá would fix us something special to eat, and we would all sit down in front of the TV.

Días de Rebelde, Días de Dolor

Unfortunately, the peace we shared at home wasn't meant to last. As time passed relationships in *mi familia* (my family) grew difficult and tense. Art and Rosa were much older than I, so they were starting high school when I was in the third grade. Those days were most difficult for Mamá. She really didn't know how to deal with "rebellious teenagers"—nor did she have the time and energy to do so. The line had taken so much out of her, both emotionally and physically, that much of her time at home was spent recovering with naps. Both Art and Rosa would get into trouble regularly. But the ones I remember fighting most often were Art and Mamá. They would have terrible fights that would often end with Art leaving the house for days. This was especially hard for me because I loved them both so much. I soon found out, though, that by crying I could make them stop fighting, and I would exploit this method every time the arguments got too intense. One day, as hard as I tried, there was no stopping them. This time the subject was a "joint" Mamá had found in Art's pants pocket. They went back and forth for at least a half an hour—what seemed to me an eternity. It ended with Mamá slapping Arturo with her strong and sensitive hand. Art glared at her in disbelief and screamed,

"If it weren't for Carlos, I'd leave this fuckin' place."

Mamá replied indignantly, "Go ahead. I can take care of him just fine." Weeks passed, and I yearned for Art to return. At times he would stop by when he knew Mamá was not home, and I would beg him to stay; he never would—until one day when Mamá caught him at home and then did something she hadn't often done in front of us. At that moment Mamá cried the deep sobs of a woman whose life was for her children and whose children were no longer her own. There was no way to predict that this foreign place would so radically transform all relationships as she had once known them. Her children were not as children she had known in Mexico, nor was her life the way she had expected it to be. It was times like these, when her emotions poured out freely, that we came close to feeling the pain she had endured in her life and how much of a struggle it was for her to survive here in *los Estados Unidos* (the United States).

Art did return, and our lives returned to normal for a period of time. Mamá was still working hard, Art had graduated and was working full-time and going to electronics school part-time, Rosa was struggling with school and friends, and I felt whole once again.

Then, all of a sudden, my family fell apart so fast that I'm still at a loss for certain details. It was 4:30 on the morning of December 22, 1977, when Rosa woke me up and told me that Art had been in a car accident and was in the hospital. I was told that there was a chance he could die. But all too soon I found out the truth. Art was in a car accident, but he had died instantly. I'll never forget the cold touch of his lifeless body in the funeral home the day he was buried. His long hair, like that of a sleeping princess, draped to his shoulders. There were hundreds of people there to see Art and to be with Mamá. I hated them all. Each one of them, with their apologies and sympathy, reminded me of exactly what was happening and the fact that never again would I be with one of the persons I loved the most.

Mamá reacted to this in a way that confused me all the more. She had her second nervous breakdown. I had been too small to really understand what was happening during her first breakdown. Rosa, who had experienced this once before, was now in her early teens, and helped me cope. Together we placed Mamá in a facility for the mentally ill. It was one of the hardest things I've ever done in my life. It had to be the worst facility in the whole county, but we knew of no other. During the month and a half of her internment, Rosa and I fought incessantly. In our confusion, we communicated our fears through fighting rather than loving—something that I regret to this day.

Once Mamá returned home, she tried desperately to convince us all (including herself) that our lives would somehow be the same, but, of course, they never would be again. In the weeks that followed, my relationships with my friends drastically changed. They changed in part because I pulled away from them emotionally, and because they really had no idea of how to react toward me after what my family had been through. Throughout my whole life Art had been the person I relied on for counseling and direction. Since Mamá was usually either working or sleeping, my care had rested on his shoulders.

I retreated from school and teachers as well as friendships. Going to school in those days was awful; I felt set apart from the rest of the kids and I retreated to a self-reliant corner by not talking to a soul during recess and not doing a bit of homework for the entire month Mamá was gone. My fourth-grade teacher responded by not really requiring anything of me but attendance (and even this wasn't that important), and when the time came I was passed along with the other kids to fifth grade. By then school no longer held the fascination for me it once had. I regularly turned my homework in late and would skip school on the days my work wasn't ready.

In time the news had gotten around to the teachers that I was a bad student. I know this because of a conversation I had with my third-grade teacher in the hall. In her very nice way she gave me a sort of pep talk on school and "trying harder." This wasn't at all strange; after all, I had always felt, throughout my primary school years, that she was a person who cared. But it was strange that no one else in the whole school had ever brought my poor performance to my attention. It was as if my fall from grace was a predestined event.

There was only one time during this period that I remember really trying hard in school. It was after having taken a standardized math placement test in the sixth grade, in which my score was quite high—in fact, high enough to place me in the advanced math course along with approximately ten other kids from my grade. The hour spent in the advanced math class each day was one of the dearest times I remember during that whole year. I worked exceptionally hard for the class while letting all other responsibilities fall by the wayside. The reward, however, was not so sweet. The following year all the advanced placement students of that class had been promoted to the eighth-grade math level, except me.

As I moved on to junior high, the issue of my ethnicity again became a problem. I remember thinking that I would be a great deal more popular if I only had Bobby's face and body and my brains. I would look in the mirror and try to imagine what I would look like. This mythical Bobby was, of course, always white and popular with the girls. This fantasy ate away at my self-esteem, and I found myself bitterly questioning why I had been born a "brown-faced Mexican." The focus of my life had markedly changed. From this point on all energies were spent on the elusive quest for acceptance by my peers— and, unconsciously, by myself.

The Weekend Ethnic

After my eighth-grade year Mamá grew tired of dealing with my poor performance in school and decided that it would be best to ship me off to a local Christian school in hopes that in this new "structured" environment my outlook, as well as my grades, would change.

There were essentially two types of kids that were shipped to this school: those children of a strict Christian household where it was simply understood that the children would be raised immersed in the faith; and those, like myself, whose parents assumed that a Christian education would help discipline, structure, and alleviate the perceived problems of the child. This school provided me with something I had been lacking in the past, a close-knit group of friends. Here I became the clown and attention getter I had always hoped to be; the fact that there were only 250 students in the entire high school helped my cause.

After two short years Mamá had become tired of wasting her money at a private school while "her son entertained himself." Again she decided to pull me from school, but this time it was for good. I was shocked. I pleaded with her to let me continue in school. I begged for her to at least allow me to finish school at the local public high school. In retrospect, I see that my interest didn't necessarily reflect a sincere concern for my future but, rather, once again a concern for my present social image. To be a class clown and a poor student was one thing, but to be a high school dropout was quite another. After what seemed to be an eternity of pleading my case, Mamá allowed for an immediate transfer to Rochester High.

The next week I found myself in the office of what was to be my high school counselor. There the counselor and I worked together to map out a schedule for the remainder of the first academic term. She pushed for the remedial courses and I for the courses in which I might find the greatest number of my old junior high friends. She won the battle over science; I would not take chemistry the term that followed. However, I won the battle for math and enrolled in Algebra II, despite my "lack of preparedness." Here I was reunited with an old friend, Todd, a fellow student of the sixth grade advanced math course. Unlike my first term at Oakland Christian, there was little chance to dedicate myself directly to the books, as I already had relationships established with a number of students. I was the prodigal son returned home, using past relationships to establish even more friendship ties with students who had attended other junior high schools. I found myself waiting in class for the bell to ring so that I could meet and greet my friends. And when the opportunity came to skip class for a "liquid lunch," I jumped at it. The race for social acceptance was on again, and all the while I found myself denying that distant and secret part of myself, *mi raza.*

At home my relationship with Mamá was crumbling. I was still incredibly angry that she had actually wanted me to quit school and start work—"hacer algo con mi vida y no nomás jugar" (do something with my life besides just playing). This kind of strict attitude would shock most people, but it was entirely reasonable for Mamá. She was a woman of character, who had worked to support not only *mi abuelita* (my grandmother) from the age of seventeen but also her drunkard husband, Luis Manjarréz, who eventually left her and the two children, Arturo and Rosa. She couldn't possibly understand someone who thought their only responsibility at age sixteen was to make friends.

Moreover, Mamá had reminded me of my distance from the other kids in my school. As she was an older Mexican woman with a heavy accent, she typified what was different about me and my Anglo friends. Mamá's very presence reaffirmed something I had so long tried to negate: the simple fact that I am *puro mexicano* (pure Mexican), and that I had a place in the Latino community, and that it had a place *en mi corazón* (in my heart). She invited me with her on her weekend excursions to Detroit or Pontiac for Spanish Mass, *quinoeañeras, el teatro, o posadas* (literally, Sweet Fifteen Celebrations, Mexican theater, or Christmas celebrations). She would often tell me that, as her child, I should accompany her everywhere she went. Together we traveled back and forth to the events that made her so happy and reminded her that she was not alone in this country. In those days I was what I call now a "weekend ethnic," attending events that were indelibly tied to my culture on the weekends, while returning to my Anglo neighborhood during the week. As a child, both of these worlds combined for me into a complex whole. But, as I grew older, I succeeded in convincing myself that these two parts of my life were opposites. My confusion is best seen in my attitude toward young urban Chicanas and Chicanos. I was awed by how they, unlike myself, felt no shame about who they were in front of their Anglo friends. They spoke Spanish in front of them and even invited them to their parents' *posadas* and Spanish Mass. It was this awareness of the distinction between me and the young urban Chicanos that convinced me that my place was back in the suburbs with the people I thought were most like me.

I saw less and less of Mamá as my social obligations of the weekday spilled over into the weekend. She tried to curtail my leaving by restricting my use of the car, but this effort proved fruitless. More and more I refused to attend her "Mexican functions" in Detroit and Pontiac so that I could go to parties with my friends. During the times we were together at home I was usually on the phone arranging another getaway.

This was the pattern right up to 1985, my senior year in high school—a year that most young people look forward to. I must say that I got caught up in the whole idea of actually being done with school and divorcing myself from a system that, as I look back, was suffocating me ethnically and intellectually. But my future choices were drastically different from those of my peers. Since I was kicked out of French class for poor attendance (to this day I have no real explanation for my taking French as opposed to an upper-level Spanish class), I wasn't going to graduate with the rest of my class.

It was at this time that I received what I think has been the most valuable and timely advice that I have ever received in my life. It came from a woman who had previously been for me a somewhat distant romantic interest. Sandra and I started out secretly searching out each other's company and avoiding any embarrassing situation in which we would be caught by her brother Steve, my good friend. So it was with this backdrop that Sandra and I developed a secret and nurturing relationship. I had no way of knowing that this small piece of advice would change my life and our lives together. Sandra said that, if I were to take the GED, I could enroll in community college without the high school diploma. Well, frankly, the idea of spending any more time in a classroom wasn't particularly appealing, but, on the other hand, neither was the option of spending another year in Rochester High School or possibly working at a local garage. So I took the test and waited for the results.

Even with this somewhat coherent plan for the future, the final weeks at school were almost too much to bear. Nothing I could do would help me to graduate on time, and I had no idea what the results of the test I had taken would be.

At home my relationships with Mamá and Rosa were again strained. I consciously distanced myself from them because of my own feelings of failure. The last thing I wanted was to have Mamá get down on me about school, responsibility, and my future. For so long Mamá had put a great deal of faith in me as her last *pollito,* the smart one, the one that didn't cause her any trouble. So, as a buffer, whenever she asked how I was doing or when the graduation ceremonies would take place, I would change the subject immediately. I'm sure she knew what was happening all along, but she was giving me the chance to tell her the truth about what was happening in my life. I just couldn't. Time went on, and the unspeakable went unspoken.

Eventually, the big day came—Commencement. I tried to alleviate the pain of that day by drinking and rejecting the convention of Commencement while secretly wishing I were involved the whole day through. With this day and the institution it represented behind me, I settled down to the project of working fifty hours a week at a local shop to earn money for the next stage of my life.

El Ultimo Pollito Votó

A few weeks later I received the results of the GED; I passed the entire series of tests, some in the ninetieth percentile. Sandy and I immediately sent my application to Washtenaw Community College (which just happened to be in the same town where she went to school). The only thing left to do was prepare for the battle with Mamá. I knew she would not go for the idea of running off to Ann Arbor at all—why should she? I hadn't proven I was serious about school since the fourth grade—why start now?

It was on the twenty-eighth of August that Sandy and I registered for my classes. I remember that day distinctly, not just because it was the beginning of a new phase in my life but also because (somewhat ironically) it fell on Mamá's birthday. At the time I had very little idea of what was going down. Sandy amazed me. She knew everything. She walked me through the process of registration, financial aid, and finding an apartment. We returned home that day to celebrate Mamá's birthday and to tell her the "good" news. She reacted nothing like I expected her to, perhaps because she already knew I had already committed myself and that there was no turning back, or maybe because she before any of us saw whatever it was between Sandy and me. It was her eyes that spoke the loudest.

> Mijo, why are you leaving me to play in Ann Arbor? You've pushed me away from your life and now you want me to be happy you're going to school. *Dios te bendiga* (May God bless you).

As we packed the last of my things into Sandy's car, all my thoughts and feelings mixed wildly. I was excited to start a new life in the company of a woman I grew fonder of each day, but at the same time I grew tense at the thought of saying good-bye to Mamá. I remember exactly where she stood when she waved good-bye. That ride was the longest I've ever taken.

Sandy moved into a house with five other people; I moved into an apartment with three graduate students from Taipei. Initially, they were hesitant to take in someone so young, but the price of housing in Ann Arbor left them little choice. Together we shared a great deal, talking about our respective cultures, growing and learning together. I shared with them who I was, where Mamá was from, and what it meant to be Chicano in the United States. But when I described myself to them, I didn't feel the same way I felt when talking about my ethnicity to my Anglo friends. The fact that they were foreign to the United States and its prejudices allowed me to open up and describe myself more freely than I had ever been able to in the past. As I spoke to them of the history of my people—something I'd always known but never before thought about—I began to really internalize that history. In a sense their curiosity sparked my own. Never again could I deny it, never again would I care to.

I began to feel in control of my life and a real part of the educational process in which I was involved. Sandy took time out to help me study, showing a kind of care and interest in my performance I had never before experienced. I was in a completely new world—a world that respected my person and recognized and accepted me as a Chicano with no preconceived expectations. As if to underscore the changes I had gone through, I was approached by my counselor and asked to apply for a Hispanic merit scholarship, at the end of my first term. This was the first time in my life I had ever heard an educator use the term *Hispanic* in the same sentence with *learning* and *scholarship*. And the most beautiful thing of all was the fact that it was directed at me.

At the end of that first year I went home for the summer to work and be with Mamá. I needed desperately to begin to rebuild our relationship and to explain to her why I had left so abruptly. But Mamá and I saw little of each other this summer. I got a nine-to-five job working with kids, and Mamá was working afternoons again. On the weekends we would sit in her kitchen and share all that had happened since I had been away, and, of course, I would accompany her to Spanish Mass. Although the Church never held a real attraction for me, I was obliged to go with Mamá (she loves to go to Spanish Mass with her *pollitos*). Slowly, Mamá and I began to piece together the relationship I had all but abandoned as a teen. But still I found myself longing to return to Ann Arbor. I missed Sandy desperately. Again Mamá knew.

It was midsummer when I learned that my good friend Steve had applied to the local state school, Eastern Michigan University, and had been accepted. After a bit of deliberation with Sandy and Mamá, I decided to give a transfer a try. I accepted the challenge of transferring to Eastern more out of curiosity—I wanted to know if they would admit me simply on the basis of my having completed one year of community college—than out of sincere interest for the school. In the back of my mind was goal was still to transfer to the University of Michigan.

I was accepted for the Fall term. There were so many classes suddenly available to me that I didn't even know where to begin. I did what every incoming student shouldn't. I took those courses that were most challenging because I was confident that I could handle them. My first term grades were a slap in the face because I knew I was capable of much more; the previous year had proven that.

In my second term I began to solidify a career plan I had previously just thought of distantly. Because of my own awful experiences in primary and secondary school, I felt that I would be particularly well suited to teach kids and motivate those who were in the same situation in which I had once found myself. I knew the difference that a serious and sincere teacher could make, and with this in mind I plotted my course.

I enrolled in the Bilingual/Bicultural Education Program because I saw it as a way of effecting change by teaching young Latino students *en la lengua de sus padres* (in the language of their parents). I became completed engaged with the idea and became a strong advocate for Bilingual Education and bilingualism in general. My course work became focused on method and theory of Bilingual Education as well as my other academic interest, sociology.

Learning of Aztlán

It was at this point that I began to seriously explore Chicano history, something I had never been exposed to in public schools. I drew strength from so many of the things I read. And, more and more, I identified myself with the people who have struggled for so long and who have been oppressed—*los Chicanos*. I found so much to share and relate to in the poetry of Corky Gonzalez, short stories of Cherríe Moraga, the art of Siquieros, and the plays of Luis Valéz. I began to piece together the anger, frustration, and confusion I had internalized as a child. I read of Chicano Marxists, Brown Berets, and militant farm workers. At the same time sociology led me to readings of Karl Marx, Max Weber, and John Stuart Mill as well as to contemporary Leftist newspapers. I was angered by the fact that such powerful thinkers and provocative ideas had been kept from me. I felt as if the pages spoke to my experience; they grabbed me by the hand and said, "Listen, Chicano, this is your story. It speaks to your life and your people's lives—to the oppression of *tu Mamá* as a Chicana and then a worker. No one can hide it from you now." I read those pages to make up for lost time; I read a history that had once been stolen from me.

In time I became disillusioned with what bilingual education had become in practice. This revelation didn't come overnight. With the attacks that public education, particularly bilingual education funding, had undergone during the "Reagan revolution," what I was preparing myself for in theory, to be a bilingual educator, was unrealistic. Bilingual education had come to mean a transitional method of teaching children English as soon as possible with the express purpose of funneling them into English-only classrooms. There was no way I was going to let myself be a party to this. So, I set my sights higher, deciding that a graduate education would better serve my needs and the needs of my people. My intent was and is that of educating future educators to be culturally sensitive to youth in both method and practice.

With every day that passed I became a more confident and self-reliant person. Throughout Sandy was there beside me. As I grew as a person, so too had my relationship with her grown. Through the years we had grown closer and much more dependent on each other than either of us had ever been with anyone else in our whole lives. We shared the newness of our relationship as well as every other aspect of our lives together. Together we had mapped out one future—our future. And in the summer of 1988, when I received notice that I had been accepted to transfer to the University of Michigan, Sandy and I were married. Never before have I felt so whole. I am confident about who and what I am, the history and the power of my people, and the power of my love for Sandy.

A History of Survival: The Study of the Women in My Family

Max Gordon

Fighters

My mother's a fighter. She fought back her father, and she fought back my father; she fights her jealous boss who constantly undermines her work; she fought my teachers through grade school; she fought against her own anger consuming her; and she fought the man in college who tried to assault her. She fights depression and hopelessness.

When we were in the U-Haul place, I thought my sister would die. Literally. She somehow seems to melt inside herself with embarrassment whenever my mother confronts someone. She rolls her eyes and looks away, unable to believe that "it" is going to happen once again. She wishes her coat could hide her; she knows everyone is staring; and she's waiting for it to end. Once it does, she takes my mother by the arm and pulls her away. My mother is still distracted by the encounter.

"You can't just do that, someone might try to fight you," Alethea warns.

My mother nods her head knowingly. "I know. I know. But what else could I do?"

The man came in and went right to the orange U-haul counter. I suppose to him it didn't matter that there were several of us standing there waiting to be helped, that my mother was tired because she had worked all day, that we had already waited for twenty minutes on our feet because we were last in line and one of the workers had left to take a break. He was a man, he was white, so I guess that meant he was first in line.

"Excuse me," said my mother.

He was a huge man with biceps burgeoning from his tight T-shirt. He wore boots and a big mustache and a menacing frown and sunglasses. He looked away from the man behind the counter slightly, as if a small child had tugged at the side of his pants then resumed talking.

"Excuse me," said my mother. "That woman was before you, and then I'm after her. We've all been standing on line."

Once again the man looked distracted and didn't acknowledge the voice nor the looks of surprise on everyone's face. He leaned in closer to the clerk conspiratorially and pointed at one of the display boxes pictured above.

"You'll have to stand in line like everyone else!"

Now he was inconvenienced and pissed. He turned away from the counter with disgust and made his way to the back of the warehouse. As he passed my mother, his shoulder grazed hers and he murmured out of the corner of his mouth, "Fucking bitch."

"AND YOU'RE ANOTHER FUCKING BITCH!" my mother shouted back at him. My sister bobbed, and she reached for my mother. I watched the man leave the store, waiting for him to turn around and give in to a frenzy of violence. If the whole thing had been a movie, the other customers would have cheered and broken into a chorus of "For She's A Jolly Good Fellow," placing my mother on their shoulders and marking the day and her effort as a contribution for human rights. Instead, they stood, mouths agape or heads nodding in affirmation. (You know how these Black women are.)

My great-aunt Shirley tells a story. She sits at the table in her home, eating a plate of greens, dressing, yams, and chitlins. In her home she is queen. She is heavy, and she wears a housedress with a floral pattern. Her hair is short and thinning, and she doesn't wear her wig because we are family and it's her home and she's queen. When she laughs, her body rocks. She is frightening and wonderful all at the same time. She swallows her bite, smiles because her food is good and she knows it, and tells her story:

"I was on the bus, and I was dressed up that day, Lord knows what for, oh—." She shovels in another heaping bite. "I had just bought a brand new outfit with my money. I was working, and I was paying my own bills, and so I decided if I wanted a new outfit I was going to have one! And it was sharp too, a little blue suit with all the curves already built in and my cream-colored blouse and the white gloves and my hat. My gray hat." Aunt Shirley turns rosy with pride and attacks her food again.

"I bet you were something else," interjected my mother.

"I *was!*" Aunt Shirley frowned, disgusted that there could be any doubt in the matter. "Nobody was sharper, honey. And I was sophisticated, too. Had my attitude and didn't mind showin' it either."

She fumbles with condiments, washes down a tremendously big bite with a can of generic diet cola, and shuffles over to the stove for another helping. We sit around the table, the story still hanging on our expectant faces. She returns, tastes the food, and smacks her shiny lips with satisfaction.

"So, anyway, everyone on the bus is watching me. I mean *everybody.*"

"It's true," my mother interrupted. "When your Aunt Shirley was younger, all the men used to stop in the street and stare. When I was in—."

Aunt Shirley's fork pauses, and her face tightens. "How am I suppose to tell my story, Beryl, if you keep adding things?" She sighs and then continues with great effort. "Like I was saying, everyone was looking at me. So I made my way to the back, and there wasn't very many seats and I sure wasn't going to stand, so I sat down next to this poor white girl. I said hello and looked straight ahead. This girl had on a sorry white dress, wrinkled and dirty like it'd been rolled in the dirt, and her hair was greasy and stringy and her face had all kinds of smudges on it. I could even smell her. She was just as trashy as she could be, probably didn't have any drawers on either for that matter—."

"Shirl—," my mother chides gently and looks over at my sister and me with concern.

Aunt Shirley is exasperated and shouts, "Just wait a damn minute, Beryl, and let me finish! So, do you know what this girl has the nerve to say to me? I'm sitting there in my brand new outfit, my brand new gloves, and my best gray hat, and I can see her frettin' out the corner of my eye, just tremblin' and twitchin' and ready to die, and finally she turns around like she *just can't stand it anymore* and says, 'I ain't sittin' next to no dirty nigger.' Then she skips her little funky ass right off the bus. I said to myself, I can't believe that some poor white trash bitch is gonna have the nerve—."

"Shirley!" my mother shouts. "Listen to what you're saying!"

Aunt Shirley looked at my sister and me carefully and then

shrugged her shoulders, concentrating on the food. "Okay, but they gonna find out sometime."

My Aunt Cora was in the drugstore around the corner from where she lives. As soon as she entered the store, the saleswoman leaped from behind the counter and followed her to the back of the store where the toiletries were located. The woman's "may I help you?" smile didn't hide her "I'm watching you, thief" eyes that shifted back and forth and recorded each of my aunt's careful movements. "I'm fine," said my aunt, and the woman, hesitatingly, left her alone. After carefully making her selections, my aunt paid in cash and carried her purchases away from the cash register. At the door she felt something moving in her pocket and discovered a white hand flapping like a water-starved fish. The hand was attached to a burly white man with a mustache. She snatched the hand from her coat, exclaimed "help me, Jesus," and knocked the man away from her. Later she found out that he worked for the store; he thought she had stolen something and, rather than asking for her to empty her pockets, tried to empty them himself.

My Aunt Rachel was married to a man who beat her. He also drank. Her hair turned gray prematurely, and she went blind. My mother says it was gradual. Slowly, her eyesight became worse and worse. Yet, despite the demands the pain made on her body, all her troubles and worries never found her face. She still possesses a child-like warmth and acceptance and a full, toothy smile. She has trouble walking now. One of her daughters died four years ago in a car accident. The man who murdered her had been drinking, crossed the median of the road, and hit her and her friend. My cousin's name was Pamela. She was my age.

And both my mother and grandmother tell the story of my great-grandmother, a tough, religious, caring woman, who's done her best to raise five girls and a boy with the support of my great-grandfather, who worked in a factory for fifty years. She was hard, even mean sometimes, but she kept them out of trouble, and they left her house alive. And when her children were grown she took care of their babies. My mother tells a story about being a young girl and playing outside of her grandmother's house, wearing dresses and getting ashy knees and being called inside by a stout, cream-colored woman with nut-brown hair, diamond eyes, and Paul Bunyon arms—arms that made biscuits, dispensed needed whacks to behinds, and helped you hold tight when your world trembled at the sides. By the time I met my great-grandmother, she was someone else—unrecognizable, untrue to everything I'd been told about her, weakened, infirm, and idle. I never understood the importance of her life until now.

That Lady

There was talk as to whether or not the children would come to the wake. They played in the family room, keeping themselves busy because they were told to do so. When they tired of television and didn't feel like sitting anymore, they made a game and began chasing each other. Their laughter was heard by adults, who quietly talked in the kitchen, and it seemed somewhat out of place at such a sad time but was tolerated. What wasn't tolerated was when the laughter became joyous squeals and the radio was turned on.

"Don't make me have to come in there," Aunt Shirley's voice called out. "Quiet down and turn that music off!"

The laughter continued and someone "almost caught" screamed.

"You all hear me in there! I brought a belt in my purse, and I'll wear somebody out if I have to get off my chair."

Grandma Mae chuckled heavily and reached for another piece of pound cake. "You are so evil," she said. "You know you ain't got no belt. Why did you scare them like that?"

Aunt Shirley took her coffee cup to the sink. "Because they only listen from the behind. I don't know about yours, but I know my grandson. He don't mind. Acting crazy like that—I promised I'd wear their behinds out if they didn't act right when we was in the car. I'll do it!"

Laboriously, she sat back down and straightened the blue jacket to her suit. Even though she drank the coffee, her hands were still trembling, and she folded them carefully, one inside the other. She straightened her back and let go of her breath. He escaped from her like she had never exhaled before.

Aunt Rachel held onto her cane and giggled. "They're only babies. Why do you think you have to hit them, Shirley?"

Aunt Shirley raised her voice a little louder than she needed to. She busied herself with her purse, reached inside, and found her white gloves. "You all say that now, now that I put a little fear in them. Just wait till they tear up your new living room like they tore up mine with that game they playin'. You'll be after 'em, too, just wait."

Everyone laughed. Grandma Mae said, "Listen to her."

He came into the kitchen and found his mother's lap. She had a piece of pound cake in front of her that she hadn't touched. He picked at the delicate cake, kicking his legs under the table.

"Honey, don't," she whispered in his ear. "You're hurting me."

"How's my baby doing?" Grandma asked with a sweet chuckle, tickling him under the chin with her thick, wrinkled finger. "You wasn't getting into trouble, were you?"

"He sure was," said Aunt Shirley, giving him a dubious look. "Probably just finished tearin' up the place."

"Don't say that," Aunt Rachel admonished. She was cutting him another slice of the delicious cake. "He wouldn't do that, would you, honey?"

He shook his head. He took the cake from her, and Aunt Cora got up and got a glass of milk for him. "Where are your cousins, sweetheart?"

"Watching TV," he told her. His mother delicately stroked his hair.

"Why don't you go back and join them, honey? Mama's still talking, okay?"

"But I want to stay with you," he cried.

Aunt Shirley said sourly, "Look at him. Already he's a mama's boy." She clicked her tongue for emphasis.

"Shirley, don't say things like that!" Aunt Rachel said, exasperated. Her voice was soft and breathy and only turned harsh when she was really upset. All of a sudden a giggle erupted from her massive body, despite her attempts to stifle it.

"What's a 'mama's boy'?" he asked.

"It's a little boy who loves his mama." His mother planted a kiss on his forehead. "Now go find your sister. You're going over to Mrs. Anderson's house."

"Mrs. Anderson. Who's she?"

"A very nice woman that I know who is going to look after all of you while the older people are at the funeral. She said that she has games and a great big television, and, if you guys are good, she is going to take you to McDonald's."

"We aren't going to the funeral?"

Everyone seemed to look around and lower their heads. His mother said quietly, "Do you want to go to the funeral?"

He whispered, "I want to go where you're going."

"Well, I'm afraid it may scare you." She furrowed her brow with indecision.

His grandmother, as always, had the answer. She took another piece of pound cake, devoured it, and said with a mouth filled with crumbs, "The boy has no business going to a funeral. Just leave him here, Beryl!"

"Mae stay out it!" shouted Aunt Cora. She was the oldest and, by self-proclamation, the wisest and snapped out commands like a drill sergeant, a role she'd played with her sisters since childhood. My grandmother, the second child, always resisted her.

"I will not stay out of it! This is none of you damn business, Cora, so keep out!"

"Now she's going to start cursing," mumbled Cora.

His mother whispered in his ear, "Go get you coat," and lifted him gently from her lap. He rushed back into the family room where the others were lying in front of the television. His sister was asleep on the couch.

"Come on." He nudged her shoulders gently. "It's almost time to go. Wake up."

Rafael snuck up behind him. He gave him a push that sent him forward onto his sister. She let out a cry.

"Come on, there's no time for that!" he said. "We have to go!"

The others were gathered in the foyer. Socks were gathered, shoes put on, hair worked into acceptable styles, and finally coats were fastened. Michael rubbed his eyes. "I'm tired."

He helped his sister with her coat. Being six, and two and a half years older than she, he was expected to help.

His grandmother was still advising his mother. "I think you're making a mistake. Those children are going to be scared."

"Only if you keep talking, Mae! Why can't you stay out of it!" Aunt Cora snapped her mouth closed with finality.

His grandmother exploded with anger. "Look at who's telling me to stay out of it!" Her great face became indignant, and her thin eyes narrowed. "Cora, you are in everyone's business all the time."

"I have to be. You all don't handle things right!"

"What the hell does that mean?" shrieked Mae.

"Both of you shut the hell up!" Aunt Shirley stomped over to the front door and slammed it behind her. Just as quickly as she had slammed it, it opened again. "If anyone is going with me, you better come on!" She slammed the door behind her again, and the house rocked.

"I don't want to drive with her." Aunt Rachel fumbled for her jacket in the closet, put it on with the help of her daughter, Joy, and finally covered her head with an ornate black hat.

"You're going with me, Mama," Joy said tiredly. She took her son's hand, who was still half-asleep, and her mother's hand. Aunt Rachel could hardly see and needed her daughter's assistance.

"Shirley drives so crazy when she get angry." Aunt Rachel took tiny steps, as though she expected a wall to meet her at any moment.

"That's okay, Mama. I got you. Wake up, Rafael. You're hurting my arm." Joy barely had a chance to put on her own coat. The rest of the family followed behind her.

"Are we going to the funeral?" He grabbed at his mother until she was down to his level. "Why is everyone shouting? Why is Grandma so angry?"

"We are going to what is called the wake. That's when they show the body, but it's not the actual funeral. People just sign a book to show they came to pay their respects, and then they leave. The funeral is tomorrow. Your Grandma is sad because her mother died and she feels bad. If she hurts your feelings, just don't pay her any attention." His mother picked up his sister and they started out for the car. While they balanced themselves on the icy snow, he thought about whether or not he really wanted to go to the funeral. He thought about his great-grandmother's body and tried to remember how she had looked.

This was the woman we used to visit when we visited my grand-mother. Her house was big and mansiony and had lots of rooms—rooms that would have been great for exploring if they hadn't looked so old and smelled so funny. There was furniture covered in thick, rubbery plastic and lamps and other old-people things. The photographs on the mantle and on the tables were old, and the people in them looked as if they had been drawn like cartoons. There was something about the strange smell I didn't like.

We visited for too long. After excruciatingly long periods of time, after I had played every game I could think of that involved one person (my sister always became tired of my games and found a place to sleep), I collapsed wherever I was, every now and then begging my mother to let us go. She would nod, but her mind was on other things. Even she seemed different.

Everything in the house was curious. The kitchen was old and musty, and I wondered how anyone could cook food there and still have the appetite afterward to eat what she had prepared. There were stairs leading up to what I knew had to be heaven itself, even though my mother insisted there were only bedrooms upstairs. I didn't understand plastic plants or stale candy on coffee tables or doors with more than two locks or old records—but, then, I really didn't understand "that lady."

That lady smelled strange and wore light-blue dresses all the time that looked like pajamas. That lady wore hair that was white like thread and that I knew was not her own, and she had soft brown skin that would crumble if touched by hands that weren't gentle. I knew this because I was specifically told how to touch her and talk to her and hold her. I knew that she was fragile. She was also boring after a while because she just sat there.

I brought her a bowl of ice cream and sat and watched my mother help her eat it. It was like watching her feed Alethea when she was a baby. Then, while that lady savored the final taste that lingered in her mouth, my mother found a record and played it for her. That lady closed her eyes to the music of a gospel singer named Mahalia Jackson and sometimes would let a sound come wheezing out of her tired body. That lady began to make me angry because she constantly changed chairs and wanted to sit by the window one minute and then sit by the record player the next. She couldn't walk by herself very well and needed help moving from one chair to the next. (Often my Aunt Cora, who lived in a small apartment upstairs, took care of her.) When we had finished putting her in one chair, she would call us over to help her sit somewhere else. She couldn't seem to make up her mind. Once she even tricked me by placing deceptively delicious-looking but stale candy on her coffee table, which almost made me sick. The worst thing, by far, was that she commanded all of my mother's attention. I didn't like her, but I knew my mother did because she always had a sad look in her eyes when she spoke about that lady, and she cried whenever we went to visit. Once, as we watched that lady across the room, she said to me, "That is the woman who raised me. If it hadn't been for her, I never would have made it."

"What about Grandma?" I asked.

"Your grandmother was off. She couldn't take care of herself. So Vannie Lou raised me." She pointed at a picture of a young woman with a determined look that might have bordered on meanness. She seemed to scowl at the photographer, as if the last thing in the world she needed was to be bothered by someone wanting to take her picture. My mother continued. "She was tough. She wasn't perfect, and she made mistakes, but I always loved her. She was always there."

She looked at the picture while reflecting on the past, and I stared in astonishment. "That's her?" I looked from the picture to the soft bubble that sat hunched over in the chair. "I don't believe it!"

"She's old. She's lived a very long life." My mother whispered. "She's sick, too, and she probably won't be with us much longer."

That lady giggled when I told her about first grade, and she said something, but I didn't understand her. I was beginning to like her music and even her a little too when we had to go. We said good-bye to her and Aunt Cora, who left to buy groceries. My mother's good-bye was long and full of whispers. She stepped away finally, wiping her eyes and smiling a trembling smile. My sister and I each hugged that lady tight. Who knew her arms were so strong? She clutched me to her as if she were trying to squeeze something inside me. I felt the squishiness of her skin and its coolness. I felt very safe. Who knew that she had safe places, too?

We stood on the front porch and waved good-bye to her. She smiled and looked up at Aunt Cora, who held herself up stiffly.

The next year we heard that she had died.

The casket was a creamy pink like nothing he had ever seen before. The handles on the sides of the casket were a shiny gold, and involuntarily his hand went out to them. He stroked the handles delicately, completely amazed. Flowers sat on top of the casket as well as along its sides, in the foyer, and near the sign-in book his mother had told him about. When they arrived, she let him sign the register beside his name. She said it was important that the family know who had come.

His mother was crying softly, and he took her hand. They approached the casket together. She stepped away finally, but he couldn't. The handle was cool to the touch, and the casket was too smooth. He stood on his tippy toes to see. Inside the casket was a soft bed made of cushiony material. He wondered how much his great-grandmother could feel. There was a soft pillow for her head, and it looked like silk.

He came closer. Her skin was like he remembered, only now it was tighter, younger looking. Her face seemed so peaceful and serene, not like when she wanted to move out of her chair or when she had gas. Her hands were placed one on top of the other and she wore a ring on her right hand. The white hair that had been carefully placed was her hair, and he thought she looked beautiful. He wanted to touch her. He reached out to feel her hand and see what it was like . . .

A hand took hold of his, gently but firmly. "We don't touch the body," said my Aunt Cora carefully and guided him back to this mother. It was as though she appeared out of nowhere. Her face was without tears, without sentiment. She simply placed her hands together in front of her and stood beside the casket. His mother said her tears would be private ones.

Drawing Outside the Lines

People were lying about the sun. Someone had the nerve to suggest that it was only yellow. The teacher, that white lady with the big face that always gave him watery kisses and stroked his head until his neck bobbed, told him to use the yellow crayon. He protested because he had already used the yellow for most of the grass, the tip was already blunt, and, if he wanted to use it anymore, he would have had to peel the paper off, and everybody knew that peeling the paper off ruined the crayon. That pissed her off. She didn't appreciate him drawing the grass yellow.

She wrinkled up her doughy, chalky-white face so it looked like a fist. "What color is grass?"

He knew the kind of grass she was talking about. The green kind of grass that seemed to grow everywhere: boring grass—the grass that grew outside his apartment; the grass that was growing in the model picture she'd drawn for the class and proudly taped to the chalkboard.

"I don't think it's yellow," she said, sounding confused, like she really wasn't sure, so he told her.

"Yes, it is! I'm drawing that yellow grass that they have on the farm!" He ran his finger across his teeth several times with deliberation before selecting the orange crayon. He was about to attack the page, when she held his arm.

"Yes, but we aren't on a farm. We are drawing what our real houses look like. Do you have yellow grass in front of your house?"

Why was she talking like that? Why had she placed her biscuits-before-baking face so close to his? What did she care if his grass were blue? Maybe he was drawing a space house or somebody's house in heaven.

"Maxie, do you have yellow grass at your house?"

She looked at him very carefully as though everyone's lives depended on the right response. He concentrated on the lines on her face, on the deep look of concern in her eyes, an almost tragic concern.

He nodded.

She sighed heavily and shook her head, rising from an awkward position and groaning because her knees hurt from having knelt beside him for too long. She had given up. He, having lost interest in her, put back the orange crayon. He changed his mind about the orange and decided on white.

He felt a hand gently touch his shoulder. Emily was standing beside him. She had long blond hair in delicate wisps that teased the edges of her face. Sometimes her face was smudged with dirt because she always played in the sandbox during recess. The sand wasn't the reason her face was dirty; while she was playing, her nose would sometimes run, and she would sniffle and wipe it with her hand. On windy days her golden hair tossed about, carelessly licking the side of her face. Constantly disturbed, she would push it aside, wipe her nose, and smear the mucus into her hair.

He liked her. She always hummed when she was by herself and didn't care if no one wanted to play with her. When she drank the punch at snack, her lips turned red.

"You color better than me," she said quietly.

She presented her picture. The colors were right: green for the grass, brown for the house, and yellow for the sun. Obviously, she had tried. There was even red pen underneath her coloring where Mrs. Peterson had helped her draw the hard parts.

"You draw okay." He concentrated on the purple he was adding to the sky.

"No, I don't." She presented her drawing again, this time with more force. "Look!" she insisted, "I ruined it!"

It was true, she had ruined it. He could see the crayon line where she had moved outside the confines of the red pen; panicked because there was no way to right her mistake, she'd tried to cover it up with a darker color and only succeeded in creating an ugly blemish that marred the entire work. Finally, in a fury she had scribbled across the entire page. Her picture was hidden under a conflagration of orange gashes that made it look like a picture of a house in hell.

"If you don't like it, start over," he advised.

She made her way back to the other coloring table. He was finished. Admiringly, he held the paper in front of his face, letting the fluorescent light come through. His picture came to life. Mrs. Peterson was obviously displeased; with disgust, she snatched her own picture down from the board. He didn't care; he knew he had drawn it his way.

His lesson had come from the time when his mother had purchased a Cinderella coloring book and a box of sixty-four crayons. At the preschool they only had one big ugly cardboard box filled with crayons stripped of their paper, crayons with teeth marks in them, melted-down crayons, crayons that had the color of other crayons mixed in with theirs from being stirred about in the box too long, and crayons too tiny to grasp effectively. It seemed like he spent hours rummaging through the box looking for the colors he needed. He hated those crayons, so his mother had gotten him his own box of eight. Now she'd brought home this box. He never knew there were sixty-four colors! He and his mother sat down that afternoon and colored. He was very proud that he had managed to stay within the lines and had incorporated several different colors into his drawing. He peered over at her drawing every now and then, but mostly he tried to hide his so that he could surprise her.

He finished before she did and watched over her shoulder. His mother's picture looked as if Cinderella would leap up from the pages. Her dress was a tapestry of colors, even more than the box provided. In some places she'd switched colors even before she'd come to a line. He was astonished. The colors were blended, scratched at, and smoothed together to produce mesmerizing effects. Cinderella's face was hazelnut-brown, and her hair was full and black. She had added an Afro and earrings, and now she was working on Cinderella's shoes.

"Wait!" he protested. "Why did you do that? The Cinderella in the book that we read at school is white."

"Mine's Black." His mother extracted a pink color to add nails where they hadn't already been drawn.

"Why are you adding things that aren't even there? Why did you draw her skin like that?"

She had drawn her prince a pea-green color. He was dissatisfied. The peach skin of his prince didn't seem to come alive like the skin in her drawing. She said simply, "They just provide the guidelines. I always do my own thing when I color. I tried to find a coloring book with Black people, but they didn't have one. So we have to make our own."

He was astonished. "But look, you didn't even stay in the lines."

"I didn't want to," she replied. "Sometimes you have to draw outside the lines. It's your picture. Draw it however you like."

When he looked up at the sky, he saw white. The sun was so white it made his head throb. Sometimes it looked a little yellow when it was starting to get late and the sky got darker outside. But even then it was much more orange than any other color. There was a little blue in the sun and some black, he was sure, but it wasn't enough so that everyone could see it, only those who had made a careful study of the sun and tried to stare it down a couple of times knew this. Thus, being an authority on the sun, he would not tolerate anyone who drew a piece of butterscotch candy and called it the sun, nor would he allow one to draw a circle and call that the sun either.

The sun didn't look like a circle to him, although, true, there was a little bit of roundness to its shape. There were also parts that ventured out and others retreated. Constantly venturing and retreating. Constantly being a shimmering light.

That's what the sun looked like.

First Lesson

The news had already reached the hallway and most of the eighth grade by the time class started. There were whispers and giggles and gasps of shock as all of the students gathered around the cast list.

"Of course, I knew Jamie would get Peter Pan. I knew it."

"Can you believe it? Tara didn't get anything!"

"Oh, no! She is going to be so pissed!"

I noticed that no one had congratulated me upon my entering the classroom. I was positive, however, that jealousy had stifled their praise, as it had in the past. I made my way to the front of the classroom, careful not to appear too confident or secure, and prepared to reveal just enough surprise at seeing my name beside Jamie's. The surprise on my face was genuine when I saw my name was nowhere near hers. I finally discovered my name at the bottom of the cast list.

"Look, Max! You got cast! Congratulations!" Someone was grabbing at my arm and pumping it up and down as though water was expected to spew forth from my open mouth. I allowed myself to be manipulated until my arm began to throb. I withdrew it and slammed my mouth closed in disgust. "Thank you."

I started to make my way from the group. Everyone crowded in tighter, making it impossible to move. It was as though they wouldn't allow me to leave the sight of my failure. I looked at the cast list one more time to make sure I'd read it right. I had. The part that I had wanted and had known was mine had been given to someone else. And I was to play the part of a pirate. Pirate #6. I had never been the number 6 of anything in my entire life.

I gathered my things and the remnants of my pride and made it to the door to the choir room. I bumped into Sam Matthews. He looked beyond me at the group of people approaching him. It was like fighting back a stampede. The girl who had congratulated me accidentally elbowed me in the stomach en route to Tom. I yielded and managed to escape into the hall. I listened to their praise and delight that he had gotten the lead, listened to how much he deserved the part, how right he was for it, and what a great job he'd do. I even listened to someone tell him that he had done so well at the open auditions that there had been no competition. That was all I could listen to. I left, miserably.

"Sam Matthews got Captain Hook?" My sister asked incredulously. "I don't understand."

She was sitting on a bar stool next to the kitchen counter. Furiously, I chopped up carrots for dinner. My mother would be home from work any minute. Every now and then Alethea would slip a carrot from the slowly growing pile.

"Can't you wait until dinner!" I dashed the carrots into a bowl of cold water. "How am I ever going to finish dinner if you eat them all?"

"Don't yell at me!" she shouted back. "It's not my fault you didn't get the part you wanted!" She walked over and got a knife out of the dishwasher. "Did you do everything like I told you to do?"

"Yes," I said tiredly, throwing her an irked glance. "I took your suggestions." The night before my audition, I showed Alethea my routine. She informed me that I was "doing it all wrong" and volunteered her direction. She stayed up very late, putting aside her fifth-grade homework, and helped me "find Captain Hook." We had both worked together, and now we shared my disappointment equally.

I savagely ripped apart a head of lettuce. "It's just not fair. I saw his audition. He was horrible. At first I couldn't believe that he'd even bothered. He seemed so disinterested! He never came to the practice meetings, and I'm positive that he didn't even get the music until the day of auditions." I took the pork chops out of the refrigerator and yanked off the packaging plastic, balling it up in my fist. "You should have seen him. He acted like he couldn't have cared less. He didn't hit one note right. Ask anybody. Everyone was laughing."

I threw up my hands, and a pork chop slid onto the floor.

"You're going to have to eat that one," Alethea said, wrinkling her face.

I washed it off carefully.

Alethea stepped down from the stool. "I'm sorry you didn't get the part you wanted, but at least you got something," she reminded me.

But I didn't just want something. It all seemed much more complicated than that.

I don't know why I felt empowered enough to confront my choir teacher. Many times in my life I had been afraid to say what I thought for fear of being punished—why should being in eighth grade make it any different? Perhaps it was because I felt so strongly that I had been wronged. If the role had gone to someone less arrogant, perhaps the whole thing could be overlooked. But Sam pimped now, surrounded at all times by his coterie of admirers, all of them more than willing to do anything he asked. By being in the play, many of them finally had something in common with the most popular kid in school. Most took advantage of the opportunity to ingratiate themselves.

Perhaps if I hadn't worked so hard and involved my family in my attempt to get the lead, I could have kept quiet. It might have been easier to do so if I hadn't seen Sam fumbling around during his audition, looking for words, searching for gestures, and generally fucking up the entire thing. But that wasn't the case. I was there when it was time for his reading, and he could barely read the words, much less find the character. I saw him charm his way through the audition. I dissolved with jealousy and bitterness. I blamed myself for being hurt. I should have seen it coming. I should have known he had the part the minute the choir teacher helped him throughout the song, waiting patiently for him to find his place, encouraging him, overwhelming him with praise while others went unappreciated and trudged out of the room discouraged. I wanted justice, but I also considered that perhaps I had misjudged the situation. I decided to give the play a try and to give Sam a chance. I didn't want to be bitter. Bitterness took too much energy, was impossible to camouflage, and was costing me friends.

I was highly aware of the fact that the only other Black kids in the play were pirates, and the three of us shared a couple of insignificant lines. We often commiserated about our small parts and heavy plights. We laughed at the others because they were awful and we knew we could do better in our many retaliatory private performances outside of rehearsal (and often we did), and we laughed at Mrs. Franklin, the director. Our laughter mattered to no one, and often at rehearsal we were both insignificant and completely interchangeable. When I began to fully comprehend how really expendable we were, rage boiled inside of me, coming up in my throat and then retreating, hot and thick. I was unable to contain it when Mrs. Franklin directed the pirates to carry Captain Hook, "like the Egyptians," each grabbing a limb and lifting him up onto our shoulders. I didn't remember any Egyptians doing that, but I followed her direction. The day of my last rehearsal came when Sam grabbed hold of my short cropped Afro for support and said, "Dude, this is great. Stay right there. There's enough friction from your hair to keep me from slipping."

After choir class I knocked on the enormous green door that separated Mrs. Franklin's smoke-filled office from the classroom. She told me to come in, and I did, apprehensively, hearing the door shut behind me.

"What can I do for you?" she asked warmly. Her voice was heavy from years of smoking, and the habit had also hardened her face. She wore a great deal of makeup and was notorious for having a visible line where her foundation ended and her real skin color began. Her ornate and zealous fashions consisting of greens, oranges, and browns only magnified her strange and frightening personality. I felt frightened and wanted to turn around and run. I didn't like the door being shut.

"I just wanted to tell you," I tried to find the words that I had so carefully practiced. "I'm quitting choir, and I'm leaving the play. I have a transfer form here. All I need is your signature."

She got up from her desk and came toward me. "Is there a problem?" She looked at me gravely. "What's wrong?"

Suddenly I felt very small. I took a deep breath. "I am not satisfied with the program here, and I have decided to pursue my interests elsewhere." Every moment was smothering me, and her perfume was cheap and unbearable.

"Why aren't you satisfied?" She furrowed her brows and concentrated on my face.

I melted under the scrutiny but met her gaze. "Because I feel that here at Rhode there is one type of student who is involved in the theater program, and, unless one fits that type then they are discouraged from participating. I feel more comfortable where a person's input is respected and more people are involved."

She put a hand to her bosom, and her chin lowered in complete astonishment. She shook her head vigorously, suggesting that I couldn't have been more mistaken. "I hope you don't really believe that because it just isn't true."

True or not, I handed her my transfer form, and she signed it and handed it back. And I never saw her again. Standing outside her green door, clutching my own hand to my chest, I realized that I had done something—however, I wasn't sure exactly what it was.

It was still early in the year, and a lot of things hadn't yet been finalized. In class we were still studying for placement tests. We took English tests and practice tests in math; we read in social studies and took more tests. The whole time I felt like I was on trial.

Because it was eighth grade there were many factors influencing our lives. Most people were thinking about high school and how hard it was going to be. Others relished in the honor of being the upper-class people of our school and for the first time in three years being able to dictate rather than take orders. Everyone had different priorities.

My goal was to get into Advanced Algebra. In some ways I wasn't too worried because I had always been on an accelerated track in most of my classes. Still I had doubt because most teachers were a little reticent about placing eighth grade students in algebra—something about the stress level. I knew I would have to do very well on my placement test to be placed in the class.

During the test I made a mistake and allotted too much time for a certain section. When Mr. Currin called time, I had several problems that I hadn't finished but would have been able to. I turned my test in, feeling confident that the ones I had finished were correct. We waited for several days for the results.

When the results came, I found out that I had just missed the mark. The score to get into algebra was forty, and I had gotten a thirty-seven. I couldn't believe it at first. I even approached Mr. Currin and made sure he had called out the right number.

"Yes," he confirmed, "you're in pre-algebra."

This was a greater disappointment than what had happened with the play. Algebra was everything. I knew it was going to be exciting.

Everyone said that, when Mr. Currin really got involved with his teaching, the class was like a party. The algebra books were a shiny, new brilliant-looking red, while the pre-algebra books were torn, used, and in poor condition. I looked at my "new" pre-algebra book. On the front cover was an ugly-looking spaceship with a man inside waving. I was destined for failure.

The classes were structured so that those students "smart enough" to be in algebra also had the same English and science classes. Those in pre-algebra and remedial math were mixed in together.

I tried to talk to Mr. Currin, but my courage seeped out of me like air from a punctured balloon. He was a small man, but I felt he was also a violent one and his heavy voice frightened me. I mentioned that I had really come close to the required score and that if he'd just give me one chance, I'd work so hard . . .

"Sorry, Gordon. You weren't the only one. If I have to choose between taking a chance of someone failing and letting someone get a better foundation in pre-algebra, I think it's best that they stay in pre-algebra. You know algebra can be stressful. Let's see how things go for awhile."

In pre-algebra I sat in the back of the classroom. I didn't say very much and didn't try to interact. My fury made me mute. I just scribbled in my book and didn't say anything. When Mr. Currin came in and got angry with the class for not listening, not doing its homework, and talking in class, I didn't internalize any of it. I wasn't a part of them. All of them, including Mr. Currin, made me sick to my stomach.

The work was easy. I began to get headaches. Potential seemed to be leaking from me, but I couldn't do anything to conserve it. Mr. Currin saw me seething and slapped me on the back with a hearty chuckle, saying, "Don't worry, Gordon. Just give it a couple of weeks."

I knew it would be too late in a couple of weeks.

Meanwhile, the algebra students flaunted, flitted, sported their books and their attitudes, and made it very clear that I was not a part of them. Oddly enough, I had been placed in the highest social studies group, a decision based solely on my academic ability (which I had already demonstrated). I had all of the "good students" in that class but none of the others. I noticed a difference, and I envied these students. They were the elite.

One day at lunch I was talking to a kid I knew about class and how algebra was coming. (If I couldn't be in it, I could at least talk about it.) We had never really talked to each other before because George really didn't talk much with anyone. His indifference intrigued me. When I asked him about the class, he told me that he really enjoyed algebra and that it wasn't half as difficult as Mr. Currin had made it out to be. I wondered whether or not I wanted to continue to talk to him. I had somehow managed to sublimate my anger before, but now I could feel it rising again.

"How's pre-algebra?" he asked.

I knew he was being polite, but I didn't feel it was any of his business. I hated the way he seemed to stress the "pre."

"Fine," I groaned. "I've already got a ninety-nine average. I think I should be in there with you. I can't believe he won't let me in. I just missed the mark by a couple of points."

"I'm surprised," he said. "I got a thirty-eight, and he told me to take it." He shrugged his shoulders. "I don't really care about math one way or the other. It's okay, I guess. I'm surprised he didn't let you in."

"Do you want me to talk to your teacher or not?" my mother asked, exasperated.

I took a deep breath. I could feel her getting frustrated at me so I tried to be delicate. "I just don't want you to tell him off, Mom."

My mother exploded. "What do you think I am? I'm not going to beat the man up. I'm just going to talk to him!"

We were in my parents' bedroom when I told my mother what had happened in math class. She was a little upset with me that it was the first she had even heard of what was going on. "Why didn't you tell me sooner?" she demanded.

"I wanted to handle it by myself. I didn't know he let some people in. I thought he wanted everyone to get a strong foundation. But I've been doing so well in pre-algebra. By the time he gets around to switching me, it will be too late." I had tried to appear calm, but panic had ruptured my voice.

"Those goddamn racist teachers. Nothing's changed. They were pulling that same bullshit with Black children when I was growing up. I ought to go up there and kick that man's ass!"

"That's what I mean!" I'd gone to her in complete desperation. "I want you to talk to him, but, please, don't cuss him out!"

My mother laughed at this remark and responded very coolly. "I am not going to cuss your little math teacher out. When I talk to him, I will be very professional. My God, when have you ever seen me cuss someone out? I may say things about them in my own home, but I never..."

"Okay, okay, I'm sorry." I felt the whole conflict churning inside my stomach. For three weeks I had been plagued by strange diseases and ailments—all math-related.

"If you want to come, you can. We will both talk to him. I'll call him when I get to my office."

The meeting with Mr. Currin was pleasant. Of course, he completely understood how I felt, but he explained to mother the trauma of being in a math class over one's head. He preferred to keep students with marginal scores in the classes in which they were most likely to succeed. Feeling that his explanation had sufficed, he began to stand, as if the conference was over.

My mother didn't move. Actually, she began to remove her coat. "Mr. Currin, I am aware that many students have problems when they are placed in classes over their heads. I do not feel, however, that this is the case with Maxie."

Mr. Currin looked over at me.

"He told me that the algebra class is the largest class that you have, and most of the students were in his math class last year."

Mr. Currin concentrated on my mother. "Yes, yes, well, this is true. It's a very large class. The selection process involved all the students taking a placement test, and only those that got a score considerably above forty were placed in that class. We made very few exceptions." He was shaking his head vigorously.

"But exceptions were made?"

"Not really,...but there might have been a few." Mr. Currin tugged at his sweater and laughed nervously. "Max did talk to me about moving into the algebra class at one point, but we were waiting until we had a better idea of what his work was going to be like."

Don't try to implicate me, I thought.

My mother crossed her legs. "And how has that work been?"

"Well, ah, let's see—." His desk was cluttered with papers and books, and he stirred around a bit before producing a manila folder lying underneath his coffee cup. "I'm a little behind." He giggled. "This early in the year I get sent all kinds of materials and new books, and the piles just rise and rise!"

My mother shared his laughter. "I taught at Eastern before I became a consultant," she said. "I remember very well."

"You taught at Eastern, really?"

"Well it was several years ago, but, yes, I did. I don't think I saw the top of my desk all year."

"I know what you're talking about."

Their laughter subsided, and Mr. Currin carefully withdrew a sheet from his folder. He nodded and passed it to my mother.

"He's done very well." Mr. Currin smiled at me. "Ninety-nine average . . . impressive."

"Mr. Currin—." My mother moved into a more comfortable position and carefully placed her hands in her lap. "I'm sure you are fully aware that institutional racism holds back many Black students. Early in their academic careers, they are denied the chances that many white students are given. This creates disparity, of course, because a lot of times minority students have to work harder."

Mr. Currin's eyes were riveted on my mother. He nodded up and down. "Oh, I know. I know."

"Therefore, when a Black student manages to transcend racism and excel academically, it is almost a miracle!" She smiled. "Are there any other Black students in the class?"

Well, actually, . . . Yes! There is one Black girl . . . female . . . Cheryl." He looked over at me for confirmation.

"I thought so. Either very few or none at all. Mr. Currin, I wouldn't be here if Maxie and I didn't have confidence in his work. I think what we need to do is see if algebra is right for him. I am concerned that he may not find pre-algebra challenging, and, as parents and educators, we do want students to be challenged."

Mr. Currin nodded and smiled. "Sure, I have no problem with that. Great! If you want to give it a try, then let's go for it!"

My mother turned to me. "Do you have anything you want to say, honey?"

I looked at her and then at Mr. Currin. His smile was beginning to tremble at the sides.

"I just want a chance. If I get C's or D's then I'll take the class over next year in high school. I just want a chance."

My mother shot me a look of disapproval then turned back to Mr. Currin, who said, "I didn't know he felt that way. My concern as a teacher is that each child has a firm foundation in math. Many of them don't do well in this algebra class; then they get to high school and find themselves in way over their heads. But if he is prepared to take it again if he doesn't do well, then—wonderful." Then to me he said, "You can trade your book tomorrow, and we'll see about changing your schedule."

My mother stood. "Thank you very much, Mr. Currin, for your time, and, if you have any concerns, please give me a call. Good afternoon."

I shut the door to Mr. Currin's classroom, and we made our way down the corridor. My mother smoothed the wrinkles in her dress. "That asshole," she mumbled with disgust. "He knew what he was doing. You should have been in that class from the very beginning."

I sighed with relief. "I'm just glad it's over."

"Why did you say, 'If I get C's and D's I'll take the class over?'" She turned and stopped in the middle of the hallway. "You have no intention of getting C's. You've never had a D in your life! Where did that come from? Why would you ever want to take the class again in high school?"

"I just didn't want him to be concerned about my progress," I told her.

"Look, that man doesn't give a damn about your progress, or you would have been in that class in the first place. You just worry about yourself and do the best you can."

My transition wasn't as easy as I thought it would be. I didn't have any more problems with Mr. Currin; he had met my mother. But most of the people who had constantly reminded me that I wasn't in algebra, who had acted as if they possessed a great esoteric knowledge that I didn't have, were not prepared to find me in their class the next day.

After the morning break on my first day in algebra, I remained in Mr. Currin's classroom. As the other students made their way to their science and English classes, algebra students began to fill the room. My arch algebra rival, Corrie, tapped me on the shoulder. "You'd better hurry. You're going to be late for class."

"I'm in class." I sat my behind down firmly in the chair to emphasize my point. Her face was astonished. She laughed. "Come on," she said viciously, "wishing isn't going to make it so!"

Others were beginning to stare.

I was finished with her. I took out my pencil and my new notebook and waited for Mr. Currin to come into the classroom. Around me I heard whispers. "What's he doing? He's not in this class now, is he?"

Mr. Currin came in, his walk brisk and energetic. At first I wondered if it was the same man. His manner was so different from the languid, pathetic way he dragged himself into pre-algebra class. I felt like I was embarking on a new adventure. The class exchanged laughter with him, and he joked about coffee stains on his tie. We were like an audience and he the comic. When he met my eyes, he looked as though he'd never seen me before.

Dear Lord, I thought. I dreamt the whole thing.

He paused in mid sentence, walked over to the cabinet, and pulled out a beautiful new red algebra book like someone would pluck a choice apple from a tree. Then he walked over to me, we exchanged books, and he continued his story in front of the class. No introductions, nothing. There wasn't any need. I knew every face in that room, and, if I hadn't recognized one, I knew it now because everyone was staring at me. Mr. Currin started class. I opened my notebook and began my first lesson.

Mirrors

There is something wrong with the mirrors here. Of course, they are intact, and, after the Puerto Rican cleaning woman has polished them, they twinkle at the corners, blinking like newly awakened eyes opening to streams of sunlight. The mirrors make black curly hair, tight and spunky, look tired and unkept—nappy, if you will. Lips look fat and juicy like dill pickles soaked in salt, or they appear dry and parched, begging for water. Clothing sags and loses its freshness. The colors appear mismatched, lack fashion, and drape as they would on a hanger—loose and unmindful. He has just bathed, yet he is positive that he can smell himself. He is perfumed, deodorized, gelled, mouthwashed, Odor-Eatered, after-shaved, and delicately lotioned. Ironically, perhaps, all of these smells combined form a funk, unlike the smell of his recently washed body. Already his mouth feels pasty. Gum takes care of that but must be replaced regularly, or it too will provide an exhausted smell one might find offensive.

The greatest crime of the mirrors is what they do to the skin. Black skin. No matter how much soap one uses, the skin looks dirty, lifeless, and greasy. Black skin may glisten after a fresh washing, emerging from the towel pink at the edges and ready for a delicate patting dry, but then something happens. The skin dries and darkens and uglies.

His class is in ten minutes. In his daily hygiene regimen he has included a new facial scrub. His mother sent the scrub because he was having problems with acne. It smells nice. He reads the shatter-proof jar: "Scrubs away dead skin that blocks pores." He doesn't follow the directions and uses too much and scrubs too hard. Then he douses his face with water almost too hot to touch and rises from a fog of steam. After scrubbing his face, he applies the cream. The cream is lighter than his skin tone, and he must apply it carefully or it will be obvious. The peroxide in the cream burns when applied, but he bears it because he can feel the dead skin peeling away. The regimen ends with the application of his own prescribed acne medicine. It burns a little too, but he knows his skin is tough as leather. He can afford a little burn for clearer skin. He can feel the ugly, dead skin peeling . . .

Soon he can see it, too. His skin peels near the eyes. Some also peels underneath the lips and above the chin. His forehead peels also. A little fearful, he changes his daily hygiene regimen. Only three scrubbings a day, and only after meals, before the oil can clog his skin. His prescribed medicine could be applied every other day, he decides. The cream remains the same as always; he has come to depend on its lighter shade for tone.

Although he spends a few minutes each morning applying vaseline to the burned and chafing parts of his face, still he notices an improvement. His skin doesn't shine like it used to in the past, and his brown cheeks have taken on a rosy hue. He never thought it possible before that skin like his could glow.

Since he already spends at least one hour a day in front of the mirror tending to his skin, he begins to experiment with different ways he can hold his face.

He wrinkles his nose and frowns and smiles. He is embarrassed when people come in to use the bathroom and see him making faces at himself in the mirror. He decides to get up in the middle of the night and practice when everyone is asleep.

In front of the mirror he sucks in his cheeks and holds them until his face begins to ache. He bites back his full lips until the lips in the mirror look thinner, or at least not as big. He begins to chastise himself for having such big lips, sentencing himself to more hours of arduous facial practice. After his lips are acceptable, he begins the challenge of changing his nose; he has been looking forward to it. He wrinkles and crinkles it, touches and pinches it, fondles it, and even picks at it (perhaps scratching the inner wall and making it smaller from within). To his complete delight he finds that, with an arrogant lift of an eyebrow and the lowering of his lips, he can lessen the harshness of his features.

Still, he is dissatisfied. He turns back to the creams. His skin hasn't been peeling as much, and he replaces the scrub, which is too abrasive, with water and alcohol treatments. The first time he washes his face with the concocted solution he feels his skin tighten and the blood rush to his cheeks. He begins to wash his face even more frequently because, in the cafeteria, they are serving even greasier food. Someone compliments him.

He notices that his skin is beginning to feel a little like sandpaper. The peeling comes back, only worse. His skin crusts, and he feels ashamed because he has to walk around with it showing. Vaseline doesn't help; it only makes his face look greasy, and *he can't look greasy.* The acne cream helps some of the time, but it hurts too much to apply it. When he touches his face, it throbs. Every now and then it looks orange with red splotches. When his skin puckers and pits and bags and wrinkles like the skin of an elephant, he thinks about going to see a doctor. He refuses to go to class, and he stops answering the door. All he can do is stand in front of the mirror, look at his ruined face, and soften it with tears.

This is when the lying deceitful mirrors finally decided to tell the truth—and, Jesus, do they have a truth to tell.

He makes his way to health services, bundled up in a heavy scarf that hides his face. He feels like a fool in the waiting room, still wearing the scarf. When his name is called, he disappears into the doctor's office, and, when the examination is over, he rushes back to this room and calls his mother. She comes to visit, surprised at the urgency in his voice. When he greets her at the door, he is wearing the scarf around his head. He feels like a mummy as he gently unwraps it from his face.

Her breath stops short for a moment, and she furrows her brows with concern. Her voice is a whisper. "Baby, I just don't understand. What happened?"

He shakes his head, unable to speak out at first. "All I wanted to do was wash my face," he chokes out and lowers his head in shame. "If you only knew how dirty it was."

Fighters

I'm a fighter. I fought my father, I fought my teachers in grade school, and I fought the racist white boy in fifth grade who called me a "nigger." Now it is I who fights the salesclerks and restaurant owners. (No, I would rather not sit by the kitchen, the receptionists, and all of the other white faces behind white counters). Daily I fight feelings of rage, desperation, and hopelessness that open up in front of me like trapdoors when I least expect it. I fight self-hatred; I fight white hatred; and I fight my feelings of hatred toward whites. Most of the time I feel like I'm fighting myself.

Someone lied to me. They told me that everything was fair, that people are protected by the Constitution, that we all have a right to free speech, that we cannot discriminate, that we are all equal but different, that white and Black are the same, that there is nothing to fear but fear itself, that Adam and Eve were the first people on Earth, that the meek shall inherit the Earth, that if you work hard enough you can get what you want, that everyone has the same opportunities, that those people who are on top are the most competent, that justice is blind, and that everyone is innocent until proven guilty. For many, these are the words that have built a nation. For me, they are anchors keeping me underwater.

(I imagine being underneath a body of water, just below the surface, high enough to feel the sunlight on my face and see what exists above. I imagine drowning just below the surface—high enough to believe I can save myself, high enough to expect to be seen by someone else and eventually saved. I imagine myself swimming with all my strength and never rising.)

I have always been warned about white people. White children will play with you and then leave you behind when their real friends come along; white people will explain basic things to you, like you're a baboon. White people will befriend you out of guilt and display you proudly when it is time to show everyone that they have a Black friend. White people have the power to kill you. White people know subtle ways to make you hate yourself. White people will laugh at your own culture and then steal it, rename it, and stab you in the back. Don't trust them.

This sounds a lot like racist doctrine. For me, growing up as a Black child constantly vulnerable to whites, it was a survival kit.

(I remember when "Officer Bob" came to visit our elementary school. All the white kids leapt and cheered because Officer Bob was a real police officer. The teacher reminded us that Officer Bob was our friend. I knew better. I knew that the gun those little white kids were delicately poking at was the same gun that could take me out of this world and had taken out others like me.)

At the same time I was always told to respect everyone, love anyone, and remember that, for all the evil whites in the world, there are some who can be just as loving as another family member. There are also Blacks, I was told, who will cut your throat in a second, and they are sometimes more hateful than some whites are. Be careful—and only judge people by who they are.

I've tried to live by all of the advice I've been given. But I realize that things, however minimally, have changed. Some of the experiences aren't the same; some of the old rules don't apply. How could I say to my parents, who had lived through the civil rights movement and histories of their families, "My God, you were right, most white people in this country are racist!" How could they understand my genuine surprise, disappointment, and dismay? Often I felt that they couldn't and carried alone the burden of having misjudged the white people around me, knowing that, if I'd only listened, history would have told me so. But things aren't the same. And everyday I give myself revised advice, build a new survival kit, and make up new rules.

I tell a story. My story is about a boy who comes to a predominantly white university and feels ashamed when he looks in the mirror. He gradually, without realizing what he is doing, mutilates his face. My story is only an allegory, and yet it happens all the time.

My Constitution for Self-preservation

I guess all this means that I feel tired.

I am tired of being judged by white people who have decided I want to be white because of my aspirations and endeavors.

I am tired of being judged by Black people who have decided that I am not Black enough by their standards.

I am tired of sexist men, of every culture, who degrade and debase women and who take advantage of those who are economically and physically less powerful.

I am tired of being afraid of groups of white men who act as if the world is their playground, or toilet, or video game. I am tired of being guided off the sidewalk by them or made to travel out of my way for them. I am tired of "beautiful" people who flaunt their blue eyes and "good hair." And rich people who spend money with no compunction and who become defensive when reminded about their privileged position. I am tired of picking up after these people, and I am tired of compensating for them. I am not expendable. I will not be taken advantage of any longer.

I am tired of questioning my right to exist and to be happy. I am tired of explaining my Blackness and my cultural differences. I am tired of chopping myself into bite-sized morsels for whites who find me too much to digest at once. No longer will I cut their meat for them because they cannot make a transition into the complexities of my life as a Black man—and, oh! contrary to popular belief, there are complexities.

I am tired of dispelling people's preconceived ideas about Black men. I am tired of quoting Shakespeare to prove that I have had a good education. I am tired of trying to prove that affirmative action isn't the only reason I'm here.

I am damn tired of apologizing for being angry, and I am tired of looking for a definition of myself in other people.

I haven't always felt this way. Many things changed when I came to this university. This year I have listened to speakers and have attended rallies and meetings on racism, sexism, and homophobia. I have sat in the audience and felt other people's anger become my own. I have begun a process of redefining who I am. I see the looks on people's faces when I walk past them, and I see the ugliness of social oppression in a way I have never understood it before. I am beginning to explore how I fit into the oppression and how I oppress others. I am becoming someone different—perhaps someone dangerous.

I never really knew my great-grandmother. All I really know is that she was a woman, she was Black, and she survived.

I have a history of survival in my family.

I'm going to be just fine.

Part 3: Breaking the Silence

Bean Soup:
A Collection of Letters

Lauren B. Shapiro

Dear Bean,

I was just looking in the bathroom mirror, trying to decide who I should address in my autobiography. I thought of God first, but too many authors, including Alice Walker and our childhood favorite, Judy Blume, have already made that kind of spiritual thematic statement. As I was washing my hands with clear liquid soap, Mom and Dad entered my mind, but I always feel like I have to balance things out perfectly for them, especially my own self-image. I knew that, if I dedicated this semester's worth of work to you, I could be myself, completely honest and even vulnerable. So, the next time you pray to God for something you may want to apologize for winning out in my sociological expedition.

I've always thought we shared a special relationship, and in the past few years I think we've grown even closer. We're no longer the nine and five year olds who stole each other's Barbie doll clothing. Now we're the eighteen and twenty two year olds who just take each other's clothing. Sometimes I worry that we're too much alike, but most of the time I just thank God that I have someone in this world who can understand me and care for me no matter how high or low I swing. Dad always said to me, "No matter what happens in life, Bean should be the most important person to you"—and you are.

I don't think Dad needed to restress this point to me so often because I think I've figured out how important you are to me on my own. I remember that all my life Dad said, "That little girl loves you more than anything. . . . you be good to her!" Well, Bean, I hope I have.

I think we were raised to avoid conflict, and therefore it's hard for us to tell people exactly how we feel about things. In many ways your support has helped me to change this weakness in myself. I suppose I always wanted everyone to like me and to think I was a "nice" person. Alas, perpetual popularity is only possible if you want to dedicate your life to martyrdom, which is how I felt for nineteen and a half years of my life. It took knowing that I could really depend upon the people who loved me the most, before I could start making changes and feeling good about myself—my whole self and not just the perfect outer image I like to project.

By the way, how did you and I get so hung up on perfection? Have you counted how many times I've used some form of, or made an allusion to, the word *perfect* in this letter so far? What a drag! I'm so much happier when I can just be and when I don't worry so much about my appearance and having to agree with everyone else in the world. I think our greatest strengths arise from the fact that we do think and feel so differently from other people. Although it may not sound so unique, I think we're extremely perceptive and sensitive to the world, which allows us to care deeply—more than most, at least. Just think back to all the people over the years who have told us we're special. There's something inside of both of us that seems to capture the attention of the masses or at least of those we love and respect.

You know how every term I go through some kind of self-realization process? ... Well, this term I'm trying to explore my "Jewish identity." I know you're probably laughing hysterically right now. You must be thinking about our long talks when we've decided that Judaism holds no great importance in our lives. For me now I think things are changing. We both hate a lot of the ritzy things our neighborhood stands for, but in some ways I think we really like it out there and have grown accustomed to the lifestyle. The question of Judaism for me seems increasingly urgent because I have to move back home in six months, and you know Dad's going to jump on the chance to take me to our country club. How depressing. I just can't deal with the country club lifestyle or the fashion shows we encounter at our synagogue. I know that plenty of nice people attend both places and that I could make some great business connections by hanging out at the club—but I just don't want to deal with it.

But if I reject the materialism that seems affiliated with Judaism, what happens next? Do I reject my religion as a whole? Will I be condemned for wanting to be myself and not just another aerobics addict at the health club? What to do? Write back soon and tell me what you think.

Love, (Me)

Dear Bean,

I was just laughing to myself about how strangely you and I both seem to deal with our male relationships. Why do we have this aversion toward Jewish men? I think we would both eventually like to marry a "nice Jewish boy," or NJBs, as my friend Romy calls them, but hey, we sure can't seem to date any. Dad must be absolutely freaking out at this point. Especially with me. I'm getting old and over the hill. I thought it was hilarious last night when you said, "Dad, I'm improving (on my taste in dates)—at least Steve Carter's stepfather is Jewish, and he knows how to say the Baruch." Can you believe it? Dad actually laughed a real long, loud, bellowing laugh. He seemed so human and so able to join in our laughter.

I love Dad so much. I just think he has rotten timing. When we were both home as kids, he worked twenty hours a day. Now that we're both at school, he's in private practice, home for dinners and even most weekends. I'm so happy that his life has begun to work out so well, but I also feel like I'm missing something. Don't get me wrong, Bean—you know I feel very close to Dad, but I wish I knew him better. I have to fight like hell to get him to tell me his honest opinion. I'll say, "Dad, what do you think of this question 'Who's a Jew?'" He'll reply, "Many different things, but let me put your Mom on the phone." Damn, it drives me crazy. I think Dad just spent too many years working on a bipartisan congressional committee because he never really lets himself go in any capacity or to any extreme.

I've been trying to relate to Dad on a new level. I mean, I'm really trying to get to know him and let him know me. I keep asking him questions, and he keeps deferring by changing the subject. At least he's been receptive to my feelings about coming home next year. I told him there's no way in hell I'll stand for him to badger me about going to the country club or participating in activities at temple. I told him that I do care about being Jewish and that my heritage is important, but I don't want it pushed upon me.

I feel I've done a lot of soul-searching in the last year, and one of my conclusions has been that I actually do like being Jewish. I mean, it's very important to me; I just don't know what I want to do with it. I don't feel like I really fit in anywhere in the Jewish community, except with other Jews who, like me, feel completely lost with their cultural and religious baggage. I know that you and I have talked about this before, but I really wonder where I'm going to go next year and who I'll be taking with me. You remember—at first I didn't even want to go back to D.C. because I couldn't deal with all the same old temple BS that I've been seeking to escape my whole life.

When I saw Caryn we talked about this a lot (remember, she and I were best friends in confirmation class). Caryn told me that she's decided to stay away from D.C. after she graduates because she's not ready to deal with all the things she readily left behind four years ago. I know exactly how she feels, and in many ways my feelings emulate hers. I just feel like it's now or never, so I might as well go back now and see how I feel.

Maybe I'm meant to be part of the Jewish scene: looked upon, admired, but never heard. Am I being too harsh, though, Bean? I mean, I feel like I'm stereotyping all these people, and it's so unfair of me, and yet, when I go home, these stereotypes always seem so applicable. I feel torn inside because I really like the ideals of Judaism. I mean, it's a religion based upon ethics. I feel proud to have my own beliefs, and I'm proud of what they're based on. I don't think enough people realize what we're all about. I mean, honestly, Bean, Jews are just as much of a minority as anyone else, and yet we choose to ignore this fact and disassociate ourselves from everyone who's not Jewish. I can't believe how many Jews I know who are racist against Blacks and all other people of color—not to mention the inherent sexism of our patriarchal religion.

Last week a large group of Jewish students organized a rally against the *Michigan Daily* paper and didn't contact any other groups on campus. Often campus groups will unite for larger numbers and support, but not us! Because we have so much power on campus, the *New York Times* picked up the story and covered it nationally the next day. You see, student protesters feel the *Daily* has been "Jew bashing." I don't know if you're familiar with this term. Let me explain . . .

The *Daily* had this editorial page, and every day they include an article that condemns the existence of Israel and all actions taken by Israelis—and therefore (some feel) by all Jews. I went to the rally with a fairly open mind. I arrived at the protest a little late, but I really was impressed by what I saw and heard. The issue on campus is still pretty controversial, but I don't feel at all sympathetic to the *Daily* anymore. I think people are really starting to feel a certain amount of support for their anti-Semitism.

The word *anti-Semitism* has always seemed so foreign to me—just a term I memorized in third grade for a history course in Hebrew school. I never knew anyone who really hated Jews until now. I guess I can't say that because I could have easily met anti-Semites before and just not known it. Even though most of us who are Jews have white skin, we're still a minority group and a scapegoat for people to exert their aggressions upon.

I'm really frightened when I watch the Cable News Network Newswatch, and the cover story is about the rise of hate groups like the neo-Nazis and the Ku Klux Klan in America. These people live to hate, and they hate people like me just because I have beliefs that differ from their own. It makes no sense in my mind or my heart, but, then again, a lot of things in this world don't. I only know that, when I hear news like that, I feel incredibly tied to my religion and my roots. The only other time I feel more religious is at a funeral or when it's Christmastime, and everyone seems to be walking around with this major glow, wishing me a "very Merry Christmas!"

I never minded Christmas when we were little because Mom and Dad let us celebrate with a Hanukkah bush. What a great time we had. I wonder if it was a mistake though for them to think we could get the most out of each experience. I believed in Santa Claus like all the other kids, so I never really had a need to attach to my Jewish identity as a child. I think this is a major explanation as to why I always felt so much on the periphery when I went to temple and Hebrew school. I didn't feel part of any one group, and I still don't. I'm starting to feel more comfortable in Jewish circles, but I'm still not sure if that's the place that awaits my presence in this universe. I don't mean to become so philosophical about this issue, but it is my life and my identity crisis...well, back to Dad (or, should I say, a major contributor to my identity crisis?).

What really drives me crazy about him is the way he gives advice sometimes. For instance, he says, "Lauren, I think you should wait to get married—maybe when you're around twenty-eight. That's a good age because you'll be established at your career and know what you really want and need from a mate. Just remember, and I don't mean to push you, but life's a lot easier when you marry someone of the same religion."

I know Dad says everything out of love, but that man can make me crazier than any human being I've ever met in my entire life. I sometimes wonder if I avoid Jewish men just to spite him. I hope not, but you never know.

So where do I place Mom in this mess? I really feel like I should include her because I know she'll probably be reading this mumbo jumbo work, and also she, more than anyone else, has made me what I am today.

I know Mom thinks she's been a terrible role model for me, but I really think she's one of the most wonderful women I know. I think Dad's a wonderful person too; he's just a lot harder to get to know. Mom's given me the freedom to find out who I am. She listens to all of my ideas—sometimes with too much interest, because I come up with some pretty insane things. I know Mom feels strange about being Jewish too. She and Dad always said that they never wanted to be part of the Jewish crowd in high school because all the Jewish kids were too cliquish back then. I don't think the cliquishness of Judaism has changed; I just think that Mom and Dad have.

They tell me to treat everyone as equals and to celebrate the differences I find between myself and others. In the same breath they tell me to go out and find a nice Jewish boy to marry. I'm told that Judaism is a religion to be cherished and that I have special traditions to follow. OK, I can relate to this. I like having just a little bit of tradition in my life, after all. But come on. When I go home to celebrate Rosh Hashana or Yom Kippur, it seems like we always argue over the most trivial things, like who broke the fast first.

Perhaps if temple were a more moving experience for me my attitude would be different. It just seems that tradition at our temple revolves around a fashion show. I've never seen so many beautiful people wearing such beautiful clothing and driving such expensive automobiles in my life.

When I'm at temple I just feel so uncomfortable. I wish I enjoyed being there; I wish I felt something. Do I need to conform to a certain image to fit in? Am I missing something? Write back with some good advice.

Yours Truly, (Me)

Dear Bean,

You know how Mom goes to the movies by herself a lot, and we think she's really strange? Well, I went to see the most powerful film last night, and I actually was glad I went alone. The film I saw, *Murderers among Us,* is an HBO (Home Box Office) premiere about Nazi hunter Simon Wiesenthal and his experiences during and after the Holocaust. Throughout the whole film I felt this sickness inside of my body for all the bloodshed and the children who died alone.

I can't remember when Mom and Dad explained the Holocaust to us. I think maybe we learned most about it in temple or by watching that TV miniseries "The Holocaust." I suppose Mom and Dad never thought the event had a great deal of relevance to our lives because we didn't lose very much of our family over there. I remember being obsessed with the Holocaust as a child though. I read all the books I could get my hands on whether they were fiction or not. The first time I read the *Diary of Anne Frank* I couldn't believe Anne was so young and vulnerable, just like us. She described her inner feelings so beautifully, and I felt overwhelmed by her imagery.

I also remember when I went to the Holocaust Memorial Center in Israel when I was ten years old. Even now, eleven years later, I can honestly say that I have never been so moved in my life. I was standing in the gardens where they've created a symbolic graveyard for all the Jews who died during the Holocaust. It doesn't feel or even smell like a graveyard because the flowers bloom in bright colors and the trees float into the sun. I remember seeing ribbons everywhere. I don't even know if they were actually there, or if I just wanted to see them. In my mind these ribbons are tied together in bows conveying that we, the Jews, are unified. We've endured and we're together in life as well as in death. I had a feeling there, standing in those gardens. It was a sense of comprehension within myself. I felt like a part of everything around me: the grass, the stones, the bees, and the old woman speaking Yiddish, who stood bent over in memory yet determined to endure. It was one of those moments in life that you describe later as "very moving."

I remember the book I got from the center that day. It had a very graphic depiction of life at the concentration camps. The cover was a photograph of the dead bodies found in mass graves. It's so difficult for me to believe that those frail and decayed bodies possessed so much life at one point. The faces were unrecognizable . . . they were all contorted in agonizing pain. I don't think it was the pain of the actual bullet searing through their brains, or perhaps their hearts. I think the pain they emitted through their screaming skulls was for their loss of faith in humankind.

Bean, can you even imagine carrying your infant child into a gas chamber? Can you imagine being pushed into one line and watching Mom and Dad shoved into another line with the butts of guns, knowing that they were going to be shot by a firing squad within the hour, even within the next five minutes? I don't know if I could have gone on after this. I don't think I would have wanted to remain in a world where people could even conceive of being so cruel.

In the movie Wiesenthal's daughter would cry herself to sleep every night because she couldn't understand why her family was so different. All of her friends had aunts, uncles, cousins, and grandparents who would visit all the time, and she just had her parents. When she was seven or eight, her dad gave her the Anne Frank diary and told her that she didn't have any family because all eighty-nine of her relatives had been systematically killed by the Nazis during the war. Can you imagine the loneliness of such a situation? I suppose sometimes we both take our crazy family for granted. Think of how often members of our family go out of their ways to make sure you and I both know that they care. I know everyone is making such an effort to be at my graduation at the end of April. I know that, if ever I were to find myself in a desperate situation, I would have at least twenty family members who I could trust with my life. I wish I could appreciate facts like this all the time. I just find myself so wrapped up in my own activities that I lose track of what really matters in life. But I know I'm not alone.

I remember asking Grandma what she was doing during the Holocaust and why she didn't try to stop what was going on. She explained that, even when she heard rumors about the events going on in Europe, they sounded too outlandish to be true. Even the Jews in America blinded their eyes to stories that were leaked out to the press. I like to think that I would have reacted differently. I would have known there was something unimaginably inhumane going on, and I would have tried to stop it.

Would I have, though?

How would I have known and what could I, as a Jewish woman, have done when no one would have listened to me? We both know women are just now being heard and credited for having voices in our society. Would anyone have believed me, or would they have just thought I was another Jew trying to make a big stink over nothing? One of the reasons we were so slow to react in the United States was because of the pervasive anti-Semitism during that time period. No one wanted any more Jews coming over to the United States, so even the people trying to escape before the horrors escalated may have found themselves without a home.

I think to myself, How do you explain what happened? Why?

How many Holocaust survivors with numbers dug out from the flesh of their arms have cried alone at night wondering that same question—WHY? When I hear about the children torn out of their mothers' arms and killed with the butt of a gun in front of their mothers' eyes, I think God made a mistake when he created us. I don't think the Nazis were special in their capacity for cruelty. I think they're just like the rest of us except that they were given the chance to act out their deepest, darkest, most remote feelings of hatred. Think of the genocide of the Native Americans when Spanish explorers arrived over here. Why were they killed in masses? Because they were different, just like the Jews. Sometimes I feel so wonderful about this world and the people I love within it. But other times I look back at history, and I look at what's going on now, and I see nothing but despair and destruction ahead. Arabs and Israelites are killing one another every day. South Africans are suffering under Apartheid and are battered when they speak out. Children are being sexually abused by their parents when they're only six months old, before they even know how to cry out for help. Sometimes I think the world is a dichotomy of good and evil, but I know this vision is much too simplistic. I fear that potentially all of us could become as hate-filled and abusive as the Nazis if given the chance. I hope I'm wrong though.

The most vivid image in the movie is one that haunts Wiesenthal throughout his entire life and one that will probably stay in the back of my mind forever. Wiesenthal is talking to his friend in the work camps as they cut stones together. Two Nazis come up and call his friend over. They put his friend back-to-back with another man and then tie them together with a rope. They tell the men to pull the rope tightly so that their bodies bind closely together. When the two men stand like one, as you and I did when we were children playing games in the backyard, one of the Nazis tells Wiesenthal's friend to open his mouth. The same Nazi then kills both men with a single bullet in the same fleeting second of time. You see, he inserted his gun into Wiesenthal's friend's mouth, and the bullet went through this man's head into the other man's head, splattering both of their brains all over the stones simultaneously. The Nazi chuckles and says to his fellow officer with confidence, "See, I told you it could be done."

Bean, how do you explain something like this? I would like to say that it is an inhuman quality and only monsters act this way. But how could millions of German, Austrian, and Italian men suddenly become monsters overnight? This is the question I struggle with. How does this happen? I've seen people I love show sides of themselves that were filled with anger and rage, but I have trouble comprehending how an entire culture of people could suddenly rationalize the mass killings of other human beings.

Why?

I don't think I'll ever know.

One thing I do know is that I will keep struggling to understand.

I will keep watching and reading and listening. I don't think I can solve whatever problem it is within our society that produces this monstrous behavior, but I can sure as hell try. Sometimes I do just want to sit back and let other people worry about what's going on in this world. But then I'll watch the news, just one half hour between five and five-thirty, and I'll hear about the seven killings in Detroit at a crack house or the three infant girls, two of whom are dead after their father slit their throats and left them in a garbage can. I'll hear about the new testings of nuclear weapons guaranteed to blow us all apart within minutes, thanks to our advanced technology. I think, No Fucking Way! I've got to do something to make a difference. I'm not just saying this to sound "politically correct." I really want to do something to help—to ensure that fewer people will be suffering the same inhumane injustices that so many have had to endure over the years. I'll do what it takes. I'll give what I can, as long as I can keep my sanity. Is that so much to ask?

With love from your favorite Martyr, (Me)

Dear Bean,

So much has happened since the last time I wrote you. I just got back from the march in Washington for Women's Rights and Equality. It was really a tremendous experience. One of the best parts of being there was that Mom came along with me. It was really great for us to spend some time together and to take part in something we both care a great deal about.

I kept thinking about a discussion we had in my sociology class about what you represent when you march or rally for a cause. I always thought I was just representing myself, but actually I'm representing women and also Jews who share my beliefs. It all feels kind of confusing, and in some ways it's easier not to even try to define your role in a march. But you know me—I'm always looking to complicate things.

Our temple sent two buses out to the march, which made me really happy. I know Jews are considered to be a lot more liberal on most issues, but the fact that lots of people actually motivated for this issue made me feel great. Mom said that there was supposed to be some kind of meeting place for the Jewish women's organizations, which also really impressed me. I sometimes feel like, in recent times, Jews have only acted on their own issues like Soviet Jewry and Israel. I know these are serious issues and that we all need to pull together and show our strength, but I don't see as many Jews supporting or even being aware of issues that concern Blacks, Latinos, and other minority groups. I feel like, as Jews, we completely insulate ourselves. We don't reach out to other people as much. I worry that being Jewish sometimes means you must exclude yourself from other people and only be seen in the right places.

One part of the march that really bothered me was the use of the Holocaust metaphor by the anti abortionists. They kept yelling, "Hitler was pro choice," and many of them carried signs that read: ABORTION . . . THE SILENT HOLOCAUST. Oh please, people, find out what you mean when you say things like this. Maybe I'm stereotyping, but I have a feeling that the people who use the Holocaust to get their anti choice point across are the same ones who make statements like "those fucking Jews." The claim that Hitler was pro choice really sickened me. They're using our pain, anger, and suffering, and they're making an idiotic comparison. This whole subject is just really pissing me off, so let's switch.

Last night I was watching television, and they did this great show about the main character's best friend's bar mitzvah. I really loved seeing this awkward-looking thirteen year old get up and say his prayers over the Torah. I remember every one of his words as he sang the Baruch before he began his Torah portion.

I never realized until recently how happy I am that I had a bat mitzvah. It was really a pain in the ass to study for all those months, and I think I was scared shitless about actually performing in front of our family and everyone else in this world—but, hey, I did it, and I loved it. I really felt this complete thrill when I was up there with the Torah rolled beneath my hand and the rabbi by my side. I suppose I had a kind of revelation. I know I was only thirteen, but I really felt this great rush when the ceremony was over. I suppose I also felt like a star for a night. I certainly had my fair share of attention. It was such an all-over warm experience for me. Everyone in the world I cared about seemed to be there, and just for me. I remember dancing the hora forever that night, around and around, floating in the air with spins of celebration. There is nothing that brings people closer together than moving together with hands held tightly while singing the song: "Hava Nagila, Hava Nagila, Hava Nagila . . ."—you know the rest. I remember watching people's faces glow with remembrance for traditions of the past while they celebrated the future life of the young Jew who just officially became a man or woman.

I suppose the traditions of our religion are my favorite part. I love to hear Grandma talk about her childhood in Russia when the

Jews had certain curfews. I can't believe she actually escaped from Russia by hiding in the back of a train. Now that woman has guts.

While I watched that show last night and got a little misty over the sappy ending, I tried to remember the time in my life when I really felt the most Jewish. Several things enter my mind immediately. Like Christmas, for instance. I really feel so alone and on the edge during this green-and-red holiday. It is the one time during the whole year when I really don't fit in with the majority at all. So, in a negative way, I feel really Jewish during Christmas, which I guess is fairly common for most Jews.

I never really understood all the traditions that went along with the Jewish funeral until Grandpa died. I do know that being with our whole family during that time, even at the graveyard, made me feel really warm and secure. I remember seeing the candlelight throughout Grandma's house for a week. With every drop of wax that hit my nightstand, a flicker of Grandpa would enter my heart. It was a sorrowful time, and I cried a lot, but I have also never felt so close to so many people in my life. I watched everyone in our family immediately adapt to take care of Grandma's needs. I think that I, of course, did the grocery shopping. Food always helps to calm my mind.

I'm not sure if the specialness of this sad time was related to the fact that Jews pull together very tightly when they experience grief or to the fact that we just have a very wonderful family. . . . I remember how sad our cousin Melissa was when she had to say good-bye to Grandpa for the last time at the funeral parlor. He had been like a father to her, and I can't even imagine the kind of grief that must have surged throughout her body during the ordeal. I'm just glad that we were all there together to show our strength for one another.

I guess I feel this way a lot when I'm with a group of Jews and I feel comfortable. There's such strength in knowing that we share a kind of bond. Immediately, I feel like I could trust these people and even rely on them. Who knows? At least I feel like my attitude toward our religious faith has been steadily improving. Well, Bean, I'll write again soon. I hope you're doing well and that you're on your toes.

Much love XOX, (Me)

Dear Bean,

I just finished writing this really interesting research paper for my English class. I wanted to write about an issue that has affected me deeply, so I chose JAP baiting. What I'm writing about are the consequences of all the jokes and harassment that the term *JAP* has been causing these days. I know that you and I used to sit around and ridicule women who we thought fit the JAP stereotype—the woman, for instance, with the oversized Benetton sweater, the skinny pants tucked into bulky socks, and high-top Reeboks, and she is wearing loads of jewelry and makeup, not to mention long red nails.

But now I'm really angry at us for acting this way and shunning people just because they choose to dress a certain way and wear their hair in a certain style. I guess we were just scared of being stereotyped ourselves, so we did the natural thing and created a division:

us and them,
JAP versus non-JAP.

I've found out a lot of interesting information through the research I've conducted while working on this paper. I guess it makes sense that the JAP stereotype began in the Jewish community. You see, coming out of the ghetto, the Jews felt really uncomfortable with their new role. They didn't know what to do with their money, but they wanted to spend. They lavished their daughters with all kinds of gifts and then called them princesses. In a weird way the Jews made their own daughters scapegoats for the confusion they felt about becoming an upwardly mobile generation.

I know the whole issue of being a JAP has affected both of us a great deal. I remember when I came to college I chose to live in a certain dorm because I heard the other dorms on the hill were "too Jappy." I knew immediately that I didn't want to join a sorority, but I didn't want to join a Jewish one especially, because I thought all the women would be materialistic, whiny people. Looking back, my rationalizations seem obviously racist and even anti-Semitic. But at the time I really didn't want to hang out with what I considered a bunch of JAPs. This sounds so awful now, and I'm so humiliated that I actually felt this way about people of my own faith. You understand though, Bean. It's so hard to be from our area and surrounded by so much wealth and then have to hear all of these people complain . . . not even appreciating what they have.

When I was home Mom was packing away old books, and she came upon the *JAP Handbook*. I was really disgusted by what I saw and read and even more disgusted that one of us actually had bought the book. It makes Jewish women look like sniveling brats whose only concern in life is to marry a man who can afford to hire a full-time maid and ensure her of weekly manicures and pedicures. No wonder you and I strived so hard to disassociate ourselves from this stereotypical image. The strangest thing about the handbook, though, is that a Jewish woman wrote it. Talk about a self-hating Jew!

I remember last year Mom sent me an article about the new anti-Semitism seen at Syracuse University. It seems that during basketball games the pep band leads these horrific chants of "JAP, JAP" whenever a woman walks by who they consider to fit the image. Shit, I wouldn't move from my seat there if you paid me. The same article also mentioned an advertisement in a Cornell humor magazine for "JAPS-B-GONE." This "Handy Information Packet for the Home Exterminator" explains how "raid Giorgio spray-kills JAPS dead!" Bean, this is sick stuff. It's misogynistic, and I'm really scared that, unless we put an end to this soon, Jewish women are really in for it—even those of us who are in denial.

To be honest with you, until this semester I never considered the word *JAP* racist, although I knew it had derogatory undertones. I remember last year when the school board met and decided that the term was offensive and should not be used on campus, I was shocked. To me the word *JAP* was normal, everyday lingo that I heard from friends (Jews and non-Jews), family members (yourself included), and even people passing by on the streets. I realize only now that I actually liked using the term because, if I could call someone else a JAP and laugh at a JAP joke, then, obviously, I wasn't a JAP. Maintaining this image seemed very important to me until I started to really feel the scare of what could happen if the stereotype is perpetuated any further.

I've started to realize that, because I didn't understand my own Jewish identity, I resented other Jewish women. I didn't want to be affiliated with the negative stereotypes of Judaism. Now, though, with a lot of work (trust me) I'm learning to find a better balance for my Jewish identity, and I'm coming to grips with many of my own insecurities. I still feel uncomfortable with the materialism I see at home, but I'm learning not to judge other Jewish women by their clothing, their accents, or their seemingly cold exteriors; we all present fronts for our own self-protection. You better damn well believe, Bean, that I'm the first one to stop people when I hear them say "JAP" or make a JAP joke. I hope you're with me on this one. I feel pretty strongly that we have to stick together to beat JAP baiting down before *it* gets *us*. Think about it.

Love to you, (Me)

Dear Bean,

I just printed out the very last part of my letters to you. I hope you enjoy reading everything as much as I enjoyed writing it all. Finishing this paper signifies the ending of this term for me. I mean, graduation is less than two weeks away. My whole life will be changing completely in less than two weeks. God, I'm scared, but I'm also excited. It has been the most wonderful four years of my life. I can't even believe how much I've grown as a human being. Every week I seem to become more aware of myself and what's going on around me. I'm so glad you have three years left at college. Enjoy it all and never look back. On those days that you're feeling really bad and alone in the world, just remember we've all been there. I made it through the roughest times of my life in college. I know you can too.

Well thanks for being my listener, as always. I could never have done this without you.

All my love, (Me)

An Individual Perspective on Life as a Black Female

Sherri Lynn Campbell

Life's Not So Simple

As a youngster, I never thought that I would have to be wary of people or wonder what they thought of me. My first experience of being used was pointed out to me by my mother. The girl's name was Terry; I really liked her because she played with me every day. Little did I know that the only reason she played with me was because of my toys. One day we got into an argument, as she was behaving roughly with a few dolls. My mother said, "I've told you time over that she plays with you for your toys." She never played with me again after that argument, and I realized she must not have really liked me.

As a child of eight, I had my first experience with institutional discrimination. I was an active child in class until my parents separated. After that I became quieter and less outspoken to such an extent that I would not participate in reading aloud. As a result, my second-grade teacher had me held back. She did not consult with my mother, nor did she bother to spend more time with me to see if I had a learning disability. It was up to my mother to protest and prove that I was capable of handling third grade.

I was not the only one it had happened to; they had flunked others, among them my cousin (his mom also protested). I cannot help but feel sorry for the other children who were wrongly held back and whose parents did not question the decision. After this incident my mother sent me to tutors to encourage and nourish my reading and writing abilities and to make me feel more comfortable doing my work.

I say it was discrimination because it happened in an all-Black school where parents' authority over their children's educations was ignored. There were other times that my mother had to come to school and stand up for me against teachers. This happened to many youngsters my age; they were discriminated against and harmed by members of their own race. They were not helped, but hurt.

I can remember the first time my mother pressed my hair. I pestered her so much. All of my cousins had their hair done, and I was the only one who continued to wear braids. My mother was dead against it. She had kept her hair in its natural state and wanted me to grow up proud of my hair. Instead, I had it pressed at the age of nine and, thereafter, had it in some form of process, be it Jheri curls or perms. Up until then I was proud of the different braid styles my mother had made for me on Sundays. I'm sure it was a relief to her to only have to do my hair once a week.

When I reflect on my decision, feelings of regret arise since it is hard for me now to deal with the way I style my hair. It is a sign of embarrassment toward the natural state of my hair. Yet, at this time I am so used to having my hair done that I would not feel comfortable with all of my hair cut off to sport a natural. Nor would I want to walk around with false hair until my own hair grew out. I would truly like to get my hair back to its natural state, but I do not think I could handle such a drastic change. When people process their hair, it shows that they do not like their hair in the same way that dyeing one's hair shows a dislike for its natural color. I wish it were not such a major deal in society for Black women to sport a naturally curly or straight style, one that is very expensive to maintain. Although more women are cutting their hair and returning to natural, I do not think it is widely accepted. I guess that letting me process my hair was my mother's way of allowing me to see my error and to live with my mistake. The terms that are used to describe Black hair are so negative: *nappy, kinky,* and *coarse.* Positive terms are used to describe the hair of whites or Blacks with "good hair": *curly, tangled, unruly,* and *windblown.* These terms have only pushed Black women to have their hair styled in a manner that fits a positive adjective.

My brother Willie and I are very much alike in terms of how we think of our roles as Blacks. Neither of us feels that we should behave in a certain manner to be Black. We befriend whom we choose, and we go out with whom we choose. It is not a problem for us if the person is Black, white, Hispanic, or, in his case, Asian. It is the person who matters; it is what that person has to contribute to us, and vice versa.

I believe this trait has a lot to do with my mother, as she always had different types of friends, depending on the neighborhood we were in and whom she worked with.

I can recall clearly a time when the IRS had sent this white guy out to talk to her about the debts my father was making and her responsibility as his wife to share the burden. She told the man to leave her home and not to bother her again. The next day they sent a Black guy out to tell her the same thing, thinking she would be more receptive to him since he was of her race. This guy also got the boot. I remember laughing at the time because I've always enjoyed seeing my mother tell someone off or put someone in their place. In many ways I wish I were more like her: she has a strong character, and she rarely lets anyone stand in her way (Black or white). That is one thing I would like to change about myself; I feel a need to become more assertive, less shy.

At Home with My Mother, My Family, and Myself

Mine was a predominantly Black middle-class neighborhood. I was not to live here long, though, because my parents began to have problems in their marriage. When I think back, a lot of their problems were caused by my father's inability to accept my mother as a career woman who came into contact with many whites—males, in particular.

My mother was always concerned with furthering her career, whether through schooling or promotions. I later found out that it was because she wanted to provide a nice childhood for my brother and me. She had been raised in a family of eleven, who barely made it on my grandmother's income from cleaning homes of whites and my grandfather's income based on a blue-collar job and yard work. She wanted more for her children. That desire extended to her allowing us to make decisions on our own, unless she thought they were totally harmful.

In those early years I'm not sure whether I realized I was Black or the significance behind it. Up until the age of eight I had grown up among Blacks. Much of my play time was spent with cousins. I'm thankful that my generation was still a part of the close-knit Black family. My mother's side of the family strongly believed in family ties. As a result, I was taken care of mainly by family members when my mother worked. This arrangement fostered feelings of belonging, which led into adulthood. I will always have my family no matter what happens between me and friends of mine. Friends come and go; family is forever. You would never hear of a member of my family being put up for adoption or placed in an old folks' home—it is unheard of. We always take care of our own. There is a trend now toward oneself; I fear that in the long run some members will not be as loyal or close.

When my mother left my father, she went to live in the town where she grew up, where most of her family lived. I can only think of family spirit when I think of my Uncle Teddy. He drove my mother, brother, and me from Ohio to California. The significant factor in this is that he came all the way from California to do that for her. Uncle Teddy was the eldest of my mother's family, and to an extent his behavior had been expected when they were youngsters, but it continued in later life.

I know to this day that with me my brother can get away with almost anything. I feel so responsible for him at times because we have been through a lot. When one feels responsible for a person, those feelings do not go away in the middle of the night; they are nurtured and expand in various ways. My mother instilled a sense of responsibility for my brother in me at a young age, and I guess it's something that I have no control over anymore.

Our childhood was never very stable since we did not live in one place for more than two years. My mother was always taking us somewhere new. It is always a surprise for me to hear of people who have lived in the same house since the day of their birth. I do not resent the moving around, only the instability of it. We were fortunate to meet many different people and to experience a lot more than the average child.

My mother was a very strong woman. Raising two kids alone and continuing with her education took a lot out of her. The stress of the two led to her illness, which I'll explain in a bit. As a result of her inability to spend much time with us, we (myself in particular) became very independent and very unruly. It was a time of freedom and adventure for my brother and me. We were able (not necessarily allowed) to do as we wanted.

There were a variety of people in our neighborhood, which was full of families and couples. We played with so many different children: white, Black, Asian, Latino, Native American, and also foreigners. I wonder if some of those kids think back as I sometimes do about the harmony of that mixture. I guess the important factor involved in the whole concept is that of childhood, a time of free thought without societal interference. If children were left on their own to grow and expand in open environments, I do not believe there would exist such extremes of racist thought.

Life with my mother was always an adventure. Though she had little time for us, the times together were of a high quality. We were always going on trips, visiting museums or going for a drive somewhere. The greatest experience for me was our trip to Mexico. My mom took us to Disneyland and L.A. to visit my Uncle Teddy and, then, to Tijuana, Mexico. I think she had a fascination with Spanish; we took lessons when we were younger and practiced with a neighbor while we stayed in California. The Spanish did not help us in Mexico; Willie and I were never ardent listeners. We were both extremely active, potentially bored children with a drive to be on the go. As a result, it did not bother my brother and me when we moved, though inside I think there were problems. I always liked meeting new people. The problems arose with adjustments to new schools. The fact that my brother and I got along so well aided us in our adjustments, as we could always explore together if my mother were absent. These times together created a mutual bond of sharing in the sense that we experienced the same things.

Our move to Maryland was the biggest turning point in our lives. My mother had finished with another degree and had landed a high-paying job. For the longest time before this job we were poor, meaning my mother did not have money to buy new clothes, toys, or expensive food; we were actually receiving food stamps. This new job was a nice turning point financially; my mother was able to buy a new car and could afford a nice townhouse where each of us had our own room. After my mom left my dad, Willie and I shared a room (for four years), which led to certain troubles because we played around too much at times. By this time Willie and I were very self-sufficient; we cooked (probably hot dogs), cleaned, and knew how to grocery shop economically.

This point in my mother's life proved to be the added cherry on the cake of stress. She suffered an aneurism two months after the move. The situation was very scary for me because I did not understand what had occurred. It was a normal morning. My mother told me to wake up, and I ignored her, waiting for the next five minutes for her to repeat herself and demand my attention. Only this time it did not happen. Instead, my mom sort of fainted, except her eyes were open. I was ten at the time and did not know what to do. I raced to my brother's room and began pounding on his chest hysterically, nervously, for him to wake up. That proved useless; he was of little help. My next thought was to call someone on the list of important numbers my mom had put above the phone. After going through three people, I called our babysitter, who lived upstairs. She rushed down in her nightclothes, scanned the situation, placed a blanket on my mom, after closing her eyes, and called an ambulance.

Everything was a state of confusion afterward. I couldn't understand why all of my mother's brothers and sisters, my grandmother, and my dad, of all people, came to stay with us. They wouldn't let Willie or me see her; they just said she was fine. In fact, she was in a coma and did not awaken for five months. My brother and I were used to sudden changes, but not those that took my mother away from us.

We did not like moving back to Michigan to stay with my dad and grandmother. We wanted our mother. It wasn't the same and never would be. My dad tried to keep us active (karate lessons every day), and he encouraged us to meet our new neighbors so that we would not think about our mother much. We tried, but we cried almost every night for about a month. It was harder for my brother because he had been a momma's boy for the time we'd spent together with our mother.

She had suffered brain damage for the time that she was unconscious before the ambulance arrived. (That fact upset me a lot when an aunt relayed that information to me about five years ago.) The damage resulted in a personality change and disability to functions on the left side (she cannot run but can now function on her left), which resulted in her inability to work or grasp information as quickly or think as clearly as before. For a while I was mad at the injustice served to my brother and me, but now I get angry over how little we were prepared to deal with this new person, my mother, because my dad and grandmother chose not to tell us anything about her condition.

I admire my mother for her strength; she has always done the best she can for us, though at times that may have created hardships for her. She has struggled with herself in the knowledge that she can never be who she had been, no matter how hard she tries. Acceptance of yourself for who you are affects how you handle yourself on a daily basis. That is one key lesson I have learned from my mother. Accepting myself as a Black woman is not a hard thing to do; it is what one inherits—what you run into as a result of who you are—that is difficult.

Life with my mother was difficult once I reached my teens. It was a time of responsibility and independence. I spent most of my time alone with relatives or my brother. I did not care to interact with people my age, though I enjoyed spending time with children and older adults.

My mother was like a child herself; her perceptions and ideas of what should be resembled, and still do, that of a teenager. It was difficult for me to communicate with her because I thought of her as my mother (an adult), not someone who might have just as many problems as I or more. As most of us know, parents are invincible. My dad and grandmother did not help in my difficulties; they only reinforced them. They were constantly telling me my mother was sick, which I couldn't see, but they never told me how I should behave toward her.

Many of the conflicts with my mother arose as I began to disrespect her in the way my dad and grandmother encouraged me to do. They always told me that much of what she said was invalid, making me question her resourcefulness as a person. I started to become resentful toward her. I was angry that she couldn't be like other adults. I was angry because she had no money, but my dad did. He would give Willie and me money to spend, while she only had money to survive. That, in itself, caused a rift between the three of us. Money was something we had easier access to than she did.

After a while the three of us were no longer capable of living with each other without flare-ups. Since most of them occurred between me and her, I moved out the summer before my senior year of high school and moved in with my grandmother. As summer passed, Willie and I moved in with our dad. For a long time communication with my mother was on shaky terms. The move was like a slap in the face, for all parties. Willie and I felt rejected; my mother blamed my dad and grandmother.

Life with My Father

Though I did not live with my father for a majority of my life, I have learned a lot about myself in thinking back on our relationship. My mom left him because he was an alcoholic. He had many hardships as a young adult and encountered racism in ways he thought he wouldn't as a Northerner.

He has had a hard time defining himself as a man and determining his role as a man in our society. He is more comfortable when he is in control; in most cases this means physical control. He is a female-beater, a chauvinist, yet he can be very resourceful in his abilities to help those around him. He has a need to feel wanted, needed. My dad perpetuates many negative stereotypes toward Black men. He has five sons, all from different women. Willie and I share the same mother, the only woman my dad married. I bring him into the picture because Willie and I moved in with him my senior year of high school since I could not tolerate my mother.

It was a huge learning experience for me. I was expected to be the female of the household, which meant cleaning, cooking, grocery shopping, and running miscellaneous errands. The only thing I was not expected to do was the laundry.

I had firsthand experience with a chauvinist. I do not like the way my dad treats women, in particular his girlfriends. But I respected the women even less because they continued with him and did what he wanted. After a while I began to associate his behavior with that of all males, Blacks in particular. I was not going to end up like these women in his life, fighting over one man. Though he did help them out in many ways, he also used them and expected them to behave as he desired.

Inadvertently, I vowed not to have any interactions with Black males since I began to view them so negatively. It did not help when incidents occurred, such as a guy being too assertive, rude, or obnoxious. It would only nurture my already negative beliefs. I would not go out with the Black guys who asked me out; I did not feel safe with them. I believed they would try to use me as my dad used his women. I found them very sexist and closed-minded in terms of how they treated women. Before I moved in with my dad, I'd had many negative experiences with Black males. (There are also some things I have left out about my dad.) I was scared of him and many Black males for a long time.

Trouble with Men, Trouble with Women

As a junior high student, I attended a fairly integrated school because of busing. Out of all of my negative experiences in school, the majority of them stemmed from Blacks. I did not get along well with the females. We were on different wavelengths. They were concerned with guys (like all other females) and fashion, but the difference was in their attitudes. Black females could be harsh and unfeeling about the things they said to you. I remember this one female wanted to beat me up because she thought I was trying to take her man. I had done nothing to the guy. He wanted me to have sex with him, and I guess my reply angered him to the extent that he decided to take revenge by telling his girl I was after him. This increased my aversion to men. I'd experienced too many sexual overtures from men whose kids I had babysat for, my dad's friends, and guys in school. The fact that the majority of them were Black made me turn away from Black men.

I never felt threatened by white guys; many of them were too shy to be aggressive. I tended to hang around white guys because I found it hard to get along with females and Black males. I felt more comfortable and safe with them. There were some who asked me out and made sexual comments, but when I said no they left me alone, rarely persisting, unlike their Black counterparts. This is not an attack on Black men, but, up until my college years, my experiences with Black males had been negative. It wasn't until my teenage years that I began to think of things in terms of Black and white and, in turn, associate behaviors to one group. I could joke around with my guy friends without fear of them thinking I wanted to go out with them.

I did not begin to like or tolerate women again until I became friends with Mary Zachariah. Before her, I'd associated with other girls who weren't so fashion- and male-conscious. When I think back, they were foreign (Asian for the most part), and, as a result, the language barrier was a problem. Mary is Indian (from the West Indies). Her family is very Christian, and thus we shared a lot of goals and thoughts. At this point my thinking was very close to that of a very hard-working Christian woman: no men, only studies. Mary and I got along fine. She liked guys, but her parents would not allow her to date unless the guys were Indian; her parents planned to pick out her mate. She could relate to many of the problems I had with Blacks since many people thought she was mixed. She was dark-skinned (it was her hair that made them think she was mixed). There were not many Indians at school, only Mary and Elizabeth (who looks more Indian). Mary and I talked about a lot of things and justified our actions. We were concerned with making it to college, not about whom we would be going out with Saturday night.

The first time I went out on a date was in my senior year of high school with Tom Arceo, my first beau. Tom was different from the other guys I had known. He was very funny and very understanding of people. It was easy for him to empathize. The differences in our skin color, race, and background never bothered him. I recognized Tom in our government class. I noticed him the day of pictures. He sauntered into class wearing flooding plaid (red and green), bell-bottomed trousers with a polka-dot tie sticking out of the zipper, a greenish-yellow shirt with a flared collar, a stethoscope around his neck, a white doctor's jacket, mix-matched red and green high-tops, and a pair of red broken glasses bound together with masking tape, and he was carrying a boom box. His entrance was greeted with laughter by the students and anger by the teacher, who took offense at the state of his trousers. Tom always struck me as a funny guy; he always made me laugh. I began to like him after we'd had some phone conversations. He constantly drilled me with questions to get me to open up. At the time I was very shy and did not like talking about myself or my problems. He taught me how to open up to people instead of holding things inside. As we began to go out, tensions began to direct themselves my way from the Blacks at the school.

Upon transferring to Powers (a private Catholic school), many of the Black females approached and encouraged me to hang around with them. I never gave them a chance to know me; I didn't trust them. I thought they would be the same as the people I'd encountered at the other school. I had found the women there very materialistic and judgmental. I figured it would be even worse at Powers since the economic level of the school was higher. I had always been lower-middle class up until my dad increased his interest in us. After being with my dad, I had a car and steady access to money. I was able to do more than in the past. But I am not materialistic, nor do I let money purposely rule my life.

I was a racist toward my own kind, stereotyping them based on past experiences. I never thought I would be truly accepted, nor did I feel I could exclusively keep my contacts with them. I understand why they were exclusive. They felt they weren't wanted, and maybe they weren't. They also felt more comfortable among themselves, given the fact that they were about 3 percent of the population.

Interracial Dating

My interactions with Tom were frowned upon and greeted with coldness. I received the cold shoulder from many Blacks, and I had the feeling I would have to go out of my way to prove myself in order to be accepted by them. Many of the Black guys who liked me wanted me to break it off. They couldn't understand what I saw in Tom. It wasn't that he was white, and he wasn't very attractive. Tom was half-Mexican and half-Polish. He appeared white. I didn't try to justify my reasoning for going out with Tom; I didn't feel like I had to explain myself. The guys who approached me in a rude manner should never have assumed I would ever have dated them. They were too crude. Sex seemed to be the most important thing to them, followed by money and appearances. I was offended by their behavior and ignored them most of the time. They would sometimes approach us in the hall and hit on me to see what Tom would say; we both ignored them.

Tom is one of the nicest guys I have ever met. It is too bad that I could not give him what he wanted but never demanded. Our relationship was not very physical. I was too much of a prude for that. I still didn't want to have physical contact with males besides hugging. It seemed to me that all males wanted sex (which is somewhat true), and I didn't know what to do, so it never came about for us. I didn't allow anyone to truly kiss me until my sophomore year of college.

The extent of our relationship was very good as far as communication was concerned. He kept contact with me constantly. Though I had a very busy schedule because of my responsibilities (such as choir, French club, and Junior Achievement) we managed to have a phone conversation every day. I finally broke it off because I felt he deserved more out of a relationship than I was capable of giving. He had feelings for me that I did not return.

Our breakup was a conversation piece since there was not another mixed couple at the school involving a white male and a Black female. I don't know about him, but I was constantly asked why we broke up. It was irritating, and it was an invasion of our privacy. But I didn't want people to think we broke up because of the issue of Black and white. Some people even went so far as to ask how much of a physical relationship we'd had.

I still date guys of different races, not restricting myself solely to Blacks. It is interesting to learn about different cultures and how they pertain to me, though it can create problems in terms of expectations. I once went out with a Columbian guy who expected me to be faithful to him while he had a girlfriend at home and involved himself in other relationships on the side. There existed a double standard I couldn't deal with. I don't necessarily date a guy based on his nationality but on what he does that interests me. When I think about the guy I will marry, I realize it would be easier to marry a Black male, or at least a minority, because the degree of understanding may be higher in terms of ethnicity.

I have observed in my own family the feelings toward interracial marriage. A few years ago an aunt of mine was dating a white guy, and the family as a whole did not take to the idea. She in turn became uncomfortable with reactions the two of them received in public. It was embarrassing for her to be noticed because she was out with a white male. She did not like the attention, the comments, or the general attitudes of many who reacted in a negative manner. I could sympathize with her because I had encountered similar experiences, but not to the extent that she did. It was different for her because of her generation. The relationship was viewed negatively by many people of her age group. For me, on the other hand, interracial dating is not exactly acceptable in Flint (a working-class society), but it seems that in public I do not face such extreme reactions to it. I did get looks when I went out with white guys at home at that time.

Nowadays it seems as if attitudes are relaxing toward interracial dating. I have personally noticed a change in attitudes and reactions since going away to college. There are more white guys from my hometown who will ask me to go out with them compared to when I was in high school. This was a surprise at first because it seemed as if all of a sudden it was okay for them to go out with a Black woman.

On the Fringes of Society

It was especially an eye-opening experience when I went to Europe. Black and Latino women were seen as exotic. There were many males of different nationalities who observed women of the different races. It was weird in a way since I had never viewed myself as a second-class citizen in America. But I realized that in many ways I must have realized that subconsciously I felt myself to be inferior to white women. (In American society the white woman is the only beauty. Her characteristics define beauty.) I didn't really know that I felt that way about myself until I was there for a while. After getting compliments from native Europeans, especially Africans, I saw that I did not think much of myself in terms of the white conception of beauty. I knew that Black males found me cute, but I never really thought about myself as attractive because I did not have those white traits. It even comes down to how hair is viewed (which I touched on earlier); white men value long, straight, curly, or wavy hair, not kinky hair. These values have become relevant in Black America also. Beauty is defined in many ways as how white one appears.

I think that this trend may be declining and there may be another rise in Black beauty or, at least, the realization that a woman does not necessarily need to resemble a white woman to be beautiful. I think the change can be seen in the number of males who would like to date me. They no longer solely regard white women as attractive. I think that the number of interracial marriages (not necessarily white-Black) have increased in the past five years. Black women, as a whole, have been given more light in the public eye in regards to beauty. There has been an increase in the number of Black women on the cover of white magazines. I think this change, in itself, has led to a loosening of ideas and a willingness to experiment with other cultures. My own mother occasionally dates white men, something she didn't do in the past, though she had many white friends. This is not to say that dating people of another race or culture is a good way to be open or show a willingness to associate with others.

My identity as a Black has been questioned many times because of my assimilated behavior, such as my ability to hang out with and date people outside of my race. When I say my identity has been questioned, I mean by other Blacks who have in their minds how a Black should behave. In terms of how some whites view me, I'm not too sure what they think. I know that some see me not just as a Black but as a person; others see me as a Black who hangs out with them, different from the majority of Blacks. I've been around whites who see me as an exception. They'll say, "You're not like the others." I used to be proud of that distinction until I realized that it put "the others" in a negative light. It seemed as if they were saying to be Black was to be something negative. When I entered college I had that said to me a lot.

College was a further awakening to reality for me. I thought that Blacks and whites could get along on a social level. That is not true. Only a certain number of both races are willing to interact outside of classes, work, and sports. That is as far as many will go. They never find out about each other, and, as a result, they continue to hold certain opinions of each other's race as a whole, never finding out about the individual. I'm not saying that they do not find out about each other; they do, but only on the surface, as acquaintances.

When I entered college, I entered it as a "bridge" student. Bridge is a program for minorities (Latinos, Blacks, and Native Americans). It was entertaining to be around solely minorities; that is what eventually happened, though there were whites around us. We went to classes together, ate together, had meetings, and hung out together. It was nice, but after a while I couldn't stand the majority of bridge students' attitudes toward whites. It was a negative attitude that categorized the whole race as bad and not to be trusted. I would be naive to think that there are no white racists and that all whites are going to be nice to me and not judge me by my race. But I didn't like much of what was said. As a result, I began to only hang out with those who rarely commented about whites and with those who got along well with them. My best friend at the time was a Mexican guy from the South, Robert, whose parents had moved North to become laborers. He was always understanding about much of what I said in regards to race, and at times he would point out situations in order for me to view things in different lights. It had never occurred to me that many in the group might take offense if I began to hang around those who were not Black.

There needs to be a reminder here, and that is the fact that I tend to hang with guys. As a result, my other male friends who saw me with guys who were not Black assumed I was dating them. This accounted for the mixed feelings I got as I began to befriend non-Blacks. Robert pointed out the reasoning behind those feelings; I hadn't even thought about the reactions that might come. In essence, I got more negative reactions from those who had an interest in me romantically than those who were just buddies, though they also found my friendship with guys outside my race offensive. This did not change my associations, and after a while they adjusted to me. I never mixed my friends. I didn't know how they would react if they were all together.

After bridge comes the reality of college life, and there I began to associate with non-Blacks more frequently than I did as a bridge student. My dad did not want me to join any organizations as a freshman; I didn't. I didn't join the minority association in the dorm, though I attended some of the meetings. I did not sit at the Black table, nor did I go out of my way to associate with Blacks. I did have Black friends from bridge, but my non-Black friends outnumbered them, and I tended to associate more with them as time went on. After a while my bridge friends told me that I was being talked about, being called an Oreo (a Black on the outside, a white on the inside).

Many Blacks thought I was trying not to be Black, but that was not the case. I did not feel it necessary to do what they did to identity or feel Black.

There is something key to this situation at Michigan, which is the fact that many Blacks come from Detroit, where they have not been around whites, nor do they desire to associate with them. They feel isolated in a way since many whites do not go out of their way to communicate with minorities, unless the minorities are very friendly. I understand why they bond together; it's because of their similarities—just like women bond together. Many women feel uncomfortable around guys. They feel as if they are always on show until they get to know the guy. This does not pertain to all women or all Blacks, just those I have encountered on this campus. I have in many ways felt ostracized by Blacks who do not know me but who see me with many who are not Black. In a sense, I have felt as if I do not belong in either world.

At times I do not feel accepted by my cousins, even those who have gone to white schools. I should mention that these cousins are also male. They feel as if it is okay for Black men to date outside the race, yet they are uncomfortable with me as I date in and out of the race. I find it somewhat hypocritical. In many ways, their attitudes are inevitable—although some of them went to white schools, they do not always speak properly, and they change their speech pattern depending on whom they are around.

I have problems with the way they judge me based on my being and my behavior. I recall a conversation I had with two of my male cousins. They asked me if I had slept with these guys I had dated. I did not reply because I felt it a true invasion of my privacy—and I have never had sex. That is an embarrassing thing to admit when it is totally assumed that you have, particularly at the age of nineteen, not to mention twenty-one.

Sex is a totally different topic. I don't feel embarrassed to admit not having had it, only when they ask why. It is a true rarity in my family—I'm actually the only member to have reached puberty and beyond who has not had sex. But when I didn't respond to the question, they took that as an affirmative. They in turn began to act kind of weird, which caused tension between us. It is a tension I notice at times but choose to ignore.

It is one thing to feel like an outcast from one's race, another to feel the same way from one's family, considering one hasn't committed a crime or become homosexual—things that would result in being cast out. In bringing this up, I do not mean that I feel like an outcast always. There are times that I feel really close to Blacks—I have feelings of home in a sense—but those times are few.

The Struggle Continues: Pulling It All Together

At this time in my life I do not feel that to be Black I should have Black friends solely. I can't do that and feel truly at ease. I would feel as if I were missing out on life. My closest friend right now is a Black male. We get along very well since our backgrounds are somewhat similar. I like having him as a good friend, yet I do not always think of him as my Black friend. I just think of him as someone who relates well to me; for all practical purposes he could have been a white guy who had the ability to put himself in the place of others. By being friends with him, I have met other males of different races who were very cool and very laid-back about racial interactions.

I mentioned earlier that at one time I did not feel accepted in both worlds. I realized I felt this way after traveling to Europe and living in France for two months. For some reason I felt truly accepted as a person there, though the culture is different from that of the United States. It didn't seem like there was much racism against Blacks. I saw many mixed couples, who walked around with a comfortable air, unlike in America, where many like couples are constantly aware of who is looking at them and feeling as if they are being judged. I did not see that in those couples. They walked around freely, unaware of other couples of the same race walking around together.

As I was saying, for some reason I felt very at ease with myself as a Black. I realized that as a Black in America I viewed myself as inferior. One cannot but help to feel that way because of the way Blacks are treated on a daily basis—from being called racist names or, more subtly, not being given respect because one is Black. I've noticed it even as a shopper. In America I am often referred to in unrespectful or familiar terms such as "honey," "girl," etc. In France I was always addressed as "mademoiselle." It may have been the culture, but I didn't see it that way because one can address someone as "Miss" here and say it in a way that does not carry respect. In many subtle ways I notice a lack of respect in the way that whites treat me.

Overall, I feel that with the combination of my schooling and the attitudes I have sensed from whites, I have gained a negative self-image as a Black and a woman. As a child, I was often put in slow tracks. But later I found out that it was only when something drastic occurred in my life that I would have a lack of attention, and it would show in my learning abilities. After repeatedly being made to feel slow, I began to feel inferior toward others. That is what happens after being labeled. It is harmful—though it may have been intended to be helpful. For the most part I have gotten over that and have gained confidence in my intelligence, but still at times I feel inferior as a result. When I say that I don't feel accepted, I mean that I feel I am being judged and treated differently because of my skin color. In general, I am able to associate with all kinds, but I cannot get comfortable if I feel that someone, Black or white, is judging me.

I want to connect the two worlds without feeling marginal, yet at times it seems that I have to be one way or the other. I have to remain solely with Blacks or solely with whites. It is a continuously confusing cycle. I never know what is correct. I don't exactly feel that there is a correct way to behave. I wish to continue to have a variety of friends, yet at the same time I don't want to fool myself into believing that everyone is similar to my friends. I believe they are a rare breed, and that reality will prove me wrong. I will always search for those who are similar to me in order to feel comfortable saying whatever I feel without being judged or offending someone because they feel I should behave in a different way.

As a Black woman in this society, I see many struggles and much confusion. In the same vein I would not change my life for the world. Although I feel confused at times, it is better to feel and experience than to never see how others live, be they Black, Latino, or whatever. A white person in America who does not associate with other races will never know how others feel and, in effect, will deprive himself of an education.

Me—Who I Am Proud Of

Leslie Riette Fair

When I was little I realized that I was Black, but I was not aware of the significance of being Black. Every neighborhood that I lived in had a very post-1960s "everything is alright now" utopian atmosphere. I vividly remember thinking that everything was OK. I did not know that people before me had paid dearly with their lives just so that I could feel comfortable in any environment. I can remember being four years old and not having any of the feelings that I have today. Little did I know that life as I knew it would change drastically within the next sixteen years.

The first memories I have about where I lived were from the North Lake Shore in Chicago. I never took the time to notice that I was one of the few Black children in the neighborhood nursery school. Sometimes I look back and think to myself that maybe it should not have mattered to me that there were so few Blacks. At other times I wonder how I would have reacted if I had asked myself or had been asked for that matter. Part of the reason that I did not think about the situation is that my maternal grandmother would take care of me at her house in Ann Arbor where people were still basking in the post–flower power stages of the 1970s.

In these two environments there was no outward signal of what was to happen to me later in life. As I think about these facts, I get disgusted with the system and how it works because, looking back, I have the feeling that I was fooled. I was fooled because everything was not alright; people just thought it was. Blacks thought it was alright because they thought that many of the goals of their battles had been achieved. Whites thought so because they had given Blacks their rights in Congress. Even as I look back, I think that people were a little more liberal then. Now I think that maybe many whites were just faking it because it was "in" to be liberal. I have no idea what was going on, but all I feel today is that I was fooled damn well. Fooled until second grade.

In first grade I was discovering that everyone was different. I enjoyed this because I was in a bilingual classroom where English and Spanish were taught. I met Laura, who was Jewish, who was to become my best friend with whom I would play and visit. She took Suzuki violin; oh, how I wanted to take it, too. I would ask my mother all of the time if I could take it. She would tell me that I could not because I did not have the patience to practice. That was true because I barely wanted to do my Español. Yet later in life when I asked why I really could not take Suzuki lessons my mother said it was because she could not afford it.

I also had a friend named Lisa. Lisa was from Puerto Rico. She had moved to the United States when she was very small. I used to like to go over to Lisa's and eat and play. The only thing that still bothers me about that relationship was that we had an argument that split up our friendship to the point that we were never close again. The argument was about television. I still can't believe it myself. We were watching television, and Lisa turned it to channel 26; it just so happened that it was the Spanish-speaking channel. Lisa had gotten the television for Christmas, and it only picked up channels 26 and 11 (which happened to be the public television station, which aired most programs in English and Spanish). Lisa was intent on saying that the television was Spanish and, being the smart-assed kid that I was, I told her that those were just two different channels that happened to be Spanish-speaking. As a result, we had a huge fight, and my mother had to come get me, but I'll never forget the earnest look on Lisa's face. Now I sometimes wish that I had not said anything because it is important to me as well as all other people to have someone or something to identify with. That is why it was important for Lisa to think that there were television stations especially for her that no one else could understand.

After this experience we moved to a different neighborhood on the North Shore of the city (we had moved about five or six times since I was born). This was, well, my first experience with being Black and catching hell for it. That year my best friend's name was Gina Mella; she was Filipino. She also happened to live on my block, three doors down, to be exact. I always remember her family as being nice and pleasant, though things were sometimes hard because they had six girls in a three-bedroom apartment. There was also a white family that lived next door. That family always struck me as strange. The mother and father were named Ron and Doris, and their three children were Ronny, Roland, and Alice. They were the most all-American family I had met until I learned that the parents fought, the dogs "pooped" in the house (which also never happened to be clean), and, though they pretended to accept us by inviting us over to their house and being cordial, they were racists.

The reason that I pictured them as no threat initially was because we, the American people, are programmed to think that the all-American family is nice and sweet, with no prejudice. It was destined that one day I was to find out the contrary; it happened when Alice and I were playing house with her Barbie dolls. She said that she wanted to grow up and be beautiful like Barbie. She also did not hesitate to add that I would not and could not because: "You're not white or blond like me and Barbie." I looked with surprise and asked her what she expected to do with her life since she was so beautiful. She answered, "Grow up and have my husband buy me bras and underpants and have kids." I said, "Well, I'm gonna go to college like my mom and dad did because it is important, and they tell me that all the time because I will need to work." She replied, "Well, if they let you in—because everyone knows that 'niggers' are the dumbest of everyone." At this reply I was infuriated; I jumped up and chased her into her house, screaming that I was going to beat the shit out of her. My mom came to get me because I would not leave until she came. It did not end there, of course, because she would call me "nigger," and I would start to chase her, and one of her brothers would start to chase me. I hated that little girl until I found out that she and her brother Roland had flunked at the end of the year.

We moved quite a bit because we lived in apartments, and my mother and her husband were always looking for a "better deal"; therefore, when the lease was up, we moved. I yelled to her, as we moved to another apartment four blocks away, "This 'nigger' is smarter than your stupid butt. That's why you flunked, and I'll be in college while you get your old bras and underpants because you will be too dumb to do anything else."

This was my first true encounter with anyone's public acknowledgment of the fact that I was Black and, therefore, that by their standards I had no power and no opinion. In fact, I was scared of the little girl because at that time I started to notice that, of the people around me who had any power, none were Black. I also had this great need to want to be around "real" Black people. As a child, I had wanted to be around Blacks in an all-Black setting to get a feeling of acceptance that I now knew whites would never be able to give me. In other words, I wanted to find myself through my people. During this time period I started to get very confused about who I was and what I was going to do about it.

My first "puppy romance" was one that reminds me that I was extremely confused as to who I was. During second grade I found that Alice's opinion of me as a "nigger" was not uncommon. I do not remember the other children saying it, but I know that it was said. As the year wore on, I started to think that this redheaded kid was cute; his name was Joey. It just so happened that Joey was white. Even when I was young I noticed that certain things were happening because I was Black, but still I chose to be naive about them. Therefore, I tended to think that everyone was nice, except for my next-door neighbors. As I began to show interest in Joey, he also began to show interest in me. He started to visit my house on a regular basis, but, whenever I asked whether I could visit him, he would tell me that I could not visit for some reason or another. The main excuse that he offered was that, because his twin brother, Todd, had leukemia, his family could not have company often. Well, I accepted what he said, but at school I noticed that Todd would give me dirty looks. I would always ask Joey why Todd looked at me like that, and he would reply, "Todd is just sick, that's all."

One day Joey came over with some daisies for me and asked my mom if he could take me to a dance that ended at twelve o'clock midnight. Well, she obviously thought that this little guy must be out of his mind. After that Joey was not allowed over often—because of this incident and the fact that my mother thought it strange that I could never go over to his house. After school one day Joey asked me over to his house. Once I was there his mother just glared at me and asked Joey if I was the girl that he had wanted to take to the dance. He answered yeah, and his mother took the liberty of telling me that they would be moving to Indiana soon. We played a while after his mother left the room, but I noticed that Todd smiled all the while with this idiot grin on his face. As I left, Joey showed me to the door, and, as I walked out, Todd said bye and waved with that idiot grin still on his face. For the rest of the semester Joey did not say much to me, and right before Christmas he disappeared. When I asked someone later what had happened to Todd and Joey, they said that they thought I would have known that "they transferred; they moved to Indiana."

Growing

When I was six years old my mother met and married a man within six months. Little was I to know that my family would be scrutinized for being "every shade of love," so to speak. In later years I was to come to realize some very rude awakenings because my mother had married a white man. To me he was white, but he wore this funny little star around his neck that he called the Star of David. He and my mom would say that he was Jewish. It really did not mean anything to me because all I knew was that he was different—he was white, and we were Black.

In the beginning my mom married him, and we were OK. The only thing that I could not understand was why we did not know his family. It was weird to have him call them because his family did not want him to marry anyone who was not Jewish. Even though I knew that she was saying that they had to keep their marriage a secret, I thought it was because Jewish people were white. He used to joke with my mom and say, "If only they knew that I was married to a shiksa." I never asked what that word meant, but I knew that it was derogatory and that I did not like to hear it in reference to my mother. It always bothered me that he would not tell his parents that we existed because it made me feel ashamed (like I had something to hide). When he would go to visit his parents, he would go alone. Sometimes he would take us to the suburb where they lived and show us their house, but, of course, we would have to duck down so that if they should happen to look out the window we would not be seen.

This little game continued until about six months after they were married. He had to tell his parents something because my mother was having a baby. Well, he only told them that he had a Black girlfriend with a daughter, but by the time my brother was born the truth was out. It still meant that when he went home he only would take my brother. It also made me start to ask myself some questions. I was questioning things because my mom was asking my stepfather whether my brother was going to be raised in the Jewish tradition. I was asking myself, What exactly is this Jewish stuff, anyway? I was starting to figure out that he was different from regular white people because he went to a family gathering for his sister called a bat mitzvah, and he brought back a funny little hat that he called a yarmulke. I also noticed that he and his family had things that they did that were different from everybody else. On Friday he would sometimes go home to participate in a religious family get-together that was for Jewish people only. The first time I asked kids at school about Jewish people, they told me that they were all rich. Well, I was thinking that this was the biggest lie that I ever heard because my stepfather never even had a job. When he and my mother were married, they had agreed to start a business together. As a result, she turned down the opportunity to be a newscaster in Rochester, New York. I also knew that he was only surviving because of the support of my mom (and whatever income he had in the bank), his grandmother, and his parents.

The parents and the grandmother were a different story, though. The parents lived in Skokie, and the grandmother lived in a high-rise condo on the lake. I started to think about reasons why he would not or did not work. I could not understand it because all of the kids started to say that all Jewish people were rich. My mom started to watch "World at War" on television. "World at War" was a television program that centered around documented newsreel footage of World War II. The focus was on how Jews were killed in concentration camps. I was beginning to realize that Jewish people were religiously different. There was also something very different about them that I still cannot quite place. It was weird because this show and "Roots" were airing at approximately the same time in my life, and I watched both.

This was also a time in my life when we started to catch the disapproval of the outside world as well as the inside. As we prepared to move, I noticed that my mom would not go with my stepfather to try to lease an apartment because of the fact that she was Black. On two occasions he signed leases, but when the owners saw my mother coming they canceled them. As a young child, I remember many an afternoon at the public defender's office trying to get legal counsel on the proper procedure to go about filing a lawsuit based on racial discrimination.

Change

As I grew older we moved quite a bit, my mom left my stepfather a few times, and then we moved to the South Side of Chicago to an almost all-Black neighborhood (with the exception of a Mexican neighborhood across the tracks). I was used to racially integrated neighborhoods and schools, and now I was in a school where there was a noticeable monoculture (with the exception of a few Mexican students, who said they were white.)

Needless to say, I did not fit in because, as I see in hindsight, I represented everything in a Black person that could have been white. I reminded the kids at my school of "a wolf in sheep's clothing." I mean, in a more technical sense, that they resented the way I talked and acted white because white is what oppresses Black people. So I was forced to learn the hard way to associate with my people in a way that did not subconsciously remind them of a race and culture that has oppressed them and stripped them of their identity.

At the time all I could see was that the other children were picking on me for acting and talking "white." I wanted to be accepted, but I did not have what it took to be accepted at the time. I did not have the clothes that were "in" because my mother had left my stepfather with just the clothes on her back. I remember washing clothes and underwear in the tub of our apartment that my mother's friend let us use until my mother got on her feet. I remember wanting just to be like everyone else. When I learned that I was in the wrong grade, no one said anything because I was keeping up with the rest of the class. I was proud of that, but, as a result, the kids chased me home every day. My hair was French-braided without beads, which was also a "no-no." My mother refused to press my hair because she thought that was too "grown." Lastly, I could not dance. I listened to the words, and the other kids listened to the beat, and therefore I was ostracized even further.

I felt lonely and isolated from the other children because I saw them as threats. Little did I know that I was the threat because I symbolized everything that was keeping us down. It is very sad for me to go over this because the more I remember the more I realize it. The last day of school was always one for fights, and a boy had told me that I was his target because, he said, "You're only a fourth-grader, but you scored higher than everyone else in the room, except four people. Well, Miss Smartass, I'm going to kick yours." Well, I did not go to school that last day. I begged my mama: "Please, please, they are going to hurt me if I go to school on the last day. Mama, you just don't know—Lloyd Smith, the biggest boy in the class, is going to beat me up." She knew that I was telling the truth, but my mother was from the old school where you hit someone back if they hit you. It took a whole lot of convincing, but I did not go to school on the last day. I still think that I would have gotten beaten up pretty badly if I had gone. As a Black person, I think that it is sad to say that the only way you can get rid of the true wolves in sheep's clothing is to drive them out.

I now look back and realize that I did not fully adapt to my surroundings until about four or five years later, but I know that, if I had not been forced to identify with other Blacks at a young age, I would have been confused as hell when I got here to the university. I would have rejected Blacks because I would not have understood—I mean, truly understood—black people culturally; the only likeness that I would have known was pigment. As an older person, I think that I would have also had a much harder time adjusting because of age and mannerisms, but all Blacks (I think) must find themselves and come to the realization that the world is not fair to us.

The Darkest One

After my family moved to the South Side of Chicago, I noticed a type of discrimination among Black people. It was the light-skinned/dark-skinned issue. It is something that most Blacks even today do not feel that whites should have knowledge of. I can defend that because whites tear Blacks apart all of the time for things that they perceive as wrong with us; it would be especially dangerous and hazardous if they knew what was troubling the Blacks among themselves. The subject is one that I was not familiar with because of my mother's action in the early 1970s in the Black Power movement, which preached that Black is beautiful, and I thought that, since I am Black, "if the shoe fits. . . ." This ideology changed as I started to mesh with other Blacks.

The white community has an invisible hand working for it in the Black communities; this hand is echoing a message that is poisoning the minds of young Black children. It conveys the message that "lighter is better." This discrimination within the race was bred into slaves by their masters. The influence is relevant to me in that there was the "field nigger" and the "house nigger." Most of the slaves in the house were mulatto, a mix of white and Black—from a slave woman being impregnated by the master. The darker slaves worked in the fields. The mentality that lighter is better is along the same lines; some Black people feel that if you are lighter you are prettier. I have found myself wanting to ask people if that is because light Blacks have more white blood in them. This concept has troubled me because I suffered a loss of social interaction when I was young because I happened to be brown-skinned. It first affected me not long after my move to the South Side.

In sixth grade there is a need for girls and boys to start being social and cool. In my school it was hard being a new student. Even though I had been there for a year, I was still the new one in the class. Alice Dora Ruggles, on 78th and Prairie, was a kindergarten-to-eighth-grade institution that people went to for their whole lives; therefore, in my second year at the place I knew that I was among some people who had been there for a while. In that grade we got another new student named Dorie Brown. Dorie was a very quiet girl from Los Angeles. Well, a "cool" girl named Tracy Stewart became friends with Dorie, and soon everyone was friends with her. This kind of puzzled me at first because Tracy was cool, but she did not end up having as many friends as Dorie. As I look back, I realize that she might not have had as many friends because she was velvety black. Tracy was never invited to all of the "in" parties that her newfound friend was to eventually be a part of. At the time I never thought of the fact that Dorie was light-skinned and had shoulder-length hair, but as we grew that year I was soon to notice and get "the real deal."

I started to notice that all of the girls invited to the parties were the ones who were light-skinned with long hair. In the immediate future I was also to learn that I was not to be a part of the social hierarchy that existed until I went to high school. The hierarchy consisted of a couple of girls who were fair and who were invited to all social events. It seemed like nothing went on without them being there. One was named Michelle Dunlap. She and her cousin, Tammy Clark, were the most sought after. I would hear how they would play spin the bottle at a party and how the fellas would freak out if they got one of them. Once I heard some guys talking about them, saying, "Damn, man, Michelle sure is fine. Look at those sandy brown eyes." "Yup, man and she got the good hair, too." When I heard conversations like this I would just get pissed. I would always want to know if there was something wrong with me.

This ideal was enforced by the fact that in my home there was my mom, who was light, my mixed brother, and my white stepfather. This caused some irritation at times for me because I was the darkest member of my family. It would not have bothered me if I had not had friends or children that I played with ask me, "What happened to you—are you adopted or something?" They would also say things like "Your mother and brother are nice-looking and have the good hair—what happened to you?" It used to really hurt because that is what I saw as beautiful all over my community. I would ask myself why I had turned out to be the brown one with the nappy hair. I once had a very bad experience in school when my mother came up to talk to one of my teachers. Everyone was in awe; they thought that my brother was so cute and that my mother was oh, so fine. Well, after they finished ranting and raving, a boy who happened to be nice-looking (in my opinion, at the time) asked me, "Why can't you be fine like your mama?" That very day I told my mother what the boy had said to me, and she explained that to her she was just a piss-colored woman who didn't take much pride in it. It made me laugh so hard, but I know that she wished that she could be brown like me. Why? Because Black is strong; it don't crack!

Teddy Blue Black

In the ninth grade I went out with this guy named Teddy. I thought that he was the nicest guy that I'd ever met—handsome too. Everyone at school thought that he was too dark and used to tease him about it. They did because he was Black. I mean, not brown, but Black. He was the kind of Black that dark chocolate is made out of. It didn't bother me, though, but we went out over the school strike in October of my freshman year. We were together all of the time. He would take me to eat every day because he had a job. It didn't bother me if I held his hand when we were in private, but I would hold no man's hand in public. Teddy understood this until we got back to school. I would not hold his hand in the hall.

Outside pressures were also taking their toll; my friends were calling him "Blackass Teddy." I had never caught that much heat for going out with someone before. In an effort to combat what other people would say about him, I would always brag about how much he did for me as opposed to what the other girls' boyfriends were doing for them. I remember someone saying, "Hey, cutie, why don't you dump Blackass for me? If you ever were in a darkroom with him, would you know where he was?" I went to my locker and slammed it around for a while, trying to figure out if he was worth the trouble. Now I look back and see that there was not really any trouble with us, just with the people around the situation who tried to influence how I felt about us. Well, Teddy called me one night and broke it off, but we remained friends until I was a junior and he graduated. The general population got to know him by a new name: "Teddy Blue or Teddy Blue Black."

What the Barbie Syndrome Has Done to My People

I was raised by my mother in a single-parent household until I was six years old. As a result, my relationship with my mother is one that is very important to me. She taught me how to be strong and have strength at times for more than one. Most of all, at a very young age she made it her business to teach me a little bit about myself as a Black child. She grew up in Ann Arbor at a time when people did not discuss issues of race—a time of avoidance. Later in her life, when she went to college during the civil rights movement and started to get interested in the movement, I think that she learned that it was important for Black children to be surrounded by positive self-images.

The positive self-image that my mother gave me was the most effective because of the fact that I never owned a white doll. I've really thought about that this week because it was just Barbie's birthday. During this analysis I figured out that I have never even owned a Black Barbie (except for a beauty head that consisted of a head attached to a dish that held makeup, and even the makeup was for a white doll). I can remember that I had an Afro doll with yarn hair that I really liked. There was also a new doll out called a Tyva doll (I guess she was Barbie's Black equivalent, but taller), which was manufactured by a Black company. I can still remember these dolls like it was yesterday, and I have really thought nothing of it until now. I wonder if other little Black girls who grew up around the same time I did played with Black dolls. It bothers me that there are not that many Black dolls today. I do not like Black Barbie dolls. My mother made the right decision when she chose not to get me one of those. In my opinion they're bad because of the implications the doll gives by being just a white doll (with white, Aryan features) that is colored Black. It gives Black children with Black features misinformation about their beauty. It gives young Black girls the misinformation that there is something wrong with their beauty.

That is where I think that the changes in physical appearance come for Black people. Barbie encourages straight hair and keen features. Those two factors play a big role in Black society. Now I notice that many Black women change their noses and straighten their hair. I straightened my hair, but I feel now that I was more a victim of the society around me when I took the step to permanently straighten my hair. My mother, who had "good hair," always spoke against it. She always felt that my hair was good enough just the way it was. Hair has also been elongated in recent years by Black women. I used to notice that some women would just wear wigs, but now there is a method of lengthening hair that is called weaving. The onset of the weave is a result of the brainwashing of Black women with the use of Barbie and various other tactics (like advertising geared toward whites, using all white women) by the mass culture. Weaving disgusts me because it is making it easier for Black women to fall into the stereotype that long, straight hair is beautiful. It is a shame, but it is true.

A very shameful thing that I did to my hair in tenth grade was that I dyed it blond. It was honey blond—but it was blond. My hair turned a fiery red-orange color. At the time I thought it was cool, and I wanted to do it to make my hair look like my friend Karyn's. Now that I look back I realize that more guys paid attention to me because of my lighter hair color. It was really freaked out, but they really liked it; I think that is the result of the way some Black men are socialized to think that lighter is better in any way or form. I thought that having my hair that color was good because of the following I was getting. Once a friend asked me how I went out with so many guys. I replied, "Maybe it's true that blonds have more fun." That comment is one that I can clearly remember because I often think about it and ask myself, "Les, what the hell were you thinking?" So, even though I can look back and see what was important to me and what was instilled in me about Black beauty, I can see what outside influences went toward agitating or changing my beliefs.

The most recent and worst thing that I have noticed now is how plastic surgery, skin bleaching, and peeling are playing a role in the lives of Blacks today. The first thing that I noticed people changing were noses. The stars came first—Stephanie Mills and all of the Jacksons. It was really strange when about two years ago one of my neighbors came to tell us that she was going to get a nose job at the end of the week. I absolutely could not believe it. Her nose looked fine to me; I wondered what she thought was wrong with it. Now, though, I have knowledge about what culturally cripples Black people. I feel that it is up to people like me to suggest that they do not buy into these demeaning stereotypes. The newest and most harmful alteration that Blacks can get done on themselves is not a nose job but lightening their skin.

Several Black entertainers have gotten lighter skin through some form of skin alteration. The most famous is Michael Jackson. Though he repeatedly denies having bleached his skin, he gets lighter and lighter. This is most dangerous because some Blacks are trying to be white to the point that they want no part of their natural selves. It scares me to think that I could get my nose and lips reduced, have my hair processed, and get my skin bleached, and I would have no trace left of who I really am. I also think that if I were to have this done, I would be so insecure that if anyone found out about me, I would panic and die. It is pathetic for a strong race to be belittled to self-alienation. Why is this? you ask—because of Barbie, of course.

Living in a Black World

As a teenager, I learned how to adjust to my environment. My first year of high school was one where I learned that all of the boys stopped going for just the light-skinned, long-haired girls. The only thing that I did not notice was that I was adjusted and living comfortably in a Black world. Everyone was Black except for my stepfather and a couple of teachers. Everything was normal; I thought that I was the center of the world. I knew that the world did not revolve around me, but I believed that Blacks who had "made it," so to speak, were being respected. Most of the kids I hung around attended all-Black or majority Black high schools. I never thought of them as ruffians or anything of the sort. Even the roughest teenagers in my neighborhood were cool with me, but now I wrestle with the fact that, in some people's minds no matter how affluent the Blacks were that you associated with at home, you were still from the city. That stigma is one that I never had to deal with until college because everyone at home was just a smaller part of everyone else.

My entire neighborhood was Black. The cab company near my house is Black-owned, and Johnson Products (Black beauty product manufacturers) and Soft Sheen (Carefree Curl Products) are right in my neighborhood. I was proud of my background because I came from one of the most prominent Black communities in the nation. Once I got to the University of Michigan I was sure that there was nothing that I could not stand up to. I felt that I was the best product that could be produced by my neighborhood. I went to the best all-

Black high school (the only one that was ranked in the company of suburban schools). The bad thing about that was once I got to U of M, I figured out that my very existence in the system was constantly being questioned. I was so used to being one of the best and the brightest without any questions whatsoever. This was the result of my having been in the presence of my own, who respected me for who I was and never told me that I was *different*.

There was a time when days were different; in high school a simple day was so much different from my life now. Generally, I woke up about 5:30 for school; no one else would be awake. At 6:30 I would be on the way out of the door to school. I would walk to the bus stop, wait about five to fifteen minutes, and the bus would pull up to pick up as many passengers as it could carry. The CTA (Chicago Transportation Authority) buses were called "big greens" by most because of their green stripes on the sides. As the door would open, I would pay my fare to a Black bus driver (they never put white bus drivers in Black neighborhoods). I would start to push and shove my way through the sea of brown faces to the nearest seat or space away from the door. I would get off at 79th and Damen and wait in the cold for another bus with more people just like me.

Once I got on the Damen bus I would run into my friends, start up a conversation, or just speak and then study. The bus would then stop to pick up and drop off people. Then I did not pay attention to the fact that I should appreciate the presence of other Black people just being around. We would all stand up to get off at school, and the bus would come to a halt that caused us all to lean forward. We would empty the bus and approach the only all-Black school that was a member of the honored city schools that accommodated the best and brightest. I would go to my locker and hang up my coat, then prepare for class and chitchat or, as always, try to get in some unfinished homework or studying. Going to class, as I remember it, was really good because we were the best, and almost every teacher conveyed this fact to their students. After the school day was over I would mill around outside of the school and wait for my friends whom I was going to take the bus with. We would board the buses that would sometimes get so crowded that everyone could not get on. (I do not know why someone created the yellow safety line for Chicago buses because people would be standing up until they were almost off the last step and out of the door.) Our realities were riding through Black neighborhoods to get home to our Black families and going home to do chores, homework, and go to bed.

It all seemed simple and realistic to imagine that people would think that my school was a good one and that I was a good student; certainly I assumed that this was true because I had been accepted to the University of Michigan on my own merits and abilities. It is sad that the world is not that liberal and accepting, even in these times. I loved my Black world because everyone there was judged on their abilities without question, and I also liked that I was in a comfortable, accepting majority.

Susu, and Men's Voices, Too

Nicole Hall

I would like to dedicate this paper to the memory of my father, Dennis Howard Hall, who did not, and could not, know me as well as we both would have liked.

Prologue

When I was young my father once said that being mixed with a multitude of ethnic origins is what makes us Black Americans. He was right. My own family is mixed with Native Mexican, Native North American, European, Portuguese, and African: these, along with my own individual Black identity, make me the Black American woman that I am.

My ethnic background is not the only thing that makes me Black. My experiences—from the day I was born through my school years, and life with my family, my neighborhood, my studies, and my friends, up until now and even beyond—have all contributed to my cultural identity. Although each experience has touched me at a different time, to different degrees, and in different ways, each and all of my experiences are equally valid and equally a part of "me"—myself and my own individual identity.

As I write about and arrange these experiences, it is necessary for me to explain why I do this. To the reader, these events may appear to be without order or cohesiveness. To me, they are the way I see myself, the way I define myself and my identity. And that, of course, is my purpose: to show those who read this who and what Nicole Hall is and how she got there.

Memories of long ago are totally disjointed, but I like it that way. You have all the factual pieces, but you can rearrange them and put them together and make the picture look any way you want. You can forget what is unimportant or too painful to remember, but you always, *always* retain the memories that are necessary for survival.

It must have been very early in the A.M., but for some reason I was always awake. Wide awake, or so I remember. We would drop Mommy off at work. I would get a little kiss, and Daddy would get a medium-sized one. The one I remember was over my head (I sat in the middle in the front seat). I thought it was cute to see my parents pucker up.

Dad used to cook, but I can't remember what. Obviously something—'cause I used to eat. I still have a teeny tiny scar on my left middle finger from some grease popping on me. Or maybe it was my right hand? The look of terror in my dad's eyes when he thought I was hurt was a sight to behold. It was an accident, of course; my dad loved me. I'm sure he did back in those days when I couldn't see over counters, say my ABC's, or write my name. One time I came flying upstairs to show him that I had learned to say the alphabet. Paris and Minion, two friends of mine who lived downstairs from us, had taught me a new song.

"Daddy, listen! I learned to say my ABC's!"

"Say 'em for me."

"OK." I started to sing in my two-year-old voice: "A B C D E F G H I J K *elemenopee*—"

"That's L M N O P."

"What?" I looked at him like he had just missed the point. That's not the way I had learned the song five minutes ago!

"You're saying it like it's one word. Those are five letters of the alphabet."

"All right," I said with an attitude. I couldn't stand it when somebody told me I was wrong when I knew I was right.

"I know it sounds better your way in a song, but, if you're gonna learn it, you better learn it right. L M N O P. Got that?"

I was still irritated, but I got it. I felt like, I don't know, really loved at that time. I didn't really fully understand what had just happened. Or maybe I did. How many parents listen intently, I mean really listen, when their kid comes in singing that tired-ass song? It takes a loving parent, someone who is willing to teach you and help you to learn, to be perceptive enough to hear the difference between "*elemenopee*" and "L M N O P" in a song, and *know* his or her child does not understand the difference. I guess I understood better than I thought I did.

He used to concentrate on combing my hair. It wasn't like he just slapped some grease and a couple of ribbons on me and let me go wild; he really took care and an interest in my hair. Now, although he had been combing his sisters' hair for years and all that, this was his daughter, and she has different kind of hair. He wasn't rough with it; he was just, uh, heavy-handed and dedicated—because my hair was, and still is, too thick for words, I used to cry a lot. He told me not to cry because that made the person who was combing my hair feel bad. He was trying to tell me that he wasn't trying to hurt me and that it hurt him to know I was in pain. I was young, but I understood that, too. I just wanted to know when the comber was gonna be concerned with the feelings of my scalp! He would even sometimes cry when he knew my scalp was hurting or he knew I was in pain. He was an emotional guy, not afraid to show how he felt, even if others thought he was being ridiculous. I think that's where I got it from. I think that was a good lesson, though: be concerned about the feelings of others, even if you are a little uncomfortable. He lived pretty much by that rule. But I think a lot of my problems in later life stemmed from this one-sided, half-taught, but good-to-know lesson about other people's feelings.

One thing I can say is that my father never ever ever tried to physically harm me. In fact, he was pretty focused on my physical comfort.

I remember once when I was asleep in my parents' bed for my daily nap. Something told me to open my eyes, and, when I did, there was Daddy standing over by the closet just looking at me. Of course, I was ecstatic because he was who he was, so I sprang up and scuttled over to hug and kiss him. I still remember his smile. Even then I thought it was strange that he was standing next to the closet just staring at me, but I couldn't say so. I couldn't articulate, and he was Daddy, so whatever he was doing was beside the point. I've always really wondered what that man was up to.

I guess I'll never know.

My mom is a big soft teddy bear—so comfortable to cuddle with. I loved it when we used to Eskimo kiss. She'd rub her big nose against my little one, and I knew I was an only child. I mean, how could she give love to another? But there was something that put a wall up between us. I think she tried emotional distance too early with me. Or maybe my dad was just getting on her nerves and she was edgy. But she loved me, and loves me, and I love her. I want to ask her what the wall is and why, but it's just the way we are, I suppose.

She once said, "We need a man to do this," while she and I were changing the outside lightbulb. How many Black women does it take to change a lightbulb? Sometimes it's like she's in some kind of a "learned helplessness" trap from the 1700s. She knows she can do anything and do it well. She's very intelligent, very articulate, and very resourceful. But she does crazy things, like tell the air conditioner repairman that she'll "have to talk to her husband first" before she does anything about getting the damn thing fixed. Now, if I were a self-supporting single woman who knew everything about cars, real estate, and that "manly" stuff that she's not "supposed" to know about, I would be *proud!* But she just babbles nonsense about "if they think you got a man there, they won't try to cheat you." I'm like "if they know I have a brain, they *can't* cheat me, and plus I get to keep my self-respect." But she is from the old school.

I learn a lot from her. Joan Hall is magical, and I find myself acting like her every once in a while. I talked to her recently on the phone for over two hours, and I now see her in a different light. She is afraid of everything that comes with being Black and being a woman and living in the inner city. She has never owned a gun, and I don't think she would have the heart to shoot anybody unless that person were hurting me. And although I cannot understand why she oftentimes refuses to see her own strengths and use them to the fullest extent, I have a harder time understanding why I do the same thing. All that stuff. I talk a big game, like "I'm The Shit, I got my stuff together, and if you can't deal, later for ya!" But I use the same survival strategies, like pretending to men, and to myself, that I need them. That's just stupid. But what does it mean? Is it a woman thing? A Black woman thing? A Joan-and-Nikki thing? What's going on?

When I was younger, around five, I realized that my house didn't have a Christmas tree.

"Ma?"

"What, Nikki?"

"How come we don't have a Christmas tree? Everybody else got one."

"Our Christmas tree is at your grandmother's house."

"How come it ain't over here?"

"How come it *isn't* over here."

"Yeah."

"Because it's over there."

"Why is it over there? How come we can't bring it over here?"

"Because it stays over at Grandma's, and we can go see it whenever we want."

"OK."

I felt kind of funny about that. Who else had a Christmas tree at their grandmother's house? Well, at least now I could honestly tell people that we had one. At Christmastime I would beg my mother to put the Christmas lights up outside around the windows so that people could see we had decorations. For a few years she put the lights up, but then she stopped. I was worried about being a social outcast. I mean, who ever heard of not putting up a Christmas tree or lights or a wreath on the door? All normal people did.

At school the teachers always talked about Christmas—the story about the baby Jesus and how his parents couldn't sleep anywhere but in some barn or another. I thought it was awful how that innkeeper didn't want to let poor Mary in the inn. She was having a baby and everything. It was then that I knew that Mary was Black. All Black people are treated like dirt. White people don't like to let them in their house.

I wondered why Jesus was white. I asked my mother why he was white, and she just said, "That's the way it is." I don't think she was blowing me off; I just think that I was too young to comprehend racism or the concept of a spiritual being. I was also too young to realize and understand how history, the white man's history, has been manipulated and changed to make white people look good and Black people look like "the white man's burden." I wondered, if God and Jesus were the same person, then how come He had two different names? How could He be the father and the son at the same time? How could God be born out of Mary's stomach if He was already born and had created the world? How old is God? Is He a hundred? If God made time, then what was going on before He made time? Did He know what time it was? How big is the sky? If God is everywhere and He lives in the sky, then how come we don't live in the sky, too? If the sky is forever and God has been here forever, then how long is forever? Who made God? Is it magic?

The concept of Santa Claus is horrible to a child's ego and self-esteem, not to mention inherently racist and elitist. But that's neither here nor there, I suppose. Santa is an American institution; to abolish him would be un-American. I remember the confusion that surrounded the annual visit of Saint Nick/Mr. Claus/Kris Kringle.

"Ma?"

"What, Nikki?"

"How come Santa Claus got so many names?"

"I don't know."

"He comes down the chimney, right?"

"Yeah."

"Well, how does he get down to our house?"

Looking up into the space that is supposed to be our chimney, I saw that it had white paint on it, just like the bricks that surrounded it. The closing was definitely solid. I pushed up on the closing to see if it would budge, but it didn't move.

"Ma?"

"What, Nikki?"

"How does he get in here?"

"He comes through the front door."

"Does he ring the bell?"

"Nope."

"Well, how do you know he's at the door? Does he have a key?"

"No, he doesn't have a key."

"Well, how does he get in?"

"It's a secret, Nicole. I can't tell you."

"I wanna know what it is, Ma! Miss Lutz said he climbs down the chimney. If we don't have a chimney, does that mean I don't get any toys?"

I was about close to tears now. I was sick and tired of being different. I was the only one in school who didn't have a brother or a sister to protect me or to take up for me when people beat me up. I didn't have a Christmas tree at my house like everybody else did; mine was at my grandmother's. I was the only one who had to lie about where I lived because my mother worked. There was no one to watch me when I got home from school, so I had to go to school from my grandmother's house, the one with the Christmas tree. Everyone else was normal, and I was strange. Now I didn't even have a chimney, and Santa had to come through the front door. That's not right! Why do I always have to be the one who does everything in a strange way? Why can't I be like everybody else? Who ever heard of Santa coming through the front door? It could only happen at my house.

Mom attempted to make me feel better. "Nikki, I promise you, you'll have toys for Christmas. Don't worry."

It didn't work. By that time I didn't care. I was used to being different, being alone. I didn't like it, but I was getting used to it. So what if Santa and his reindeer didn't come to my house? Everyone would laugh at me and say I was bad.

I'm not bad! I didn't do anything wrong! I'm good! Santa, please come to my house.

I think my mother saw the pain in my face. I looked like I didn't have a friend in the world, and I felt even worse. I began to cry, but I didn't really know why.

"Nikki, don't cry. Everything'll be all right."

"You always say that! Forget it!"

I ran to my room and cried. My mother just didn't understand. It seemed like she wanted me to feel miserable. It was her fault the Christmas tree was at Grandma's. She could have brought it over to our house and made it be normal. It was her stupid fault that I couldn't go to the same school as everybody else on the block. I had to go to Brady, from Grandma's house, the one with the Christmas tree. If I had to go to someone else's school, why couldn't I go to Roosevelt from Grandma George's house? And where were my brothers and sisters? Everybody at school had brothers and sisters. Sometimes they even went to school with their families. I didn't have anybody. It was my mother's fault. Maybe she likes to watch me suffer. Maybe she doesn't care if I feel like doodoo. Oops. God heard me! I'm sorry, God. Don't strike me down. Please.

Someone said that Jesus was God's son and that we are all God's children. I was happy about that because, if Jesus was God's son and I was God's daughter, then Jesus was my brother. Aw right! Now I finally have a brother like everybody else. Maybe if I asked my father God for a Christmas tree and some brothers and sisters then He would give them to me. But . . .

Wait a second! I already have a father. I know, I've seen him. But I have never ever ever seen God come to my house. How do I know there is a God? Oh no, God heard me again. I'm sorry, God. Please don't kill me and send me to Hell. Oops, that's a bad word. I mean, to the Devil.

I eventually fell asleep. I'm more than sure that by the time I woke up, I was on another set of questions that no one could answer for me. Of course, I got Christmas presents—probably my Baby That-A-

Way or some Barbie camping set, that one with Skipper, Ken, and Francine, I think. Anyway, as I look back, I realize that children are put through hell to grow up, only to be put through more hell when they get older, and perhaps to burn in Hell when they die. What about children whose Santas don't have money? And why would you tell a child that God can take his or her little life away at the blink of an eye for no apparent reason? Why the hell do Black people cling to a religion that has been manipulated to support their subordination and oppression? You know, that God-made-the-system-and-that's-the-way-it-is, that suffering-on-earth-puts-you-closer-to-heaven crap. Why do people buy this stuff? Why is all the fear and the alienation necessary? Or, once again, is it really just me?

My first lesson in responsibility came from the person I wanted most to impress. I felt like I was always performing for Daddy's family, trying to earn their love. I was so uncomfortable and so on edge all the time around them. It wasn't like a family; it was like a proving ground. And I always seemed to fail.

Auntie Judy, her daughter (my cousin) Alburene, and our cousin Denise, and I went to Palmer Park. Denise let me wear her sun visor. It was a white hat with elastic and a string to tie in the back; the visor part was green. It was so pretty. I asked her if I could wear it, and she said yes. Denise is great. She's my father's first cousin by marriage—my grandfather married Denise's aunt. Anyway, she was grown, she was on my father's side, and she liked me. Unlike Judy, she wasn't always scolding me for something.

I felt good on that sunny day. It was strange to only have Alburene to play with. She was little, five years younger than I was. I was eleven, and she was six. And we were having a great time.

I don't have any siblings, and my mother took care of my every whim, so I couldn't even spell responsibility, let alone know what it meant. I knew I hadn't done it on purpose, but I left the hat in the sandbox. Actually, Alba left it there. We were on the monkey bars, and I got tired of holding it, so I let her wear it and forgot about it. When it was time to go, Judy asked me where Denise's hat was. I explained to her that Alburene had it and that I didn't know what she had done with it. She yelled at me for losing the hat. I tried to tell her it was Alburene's fault, but she said it was my fault. I was mad as hell, but mouthing off to one of my aunts is asking to be killed. She said, "You was responsible for that hat. Denise gave it to you to wear, not Alburene. You was supposed to take care of it." It made sense, but I still didn't get it. If Alba left the hat in the sandbox, then *she* put it there and *she* left it, not me. So why was I getting my behind chewed away bit by bit?

I felt small and stupid, but nothing makes me feel as bad as when somebody compares me to Kelly. You know, Judy just had to throw it in to Denise that "Kelly doesn't do stuff like that." Everyone loved Kelly. My own family seemed to like Kelly more than they did me, and that made me sick. See, Kelly is Alburene's half-sister on her father's side; in other words, she's no relation to me or to my father's family. Yet her "valued attributes"—being so cute and ladylike and all—got her a place in my father's family that I never had. Because Kelly did what she was told, and she is "responsible." And I was not, at least according to them.

Although I was angry at the time, I realize now that the first lesson was for my own good. As a woman, and especially a Black woman, with our family's history, it's up to me to be responsible enough to run my own life. I cannot and should not be dependent on my mom, my dad, or my husband to take care of me. What happens when they die? What happens when my kids need to be fed? What happens when I start having sex, and diseases are going around, and Negroes don't wanna tell you they got a disease and shit, and I get pregnant before I can support myself, let alone some kid? What happens when I borrow and ruin something that belongs to someone else that I can't afford to replace? I have to not only be respectful of other people's property but be respectful of myself, and be RESPONSIBLE for my own actions.

Who knows? Maybe I was loved a little more than I thought.

For some reason, wherever I go, people think I'm some kind of a slut or a sex maniac. This has been going on forever. I'm always accused of doing something or other with somebody's man other than my own. I've been called a "highly sexual person" by a man who never bothered to ask what pleases me and what doesn't while we were seeing each other. I've been called a "hoe" (meaning "whore"). It's been said that I've been with men I don't even know (literally and figuratively), and somebody put the word out that some guys "ran a train" on me. I'm here to clear my name: most of that is not true.

When I was in seventh grade, people realized I would never fight back, so, of course, they picked with me until I could do nothing but take it. I want to blame it on age, peer pressure, and lack of maturity, but I think it's me. I have always been a sap, probably because I have never had to fight too hard for anything in my life. Or maybe people thought I liked myself a little too much—you know, with the good grades and the "good" hair and being an only child and keeping to myself. But the thing is, people never bothered to ask me how I felt or what I thought about anything. If they would have bothered, they would have realized that I answer all questions asked of me honestly, because that's just the way I am. But no one could find anything good to say about me unless they really knew me. I don't mean people that I hung out with, talked on the phone with, or told my business to—I mean, people who really knew me. To think you know me is to hate me; to love me is to really know me and who I am, not what you perceive to be me.

In middle school "heffahs" couldn't *wait* to steal my boyfriend. Any little thing and all five of them were on the scene, ready to hook Ron up with someone else, preferably one of *them*, my so-called best friends. I'm still not sure what it was with them. See, the six of us, plus a few others, formed the "smart kids" clique in middle school. We all had the same advanced English and math classes for three years, and, when you get tracked, you end up being with the same folks year after year. In sixth grade we were all friends, and everything was fine. But in seventh grade they began challenging me on everything. "Why are you friends with that slut So-and-So?" was their favorite, when, in reality, So only had one boyfriend, and they all changed guys like shoes. *They* would try and say that I did the same things as So did, like skip school to sleep with her nineteen-year-old beau. Because I spent time with So, I was "getting the bad rep." By the time I started dating Ron in eighth grade, I was a slut because I still hugged my male friends when I saw them in the hallway. Somehow they pulled something sexual out of that, too. And, of course, it was up to the girls, who all liked Ron, to save him from trampy old me, at age thirteen. It was chaos.

I was miserable. Now, had I stood up and said, "All you bitches are scheming little liars with nothing better to do besides cause trouble. The next one of you hoes who steps out of line to start some shit with me gets her ass whupped," and followed it up with a swift kick to someone, I would have gotten some respect, or at least I would have been left alone. But, as it stands, I never did. If you don't stand up, you'll be lying down, like a doormat, and folks will step on you every time.

The nightmare grew worse in high school. People made up stuff out of the clear blue specifically to make me look bad. I mean, people

I didn't even know, had never even had a conversation with, had never seen before would spread lies about my alleged affairs with other people I didn't even know. I couldn't even keep track of who said what about me and whomever. I was supposedly doing it in the bathtub (which held a grain of truth, but that's beside the point), on the washing machine (which was a lie unless kissing counts), and on my dishwasher (which is totally unfounded because we do not and never have owned a dishwasher). Now, if the stories were true, it would be one thing. But why would people go out of their way to make sure that I, Nicole Hall, one student in a whole class of two hundred and a school of eight hundred, was hated by the entire student body?

One person in particular (I'll call him Peter) and his cohort ("Donna") used to take immense pleasure in seeing me hurt. Once a friend of mine and I were writing notes to each other. My "friend" (Ed) had wanted me for my body, and I had wanted him to be my boyfriend. No deal had been struck, so we were just friends. Now Ed was silly just like me; he'd say anything to get a reaction or to see how far he could go. In the note he wrote something to the effect that he wanted to "eat me out." He made it sound trashy, and that's exactly what I wrote in the note. "That's disgusting!" was my whole part of the note. Near the end of the note I said that he couldn't do it because I was "on the rag." He wrote back that he didn't care. I wrote, "OK, but don't be mad if I bleed on your pearly whites!" Peter's low-life ass went into the garbage can three days later and showed the note to everyone. Now anybody with any sense could see that the whole thing was just a sick joke. But Peter went out of his way (actually, garbage *is* his way) and tried to make me out to look like him (trash).

Now let's reflect for a moment. Ed had asked me to let him have oral sex with me, and I said no. He asked me several times in the note, and I told him several times how sick I thought he was. To make him laugh, and to give him a taste of his own disgusting medicine, I wrote something about dental stains. And *I'm* the slut? What about Ed? He was the one who asked to lick my private parts without an invitation. Why am I to blame?

Perhaps Peter really liked me. Perhaps the young women involved were simply jealous and didn't understand me as a person. And maybe Michael Jackson didn't really have that plastic surgery. Just thinking about this, I realize that it was not simply a growing up process: it was an initiation process. To be a real "bruthah" or "sistah" you gotta be able to hold your own. You gotta be willing to stand up for yourself. In middle school the young women were only reacting in the way they had been taught to react toward other Black women whom they saw as a threat: intimidate and retaliate. How many times are Black women taught to go up to each other, introduce themselves, and offer to be helpful in a "competitive" situation? In competition for jobs, grades, teacher admiration, and men, Black women (and all groups of American women) are socialized to be cutthroat. I don't know how many times I have seen gangs of young Black women threatening to "kick that bitch's ass if she don't quit trippin'." But what is trippin'? Usually it's looking at somebody wrong, walking past without speaking, saying hello to someone's boyfriend—minor things like that. It hurts to think about it in these terms, but that's the way Black women are taught to behave.

All this junk about how Blacks are taught to stick together and pool resources through the extended Black family is something that book-headed scholars made up to explain things they don't understand. Of course, if the Black woman is in your family, she's automatically "your girl" to a certain extent. But, in general, "random" Black women are so jealous and so confrontational to each other at that age that they don't take time out to communicate and share and grow from the experience. Instead of sticking up for me as a fellow female, girls were the ones who spread most of the rumors about me! It wasn't the boys who were making up lies about being with me; it was the girls that took it upon themselves to lie for them. And when the boys had something to say, they didn't do it behind my back like the girls did. That, to me, fully demonstrates the phrase "stabbing her in the back": the pain comes from behind where you can't see it, and the perpetrator is not willing to be identified. Sneaky and low-down is really what it is.

Right now I'm different. I stand up for myself, I mind my own business, and I don't let what other people say bother me. I have learned that, in spite of my "Black female relationship socialization," I can be better than that. Now that I'm older I see other Black women who have gone through similar traumas and have changed their behavior and perceptions of our sisters. We know how much it hurts to have your own sisters treat you like some bald-headed stepchild with two different color eyes and a wooden leg with a kickstand. And, looking back, I can identify and relate to the characteristics in Black females that I have learned to respect: take care of yourself and of your own and always, always be up-front. It's one thing to say "none of your goddamned business, bitch," or "I don't have to answer that" instead of lying. Being a backstabber or a rumor starter is the same as being a coward; if you got something to say, say it and mean it. That's really where the strength lies: in assertiveness and being for real, not playing games.

I have learned that. I hope *they* have, too.

Lately I have been getting sick and tired of hearing about the issue of skin shade in Black America. A person can talk about it for years on end and still never come to any conclusion or any solution. It gets exhausting just thinking about the whole issue: where it comes from, who the hell started such nonsense, what definitions are incorporated into skin shade stratification, how much of a problem is it, if it is a problem, if it affects women more than men, the media's role in the scam, who sets the standards, what's the point, etc. Although this subject makes me sick, I still have to keep coming back to it. You see, my skin shade has always defined the way I look in the eyes of others. And over a twenty-year period I have learned to use shade to define myself. I'm getting ill just thinking about it, but the reality of it is that, if I can't admit it, I can't solve it.

My thoughts on the whole issue are totally incongruent. Not only do my own thoughts and opinions contradict themselves, but they contradict everything I believe in, and that pisses me off. I can't tell if it's my own belief system that needs an overhaul, or if I am simply a product of my environment. Who knows? Will I ever know, really? Shit, if I knew that, my life would be a lot easier in general. But that's irrelevant.

Being as politically aware as I think I am, I know that socialization, institutional oppression, and interpersonal conflicts play into the perpetuation of stereotypes. See, look at that language! Are those my own words, or is that some stuff I picked up in women's studies that I think I'm supposed to believe? Actually, the truth is I realize that, although the syntax and idea expressed in that sentence are indicative of my emergence as a member of a "privileged" and elite class (one of a handful of Black U of M students), the idea is one that I have lived with all my life. As a young child and an adolescent, I knew that Black people were not poor because they were lazy. I knew that women were not raped because they asked for it. I knew that being gay was not an illness. I knew that something was wrong with American in general, but there were two problems that prevented me from speaking out. One was that I could not articulate my feelings (who learns about institutionalized oppression in eighth grade?), and the other was much more pressing: I was buying into the very things I knew were wrong. And this has been eating at me since I was four years old.

My mother's family is light and dark. I don't know what I've been comparing the shades to—probably to each other. My mother, I realize now, is medium-brown-skinned. She has a beautiful complexion—very smooth with a reddish hue. I think she has gotten darker with age, or maybe I have set different standards for skin shade as I have gotten older. Whatever. My aunts Barbara and Valencia (Bootsie) are about the same shade—kind of light but not "high yellow." My grandmother is dark-brown-skinned, and my grandfather was light, I think. I can't really decide about him. Sometimes I think he was dark, almost as dark as my grandma, but then I think he was light. He wasn't as light as I am. But am I light-skinned?

My father's family are a bunch of light-brights. My paternal grandfather was of Native North and South American descent. I hear stories of his Indian and Mexican relatives and things, but I never saw any of them. I never saw him, in fact, except in his casket. The world is a better place with him in there instead of walking the streets continuing to make everyone's life a living hell. (Please, God, forgive me, but you know what he did and how wrong he was. Why do I have to include him as a member of my family? I feel bile coming up. . . .) Anyway, my biological grandmother was fair-skinned with long, wavy, dark hair. My dad looked entirely too much like her. I saw a picture of her, and they looked almost like twins or something. But anyway, she died in childbirth with my father's sister, Dorothy, who was named after my grandmother. My father's father eventually remarried my Grandmother Georgianna. She raised my father from a very young age, so, as far as anyone is concerned, she is my paternal grandmother. She is very fair-skinned also, with long, wavy hair. I think my grandfather was color-struck as far as women went. So, of all the children my grandfather had, most were light-skinned, including my father.

As a child, I was told stories of when I was really young and just learning to talk. I believe the stories because they sounded a lot like my color-struck subconscious. I used to call my uncle Carl and my cousin Kevin things like "Chocolate," "Blacky," and all the awful names that a two-year-old picks up from wherever. Of course, none of my relatives wants to take responsibility for teaching me those derogatory terms of color-consciousness; they all want to blame it on me. Do you think a baby can pull color barrier-linked derogatory comments out of the sky? I had to learn them someplace. Since no one realizes where they came from, it just makes me see the extent of the internalization of color difference. People say horrible things about members of their own families and don't even realize they're saying them! That's really bad.

While I was being babysat by Mrs. P—, her daughter, Rochelle, let me play with her dolls. She had a white boy doll and a Black girl doll, who were twins. I hated that Black doll with a passion. She was ugly and deficient. The white doll was more fun and easier to look at. I wanted to have a baby that looked like him and not like that other thing. Suddenly, one of the twins started to cry.

"Nikki! Your baby's crying," Rochelle challenged me.

"I know, I can hear it!" I said with an attitude. Rochelle was mean and got on my nerves. But I didn't have time to think about her; my baby needed me.

"Not that one! The other one," she said.

"No it ain't! It's this one!" I said, holding my baby in my arms.

"You always pick that one!"

"So?" I was a smart ass when I could get away with it.

"You make me sick! You don't like the other doll 'cause she Black! Gimme my dolls!"

Rochelle was mad. She didn't like me, anyway. She could never find anything nice to say about me, and, just because she went to school and was older than I was, she thought she could boss me around. But I was in her house, so I had to accept it.

School wasn't any better. Everyone tried to break my spirit under the guise of keeping me from getting "the big head." Students, teachers, everyone had to have an opinion about me. I couldn't be anonymous. Oh no, every teacher knew who I was, whose class I was in, and that I was "spoiled." Why was that? I have always been very sensitive and self-conscious. But does that come from my past experiences or my own insecurity?

Mrs. Brown, my first- and second-grade teacher, read us a book about what it means to be Black. This was in the mid-1970s, when folks were wearing Afros, and everyone owned something with a Black fist on it. There were pictures of different children with varying skin shades. I can't recall the name of the book, but skin shade was the whole point. We sat in a circle and looked at the pictures while Mrs. Brown read the story. I remember a picture of a light-skinned girl with "good" sandy-brown hair. I wanted so much to look like her; I thought she was the prettiest girl in the whole book. Her name was Saundra. I wondered if I was as light as she was. No, I wasn't. Her hair was good, and mine wasn't. That made her prettier than me. I knew I was light and considered pretty, but everybody still hated me, or so I thought. I thought that maybe if my hair was like Saundra's I would be prettier and more people would like me. Then Mrs. Brown asked a few of us to put our hands in a circle. I wondered why she took so long thinking about whose hand to put in and whose hand to leave out. Now that I look back, it's for the same reason I take so long to decide whether someone is darker or lighter than I am, or dark or light period: the standards vary as much as the skin shades do. I was proud that she asked me to put my hand in, but at the time I didn't know why—just to feel superior and to have something to do. After some people's hands were in the circle and others weren't, she told us all in her strong voice that we were all Black and not to forget it, to be proud. I realized then that she had put the light-skinned people's hands in the circle and left the dark people out. If I am remembering correctly, I think she brought it up to help the light-skinned children in our class feel more sure of ourselves—kind of like in self-defense against darker-skinned kids calling us names and claiming we were not Black.

Since then I have had a complex. I have worried that I am not light enough to be considered light-skinned, which has kept me in a panic for years. Mrs. Brown took a little while to decide if I was light enough to go in the circle. Had I looked like Saundra, she would have been quicker about choosing me, and I would have felt a little better about myself.

Throughout my adolescence and late-teen years, the skin color thing has been hanging around my neck like an albatross. You wouldn't believe the things I used my skin shade for just to get friends. It's sickening to think about it. The self-hatred involved in deception and denial makes me want to cry. But, with all the pain it causes me to think of it, at least I learned something from it.

When I was in YMCA day camp, I met a little friend. She and her brother were the only white people in the camp, and probably the only white family in the Detroit inner-city suburb of Highland Park. She was nice. She didn't say anything about skin color or race; I did. I suppose I was about three or four years older than she was, and I was just curious about how it felt for her to be white and me and everyone else to be Black. I think she said she didn't care. I was the one who cared.

I told that little white girl that I was a white girl with a dark tan. And she believed me.

Why would I do that? It wasn't to be closer to her; she didn't care one way or the other. I just wanted to have a place where I could be white. I was white with her. She thought I was white. Had my skin been darker, I wouldn't have been able to pull that off with her. But I did, and I felt good at the time. White was right, right? And I was white, so I must have been right.

In high school I had a clique of friends. My high school was so clique-oriented; you had to belong to a group. For some reason I immediately formed friendships with the white girls in my school. To me they seemed less confrontational than the Black kids, who wouldn't give me a chance. Or maybe I wouldn't give them a chance. I don't know. But, anyway, the pain started when I began to deny to my friends, and to myself, that I was Black.

My closest friend came from a liberal-minded, woman-identified background. Her white family showed no overt prejudice toward me, but, now that I look at it, the little things count. We would go to the beach, and Sheri's whole white family would compare their skin color to mine to see if they were tan or not. That made no logical sense: not only am I darker to begin with, but I tan faster than they do. But the denial came on my part, when I began to see myself as lighter than I was. I would lay out in the sun because my white friends did, but I would get indignant when they would say shit like "girl, you are gettin' *black!*" I didn't want to be Black. I overemphasized my multi-ethnic background in order to be closer to white, to be closer to them. "I'm mixed" was my motto; it wasn't white, but it was as close as I was gonna get. Sheri caught me without a relaxer a couple of times and commented on my "nappy" hair. What can I say? We were both victims of socialization. She was hating, and I was self-hating. It was disgusting. Now I see these same people, and they feel a little put off by my "newfound" Black identity. When I talk about racial oppression, they lose their liberal footing and get defensive. But that's the way of the world, I suppose. I think they're noticing I'm getting darker as the years go by.

Today is a different story. There has been a long series of events that have led to my opinions of my own looks today. I will admit that I have wanted to be lighter-skinned than I am. I think it's because I want to be one or the other; that's the way society sees things and categorizes them. No areas of gray, just right and wrong, white and Black (respectively). And with the everpresent color consciousness in the Black community and the daily harassment that comes with it, I figured I may as well have wished for valued assets. I don't think I could stand the pain that I see dark-skinned women go through at the hands of their own brothers, father, friends, and lovers every day. No, I don't think it's right. I think the whole thing about beauty standards and socialization is bullshit. Why can't she or he have nappy hair, a wide nose, thick lips, and dark skin, and still be beautiful? What, do we all come out of some kind of mold or something, where there is only one way to be beautiful? I don't understand how some Black people can stand up there and spout all this shit about Black power and say, "racism has got to go," while they're out there breaking their necks to get with "some light-skinned babe." Don't they see that they are preaching hatred of themselves every time they "diss" a dark-skinned brother or sister for a lighter counterpart simply on the basis of skin shade and socialized color standards? It seems pretty clear to me, but every time I speak out against color consciousness, I see another area where Black people are discriminating against each other because of their skin color. It makes me really sad. What's even more sad is that I use the pronoun *they* like I'm not a part of it.

A page ago I just said I wanted to be lighter-skinned. I might be aware, but I am not immune. This is a vicious cycle, a cycle that I know is totally wrong but that I can't break out of, and it makes me sick, really. Skin-shade stratification in Black America is a nightmare. I hope we can wake ourselves up in time. . . .

The concept of "being Black" has been on my mind lately. This is the first school term that I've taken Afroamerican studies, and I'm really excited. But in my natural state of curious and questioning mind some things about Black identity confuse me.

I was having a conversation with a couple of brothers about what it means to be Black. I was telling them ("Sam" and "Earl") about how this older man in my Black family class keeps using the phrase "real bruthahs." This man (I'll call him Mike) has spent time in prison for various crimes and comes from an economically disadvantaged background. In his eyes we college Black kids aren't real bruthahs. We get money from our parents and don't care about the community or each other. And we talk that "white folk's talk." So, in essence, since we college students are in college, and we aren't poor, and we date white people, and we talk "proper," and all we want to do is make money, then we aren't really Black. Why didn't he just throw in a "we all wear matching underwear" for an even broader sweeping generalization?

Mike and I used to argue the point periodically in class. I told him to shut that shit up and stop alienating middle-class Blacks on the basis of economics. He told me I talk proper, that I ain't never missed a meal, and just because I'm from Detroit does not make me "really Black." He kept throwing the "N-word" around like it was nothing. Niggahs this and niggahs that! Niggahs don't wanna do nothin', they don't know how to act in public, places in Ann Arbor gotta put up metal detectors when the niggahs come out at night, etc. But the same people he was talking about, the "bad elements in society," were real bruthahs. What the hell, do I have to be a repeat offender for grand theft–auto, on welfare, and functionally illiterate all at the same time to be Black? Do I have to speak "the dialect" to be a real bruthah? What's wrong with the way I talk? People understand me, don't they? That's what language is for. Do I have to know that Too Short, 2 Live Crew, and Big Daddy Kane are all rappers? Do I have to know the words to all their songs to be Black? Does my radio have to be parked at 97.9 WJLB "24–7" to be Black? Am I not allowed to define myself? Aside from the ethnic factor, what else makes us Black?

Sam and Earl said some shit about learning to "come down to their [meaning "lower" Blacks] level" in order to relate. Down? Where am I? Whose standards say I'm above them? Talk about self-hatred! Sam started complaining about how I'm such a stickler about language. But, in my opinion, if you don't think about what you're saying, then you're not communicating, and you're wasting other people's time. You may as well be "talkin' out cho ass," as the real bruthahs say.

Every time I think about what it means to be Black, I think about the Kentucky Fried Chicken scene in Spike Lee's movie *School Daze.* Six Black college men went to have a bite to eat at KFC for lunch. As they sat down, four Black men from the community in which the college was located began to harass the students. All the college boys asked for was the salt, and all the city men said was "I ain't cho *bru*-thah." After a few minutes of harassment, the symbolic confrontation between the politically conscious, middle-class, college-educated Black man and the bag-wearing, Jheri-curl, unemployed, inner-city Black man took place.

"You college boys is niggahs just like us" (not a direct quote).

"You're not niggers" (direct quote).

The power in the scene lies not in the acting but in the content of the scene. It questions everything we are taught about each other. It was no accident that the college men walked away from the fight (they're educated and have some sense; they're above that type of behavior, right?). It was no accident that the city men tried to test the waters and assert their manhood (after they have been emasculated by the institutional oppressiveness of racism, right?). But people like Mike, Sam, and Earl don't see it. People who use the N-word and fling it around like it's a part of the air don't see it. People who foam at the mouth over a light-skinned partner because s/he is not ebony-skinned don't see it. Young Black people who sell drugs to each other and shoot our beautiful Black children down in cold blood in the streets don't see it. Black people who would rather fight each other than unite among themselves, among ourselves, do not see it. They don't see it. We don't see it.

And it keeps ringing in my head: *YOU'RE NOT NIGGERS.*

Whatever we are, whoever we are, we're not niggers.

It's time we stopped treating each other like we are.

Epilogue

As I read, I see disjunction. For those who don't know me like I know myself, it's hard to see just when and where my Black identity comes from, what its definition is, what's going on. But you're not reading it wrong. It's supposed to be that way—linked enough to know what it means but separate enough to leave room for more growth.

I don't know when I decided that it was time to stop hating myself and stop hating my own. I still don't really know how to communicate my thoughts to others without someone getting the wrong idea. I still get stares and whispers about being "uppity," accosted by my roommate about being "high-yellow," and mentally undressed by men who have decided that I'm an easy lay. But the difference, the element of growth, lies in self-perception. I'm me.

As Maya Angelou says, "I'm a phenomenal woman." I don't remember the direct quote, but the poem the line comes from was something to the effect that being Black and female is empowering in itself. It's an inner beauty that comes from inner strength—something that no one can touch. I saw Oprah Winfrey say it on TV today. Phenomenal-as-Black-woman is a womanist (in the words of Alice Walker) perspective; it incorporates a sisterhood of Black women that I've just begun to see, where before there was blindness and confusion. And maybe, just maybe, if I think of myself and my abilities in the same way that Maya and Oprah think of theirs, I will be phenomenal by working up to my own individual full potential.

And to me potential, drive, self-respect, and dignity are what make me, just me, a Black American.

A Conflict of Soul

Andre Reynolds

As with most humans the biggest factors that mold their character are peer influence, parental influence, and environmental influence. For me these factors were magnified twofold since I lived my childhood and adolescent years in the same community. I am an African-American male who lives by the religion of morals and judges a person by the content of his character. I've always gone out of my way to understand others, but I've always skipped the most important person—me. Unfortunately, I never gave much thought to the reality of being an African American because my community didn't have prevalent racism, my friends ignored the issue (or they didn't think about it), and my parents (who I think innocently committed the biggest injustice to me) never successfully opened my eyes to the injustices that African Americans are living with and, more importantly, have lived with in the past. My complexity is one thing that has constantly discouraged me from really delving into my person. I'm complex to the point that I even consider myself strange—not strange in that I'm a social outcast, but strange in that I see myself as a person from the future trying to maintain a personality that can't exist for another one hundred years. So now I will attempt to understand the reality of not only being African American but also of being me—Andre Pierre Reynolds.

The Wonder Years

Chicago was my first home, and in 1968 Mae and Jesse Reynolds brought me into it. Since I was born my father has preached the importance of education. He was only twenty and had himself struggled for an education. It never came easily to him, but he always maintained perseverance and determination. What came hard for him he didn't want to come hard for his only son. He began saving for my education when I was born. Even though he couldn't afford to maintain the saving, he made sure that the goal always stayed alive in my mind. He would stay up endless nights tutoring me in math and making me read stories. When I didn't pay attention, he made sure that my butt reaped the consequences and not my mind. Nothing was left undone. We went through numerous amounts of workbooks outside of the ones that were assigned in school. As a result, I was always ahead of my class, but that wasn't enough for my father. Needless to say, he was always telling me that I wasn't doing enough, but for some reason I always knew he was proud of me and for some reason I always knew I was proud of him. However, neither of us ever told the other how we felt.

My father and I rarely relayed emotions to each other. We were the masters of disguise. If we weren't hiding our feelings, we were pushing them aside. Unfortunately, I got used to having a disguise and allowed it to carry into society. I learned to be cold and sometimes emotionless toward people. Most of the time I pushed my feelings aside. When I was alone, however, I cried endlessly. At times it seemed as though it was easier for me to cry because I'd held it in so many times. I hated showing emotions and always tried my best to maintain peace of mind no matter what the consequences.

I always had my way—as long as I did my schoolwork. My most mischievous times were after good report cards. I was king then. Not only did I not care about anything; no one else cared if I did. I did anything I wanted to and begged for anything I wanted. Yeah, I was a brat; however, I learned to relate good things with a respect for education and bad things with anything or anyone not associated with education.

From kindergarten to third grade I attended private schools. The second and third grades were predominantly white. More than anything, I can remember going home to my all-Black community and being teased about my speech and behavior. I hated to be teased about that, and I hated the children who did it. By the end of my third-grade year, I didn't have any friends around my home and spent most of my time with classmates and relatives.

Ironically, my mother never stressed education, even though she was well educated. Religion and discipline were her main concentrations. Unfortunately for my mother, those were the two factors of my life that I hated and never understood. I was a very inquisitive child, and the one thing that always puzzled me was that my mother never had any concrete answers to my questions, but she so adamantly believed.

"Why don't we see or hear God, Ma?" I would say.

"Because you're supposed to believe," she would answer.

"But what if you don't believe?" I inquired.

"Don't talk like that, and do as I say!" she so commonly replied.

It seems like that scene was repeated a million times with different questions and ambiguous answers each time. Although I was a bad child, I never understood the whippings I received. I could understand spankings, but I would have welts on my legs for two and three days at a time. No child deserved whippings that bad, and I knew it. However, I never stopped to realize the added stress I put on my mother when I didn't listen to her or ignored what she said. By the time I was four my parents had divorced and my mother was stuck with the task of raising a child, working, and attending night school for her bachelor's degree. Even with the heavy load, she always expressed her love for me through time shared and other very obvious ways. Nonetheless, whippings from my mother only weighed down the already uneven balance of my respect in my father's favor. A lot of my character is just a modification of his. Understandably, I have tremendous respect for my father, but I have more love for my mother.

The foundation of my character can be attributed to my parents, but once I moved to Evanston, Illinois, the effect of my friends and the environment were the prevalent factors. I was in the fourth grade and was a little nervous about entering my new public school. Little did I know that this school would play a major role in the development of my character. I used to wonder why I remember the events of fourth and fifth grade so clearly. Now I realize that it was the drastic change in culture. Not only was it strange to see intermingling among races within the school, it was even more strange to see the coexistence outside the school. While in Chicago I never felt comfortable in school or in the community. In Evanston I felt relaxed in both places. I recall it took little or no time to incorporate myself into the scheme of things, and after only two weeks I had accumulated two best friends. They were a major reason why I began to react to a person's character and not to his color.

Craig Stone and John Osako lived down the street in the same building. Craig was Jewish, and John was Japanese. They were both proud of their ethnicity, even in their youth, and they openly shared their beliefs. John had only been in America for two years, so he still had a lot to learn. Craig was dedicating all his time to helping John out and was more than willing to help me out. John would show and give us Japanese comic books, and we would show and give him Superman. He taught us Japanese games, and we taught him how to play checkers and football. He showed us pictures of family at home in Japan, and we showed him Ma and Dad. It was so easy to believe that Craig and John weren't any different from me other than the fact that they came from different backgrounds. I learned to respect them because they respected me, and we got along great.

I wanted to be "cool," however, so by the middle of fourth grade I made friends with some boys who I thought were popular. It turned out that they weren't as popular as they were silly, but that was OK because I was silly also. We were like a gang, except we weren't African American, Latino, or white; we were all races. There were six of us, and our race setting was so unimportant that I can only remember that three of us were African-American. This gang was always changing, and at times it would be as large as nine and as small as four, but through fifth grade the leader was always Marlon Gallimore. I admired him because he was funny and could "cut down" anyone, but I couldn't respect him because he wasn't into school. Marlon made me aware of even more unusual patterns in the community because Marlon was a dark-skinned African-American boy who was looked up to. In my old community there was a pecking order of admiration. Although it wasn't a blatant reality, there was an underlying thought that light-skinned African Americans were of a better breed. I never really thought about the issue because it was so interwoven into everyday life.

Marlon, however, destroyed that lie, but in the process he and the rest of the gang passed on another lie. The gang often talked about the cute girls, but it never occurred to me that most of the cute girls happened to be white. At the time there wasn't a problem with it, but in my mind white women were more attractive. It wasn't that I thought African-American women were unattractive; it just seemed that white girls were the main attraction. Since we weren't hung up on the difference in race, I believe we were prey to other social forces like TV and magazines. It's ridiculous how the most beautiful women in this country are represented by white women. It's also ridiculous that, when a white woman tries to look like an African-American woman, it's a new kind of beauty. Nonetheless, I became a victim of the lie. At first it was weird since I hadn't experienced anything close to interracial dating, but I soon got extremely comfortable with the idea. I dated Peggy and Andrea and liked Rachel and Aska. If it weren't for my mother, I think I would have been more engulfed by white girls.

My mother and father wanted me to do what I wanted as long as I didn't hurt the next person. Whenever my mother would point out pretty girls to me, however, they would be African-American every time. When I pointed out cute white girls that I liked, she would smile and give a silent "oh." I think that little hints like that from my mother kept me slightly aware of my ethnicity; otherwise, I would have been completely headed in the wrong direction.

When I entered middle school I found new friends, and I really began to tune into school with the help of the most influential peer I've ever had—Ciaran Fox. Ciaran had all the characteristics I learned to admire. He was silly, cool, and, most importantly, he was into school. I didn't meet him until seventh grade, but we immediately hooked when on the first day he asked me to be his locker partner. We often joked around and quickly raised our unknown status to that of class clown. Even class clowns earn some respect for being funny. We didn't get any respect in that department, but when it came to books we got it all. In fact, people hated us because we were able to goof off and still get good grades. Ciaran was an Irish white male and was distinguishable by his short stature. We were an odd combination, and, if you'd placed us in the middle of an average town, we would have gotten a lot of stares. Evanston wasn't like that, however, and we fit right into the weird mesh of people.

We did a lot of strange things that at the time made us perfect candidates for the term *nerds*. I laugh whenever I think of the times we ran around the halls of school emulating Benny Hill or telling the worst jokes that we laughed at the hardest. After a while people would just laugh at us, and we would laugh right back. We spent a lot of time together in those two years, but when we were together we were studying or trying to study. Ciaran was smarter than me at the time, but he would always go out of his way to make sure I understood our work before we proceeded. As a result, I learned to trust Ciaran as well as he trusted me.

My close friendship with Ciaran was a major addition to the development of my thinking. Because of him the gap widened between the respect I gave to people who were tuned into school and the respect I gave to people not in tune to school. Unfortunately, my analysis of those tuned into school was based on the grades that students received. In general, white students received the best grades, and African-American students received the worst grades.

This was the beginning of a mind frame that would haunt me for a long time. Why couldn't I realize that there had to be something behind the fact that African-American students weren't doing as well as white students? I wish someone would have helped me think about the reasons why this occurred. Consequently, I did all of the thinking for myself. The first thing I did was equate the opportunity level of other African-American students with that of mine—mistake number one. Second, I assumed that other students had the same parental guidance as I did—mistake number two. Third, I assumed that their chances of getting shuffled up the ladder of success were the same as mine—mistake number three. There was one major difference that I had failed to see. Those who were victims of this institutional-ized racism identified strongly with being African-American, and I, on the other hand, was one step away from complete assimilation. Thus, they were more susceptible to racism and prejudice. The proof is that when I look back on those years most of those African-American students who were successful were in some way assimilated.

Unfortunately, I didn't realize that fact back then because of an underlying thought that African Americans weren't as interested in school as whites. I never acted on this thought, but it caused me to form prejudices that would play a factor in the determination of my close friends. If there hadn't been other African-American students who had somewhat assimilated, that would have been the last step to complete assimilation. Unfortunately (for them), there were others like me, so I was able to maintain respect for my people as a whole.

In this day and age assimilation does a lot of harm to young African-American minds and African Americans as a whole. The more assimilated the child is the less he or she understands and identifies with his or her culture. Consequently, a lack of pride in one's race results, and the negative effects can be numerous. This is a time when an African-American person needs to be strong in char-acter because we are always tested and tried by others because of our color. Like me, the assimilated child grows up believing that he is a new genetic form of an African American, and that allows whites to take advantage of the situation. Assimilated African-American chil-dren allow whites to make biased (racist) distinctions between "good" and "bad" African Americans. I was a "cool" African American, and those African Americans who closely reflected our culture were es-sentially "niggers."

Utopia in America?

The effects of my adolescent years had a major impact on the development of my character. My friends, in particular, helped shape my character. To give a good understanding of my mentality and the mentality of my high school—my best friends were white, African American, Black Venezuelan, and Jewish. I didn't realize that until I got to college. It never really mattered to me or to them. We were people, and, more so, we were friends, and all we asked from each other was attention and fun from any friendship.

We would do everything together, even if it meant just hanging out in Sean's room (as we did so often) and drinking some beers, talking, laughing, and listening to "house" music all night. Even when we went out, no one was left behind, and wherever we went reflections of our relationship enhanced the copacetic nature of our community. Integration was everywhere and in all different forms: African American and white, Asian and African American, Jewish and African American, Jewish and Asian, and the list goes on. It didn't matter if you were male or female, child, teenager, or adult. It just didn't matter. Those who had a problem with it (mainly newcomers) were systematically ostracized without the issue ever being allowed to blow up.

Consequently, I never learned to open my eyes, and thus I was naive to racist attacks and prejudiced overtones. To me everyone who wronged me had a rational reason, and usually I would work overtime trying to figure out the things that people said or did. For that matter, I would often excuse prejudiced phrases unless they were blunt. I don't believe that I was just naive; I think I was afraid that I would be blowing things out of proportion. Sometimes I would comment on prejudiced phrases, and most replies would be "I'm just kidding! Settle down." Or: "You know what I mean! You know I'm not a racist." Maybe the comments weren't racist, but still they were promoting stereotypes and subtle prejudice. It bugged me, and I didn't know how to deal with it, so I dropped it.

Luckily, it rarely occurred in high school. Once, however, it hit me head-on when a friend of mine (who happened to be a "newcomer") referred to a group of African-American boys as niggers. I was completely shocked at the casual nature in which he used the word. When I confronted him, he promptly replied that he didn't mean me and that I was different. So I tried to explain that it hits me has hard as any other African-American male. For two hours I tried to explain the impact of that word when used by a white male, and he continuously refused to understand. Incidents such as this were few, and the effects on me were always short-lived.

I never let things bother me. Like any other human, I lived for peace, and, if I were able to achieve it, nothing—and no one who couldn't relate—concerned me. I often considered my community a Utopia, and I never wanted to relax that image in my mind. I could be friends with anyone I wanted. I could be assured that I would be given a fair shake from any of my peers. My community, however, wasn't perfect, but, if you wanted to find peace and equal treatment, you could find it—and I did.

When I first entered high school, issues of race rarely entered my mind. There was one general trend, however, that made me think about the issue. The difference in the actions of African-American students and white students was becoming more noticeable. I found a group of friends that stood right in the middle. There were about ten of us, including girls. The friends I chose weren't brilliant but had a respect for school and at the same time enjoyed going out and having a good time. Four of the males were African-American and two were white. The four girls were white. Three of the girls were Jewish (that fact was completely irrelevant since they didn't identify with being Jewish). We mingled and hung out and never thought twice about the issue of race. In fact, I can't remember any one of us feeling uncomfortable or anyone outside our group feeling uncomfortable. Our cultures blended in a coincidental way. Although we would drink beer and play drinking games a lot, we would also listen to house music and dance a lot. We did what we, as a whole, thought was fun, regardless of what culture it may have come from. I wish people could share themselves and their cultures without maljudgment, as we did. It's too bad the human race isn't mature enough to handle that yet. It makes you realize that we have a long way to go.

Although it wasn't pertinent at the time, I never developed a strong sense of who I am because of the environment I was a part of. Prejudice and racism force a people to strongly believe in themselves, or deterioration is inevitable. Because of the extreme racism and prejudice toward African Americans, there is an immense pride within the African-American community. Unfortunately, I wasn't brought up having to deal with these forces and thus quickly found myself a victim of the double lash of semi-assimilation and a lack of strong pride. I was never ashamed of being African-American because I didn't feel there was anything to be ashamed about. On the other hand, I was never strongly proud of being African-American because I didn't think there was anything to be strongly proud about. That's why white America must understand that it isn't fair that the perception of history is all white and the only African-American history pertains to slavery.

There's a lot of damage done to the mental stability of children when they can't find reason to believe in themselves. I learned about Martin Luther King, Jr., but I was never taught that Martin Luther King, Jr., enhanced a struggle that needs to be continued. I was never reminded that my brothers and sisters in the city are being oppressed, and their right to equal opportunity is consistently snatched away. I was never told that I was living a lie when I defended the actions of white people who showed me little respect. I was never told that I was living a farce that will exist as long as white people continue to deny the rights of the people that I am a part of but have known so little about.

I think I should explain how I define assimilation and how it pertains to me because the definition varies among different individuals. I never perceived myself as being white, nor was it a close thought. I never wanted to be white and was happy that I am African-American. When I refer to the degree of assimilation, I am referring to the amount of association with African-American culture as opposed to white culture. Of course, there aren't rigid lines in the definition of cultures. So, consequently, there aren't rigid lines in the amount of assimilation that one has incurred. It is obvious, however, that the behavior and attitudes of African-American and white people differ more than they overlap, and thus, when an African-American person possesses more of the nonoverlapping white behavior and attitudes than those of African Americans, then she or he has to some degree assimilated.

There is one important point I'd like to make about assimilation. Although it is perceived as negative, there are many situations in which the transition is completely innocent or by coincidence. It's not until a person purposely chooses another culture over his own culture that the results are negative and harmful to oneself and one's ethnic group. My assimilation at the time was definitely of an innocent, coincidental nature.

The fact that I was somewhat assimilated was never apparent to me until I got to college. I just perceived myself as different. In college the differences between cultures are great, and there is barely any overlap. Since my community had a large amount of overlap, assimilation wasn't an issue. As a matter of fact, even though I was partially assimilated, most of my behavior could be placed in the overlap. The behavior that I refer to includes the manner in which I joked around, the intonation of my speech, and other minor things. On the other hand, there were things that I did that were strictly related to African-American culture. My assimilation was a result of the people I was around the most. In my four years of high school I only had five classes in which there was at least one other African-American student, and only two of those classes had more than one other student (even the most liberal of American towns are victimized by institutionalized racism). At least six hours of my day, five days a week, were spent exclusively with white students. Since I had assimilated as much as I was going to, I never got worse because of my situation, but I never got better.

I never got slack for my partial assimilation except when I visited my cousins in the city. They would mock my speech or laugh at me instead of with me when I joked with them. I had to learn to adjust to them or I would get cut up all the time. Like a chameleon, I learned to adapt to situations in a matter of seconds. Although I was uncomfortable with the fact that I varied my character when it was barely nudged, I was happy because doing it allowed me to keep up somewhat with what was happening in the "hood."

I never really thought about the fact that my character fluctuated in different situations, but I know that it played a major role in the development of insecurity in my character. When I stepped out of Evanston, I would often feel worried that my actions weren't appropriate for certain situations. First, I was worried about acting correctly in a situation dealing with African Americans. Later, I was worried about dealing with situations correctly in a white setting. Although my feelings weren't obvious to others or even to me, they were there in all degrees. I remember that I hated to go outside of Evanston. I would make excuses so that I could stay in Evanston, and sometimes I made myself believe some of the excuses so that I didn't have to deal with reality. My character seemed to be weaker the further I was from Evanston. My problem almost elevated to a point where I didn't want to visit my cousins, fearing that they were going to bury me in the sand.

A major turning point in the development of my character was over the summer after my junior year. My math teacher chose me to attend an actuarial summer program at Howard University, a predominantly African-American college. The program lasted for five weeks, and the experiences were endless. There were fifty students in the program, and the respect I had for them as bright students was immense. They were all achievers, and often they bragged about their achievements. I hated the bragging, but I admired the perseverance they each maintained. Everyone came with the intention of learning as well as having a good time. Any idea I'd had that African-American students were not in tune to school was demolished.

When I first got there I was extremely scared that they would treat me like the others had. I didn't give anyone a chance to prove that they were sensitive. I figured there wasn't any African American there that could understand why I was different. As a result, I didn't talk to anyone on the first day, except for one of my suite mates, even though there were numerous efforts by others to meet me. Finally, it took an episode with the most beautiful African-American woman there to loosen me up.

On the second day, still in my introverted state of mind, I got in the elevator of my dorm, followed by Delaina Sanders. The next thing I knew there was a teddy bear in my face and a woman saying, "My teddy bear really likes you."

"I really like your teddy," I surprisingly replied. (I was also a shy person.)

"My teddy wants to give you a kiss."

At that point I was thinking she was wacked or I was meeting the freak of the year. So I gave teddy a kiss, and she said that teddy really liked it. The doors opened and I gave a sigh of relief, only to find that she had followed me out of the elevator and wanted to go to my room. Yes! I thought to myself, this is where the fun begins. I was wrong. That was where the learning began. She came into my room, and we talked for three hours. Afterward I was happy we had. She opened me up to an entirely different world, and I opened her up to mine. She made me realize that people, especially mine, weren't always as insensitive as I'd thought. In Evanston I'd judged the individual, and after the program I extended my scope to everyone. Later I learned that every student in the program had different experiences since we came from all over the country. Thus, we were all open to the behavior of others. As a matter of fact, there were a few students who I would consider more assimilated than I was. At the beginning of the program I thought I would have to go into a telephone booth and put on my Super-chameleon outfit, but by the middle of the program I was confident enough to throw it out.

The most important result of my having attended the program

was that I felt a new pride and confidence in my people that I had never felt before. On top of that I have never felt as comfortable or had as much fun with a group of students. I even felt close to those students that I didn't like. As I said, I don't like to cry in public, but on the last day it seemed as if I cried more than anyone. Most of my cry represented the thanks I wanted to give for the new feeling they'd unknowingly given me. Howard University provided me with the best experience of my life, but Evanston, the "utopia," threatened to undermine it—and to a large degree succeeded.

When I got back to Evanston I was more than aware of the presence of African Americans. The first people I called were my African-American friends to tell them what had happened. They were happy for me, but at the same time they were leery of my change. When we all got together I would tell them stories, and sometimes I would throw in the importance of African-American unity and my feelings on the importance of dating African-American girls. They couldn't understand why I had changed so drastically. They thought I had gone through some radical change. It took them about a week to say something, but one of my white friends finally spoke out, and the rest followed.

"What's gotten into Andre?" they would say. "You're acting as racist as those white racists who want to segregate everyone. We want unity for all groups, not just one. If we keep separating people, nothing will ever get done and no one will ever get along. What's wrong with dating anyone you want as long as you love them?"

I knew I was right, but what they were saying sounded so peaceful and beautiful. Only five weeks before I'd lived that attitude, and it wasn't likely that I'd just throw away that frame of mind in a second. After weeks and weeks of criticism, my newfound attitude began to deteriorate. I didn't completely give up my philosophy, but I ended up adapting it to fit into my original philosophy.

At that point in my life the structure of my views was very unclear. I couldn't really decide how I wanted to approach issues and how I wanted them to dictate my life. I'd want to date anyone I wanted, but when I did I'd feel guilty if she weren't African-American. I thought it was good that I could feel comfortable around any group of people, but I began to mildly isolate myself in all-white settings. I was happy that I was asked to go to the prom with one of my closest friends, who happened to be white; however, I didn't really want to be seen out in public. I had to make some quick decisions. I hated my behavior. It didn't make sense, and it was annoying me and everyone around me. I thought I had to choose between the two views. So I decided that I would be more comfortable with my new-found view. That's the way I wanted it. I was going to enter college with a new frame of mind. I wanted to get involved with all African-American activities and maybe even join an African-American fraternity. Along with this, I wanted to maintain my friendly nature and ability to get along with others, regardless of race. While the latter occurred, my other desires slipped away because of a few minor confrontations in the early part of my college years.

Are You In or Out?

I was extremely happy entering college with my new attitude. My first priority was meeting as many African-American students in my dorm as I could. I only ended up talking to four of them before school started. One fact stood out more than any—I was very different in attitude. I sensed a lot of hatred toward integration. Even though I decided I was going to take a stance, I realized that at heart I was still an integrationist. There were other minor differences, but there was an overall difference in the way we were. Who am I to think that they had to be like me? It's stupid, but I had expected something close to that.

The more I look back on it the more I realize that they were like me in the most important way, and that was in the fact that they were African-American and wanted to get through this school with respect and equal treatment. Nonetheless, I was intimidated because of my ignorance. I did meet an African-American woman who was willing to debate and discuss some of the issues without trying to totally change me. She preached some of the same things that I had learned at Howard, and once again they made sense, and my views were starting to be where they should be. Conflict began to occur, however, when I tried to blend my friends on the hall (who were white) with my African-American friends.

The white male friends on the hall were the first people I met and hung out with and, therefore, befriended. I didn't care that they were white; I just cared that we got along—and that we did great. We would always go out on the nearest field and play football, basketball, Frisbee, or just goof around. Most important, the friends that I hung with most were silly and loved to laugh like me. They weren't uptight, and that was very important to me. I don't like to be around people who are always critical of what you say and do. Nonetheless, they were not like that, and they laughed at the weird things I said and did, just as much as I laughed at the weird things they said and did. They were also open-minded and learned to like some of the things that I liked and they weren't used to, and I tried to do the same. I spent a lot of time with them, and, before I knew it, my closest friends were white. This didn't occur because I thought I couldn't get along with African-American students; it occurred because I had an unbiased character, which had been developed over seventeen years. Not realizing that fact, I still felt guilty that I had contradicted myself.

I decided to try to introduce my African-American friends to my white friends and hoped that everyone could get along. Why not? It had worked in Evanston. Well, I quickly learned that the University of Michigan is not Evanston. Only days before I decided to try my idea, one of my African-American friends surprised me with an up-setting statement, questioning the number of white friends I had. Obviously, in her experience the races didn't intermingle that much, but I perceived her comment as an attack on a very sensitive part of my personal life. I overreacted, and we stopped being friends. I think that my overreacting was a way of justifying having all white friends. However, it didn't work, and, if anything, it made things worse.

At this point in my college career an old bothersome flaw in my character reappeared in great proportion. All of a sudden I felt that I was being judged by African-American students. I was seriously paranoid. All my wants and desires to get involved were washed away by blind fear. It thought that I would be rejected and hated because of my association with more whites than African Americans. Once again, however, I was overreacting; the best year of my life was about to ride over that paranoia.

By the second semester of my freshman year I had accumulated four of the most laid-back friends I have ever had. On top of that, each had an attitude and physical diversity that reminded me of home. They were white, Jewish, and Asian. The physical diversity wasn't perfect, but their caring, peaceful, fun-loving attitudes were the perfect anecdote for the insecurity I was feeling about the Afri-can-American community. I didn't really think much about being apart from the African-American community since we didn't stay in Ann Arbor that much. Every weekend we took trips to other colleges; otherwise, we did things among ourselves. We had a memorable time that semester, but by the end of it my bond with the African-Ameri-can community was weak.

Over the summer I didn't do much thinking about my dilemma,

but by the end of the summer I decided once again that I was going to get involved. Again I felt a bit intimidated, and, in addition, I began to get into the same groove as in the previous semester with the same four friends. I was having a lot of fun, and was anything wrong with that? Therefore, the combination of fun and intimidation left no doubt in my mind about who I was going to hang with.

Now I'm in a predominantly white fraternity. How can I decide to be in a predominantly white fraternity when some of my beliefs contradict it so heavily? Why? Because some of my beliefs support it heavily. That's where I stand. I have two sets of beliefs that clash only because this society isn't mature enough to handle them. I am proud to be African-American, and I strongly agree with most pro-African-American platforms, but I have developed a character for over twenty years now, and I'm not going to and couldn't change it overnight.

Thus, I am living with a dilemma. My dilemma, however, is a dilemma only to this society, and the more I think about it the more I come to understand that I'm not in the wrong—this society is in the wrong. This country demands that we remain racists, sexists, homophobics, etc. Is it right? Of course not. It also demands that people blend into their "proper" categories, depending on their color or sex, and be "normal" within them. This country seems to impose strict definitions on normality. Quite often, I find people who try to strip me of being African-American because I'm not normal. Quite often, forces work to pressure those who aren't normal to be clones of a put-together category. Unfortunately, they work on most of us. So those who aren't normal tend to stand out and stand alone. I've fought these forces for twenty years, however, and I'm not going to give in after coming this far.

I will continue to be the way I am and think the way I do while at the same time being open-minded and willing to learn. If that's a problem for those normal thinkers, *c'est la vie.*

Part 4: The View from Inside

Inner Strength: Being African and American

John B. Diamond

This essay is dedicated to my family.

My grandmother was frail now. Her once strong body had withered to practically nothing, and yet her inner *strength* remained. Inside her was a passion so powerful, so beautiful and enlightening that her touch warmed my heart. She had a quiet confidence about her—such confidence that, even in the face of death, hardly able to speak, she reassured me with her smile. I stood by her hospital bed for the last time knowing I would never see her again. As I prepared to leave her room, I kissed her cheek, fought back the tears, and forced my face to mock a smile. She looked at me, balled her fist, and told me to never give up.

I often wondered how in the face of death she had found such strength; how, as her life was coming to an end, she had urged me to never give up on mine; how a seventy-pound woman could be, in my eyes, the most powerful person in the world. I realize now that nothing is more powerful than inner strength—the inner strength that overcomes adversity, that quietly demonstrates pride, and that she instilled in me in life and death.

Lansing, Michigan

I was five years old when my family moved to Lansing, Michigan. We moved from Saginaw, a town torn by racial hostility and divided by segregation. The move seemed like a welcomed one. My parents were proud that their search had landed us (my parents, my sister Kim, and me) in a liberal and somewhat racially harmonious city. One characteristic of my parents, and seemingly other members of their generation, is their optimistic outlook concerning racial issues. My parents seemed to feel that because life is better than it was years ago maybe time is in our favor as Black people—that maybe there is a natural progression from bad to good or from worse to better. They saw Lansing as an example of progress. It seemed to be an example of Blacks and whites living in harmony.

In 1974 the area into which we moved was mostly white. My family was the second Black family on the block, and we seemed to be well accepted. As more Black families moved in, it seemed that a tension began to mount. It was a tension noticed by some, ignored by others, and acted on by a few. One way it was acted upon was through the denial of access to certain luxuries. Slowly I began to realize that, as a Black child, there were certain things I was not allowed to do.

Our next-door neighbors, the Minelli's, were a large family with six children. They were a good example of Lansing's closet racists. Although they did not overtly express racial hatred, they would always tell me to get out of their yard if they were not playing with me. The problem escalated to the point that they felt it necessary to construct a fence designed to keep me and other "undesirables" out of their precious yard.

The Minellis were members of the Elk's Club, which was about a mile away from our block. One hot summer afternoon some neighborhood kids were going there with the Minellis to swim. It sounded like a good idea to me, so I asked Mark, the Minellis' youngest son, if I could come along and swim. Mark looked at me as if I should have known better and simply said no.

I was shocked. Why couldn't I go when so many others could? I was his friend, too. When I asked Mark why I couldn't go, he matter-of-factly stated that Blacks were not allowed.

The people in my neighborhood and town were constantly trying to protect its image. I felt like I was welcomed as long as I knew my place. Comments like "you're not like the rest of them" or "you're one of the good ones" were common. The whites in this area made a habit of thinking of Blacks who didn't fit stereotypes as exceptions. They were not racist against the "good niggers," only the bad ones.

In Lansing the racial tension was there, but the false feeling of harmony still existed. I tended to ignore the racism, hoping that things had changed, hoping that people could live together without hating one another. As I grew older, the integrated environment blinded me to reality. It made me buy into Lansing's big lie.

Sticks and Stones

Sticks and stones may break my bones, but names will never hurt me. This oversimplified statement which is used to train children to avoid acting violently, is one of the biggest lies taught in elementary schools. True enough, words cannot harm one physically; however, they can harm one emotionally and even change the course of one's life. The words that are used by those in authority during this period of one's life sometimes determine a person's future. Those important words that are not said may blind us to our past or deny us a bright future. Thus, in a real sense, words can destroy us. They can destroy one's self-concept. They can take away our self-confidence and feelings of self-worth. Unfortunately, they can harm us in ways much deeper than broken bones; they can destroy our dreams.

Harmony and Togetherness

One of the first experiences with white children was in elementary school during the first grade. I remember this period because little white girls would always want to feel my hair. They were so fascinated with me because I was different, and their fascination made me a showcase, a novelty of sorts. Being the center of attention is not usually negative for a child, but I began to feel as if something was strange about me—that maybe my differences made me better or worse than them—and, because they were the ones in the majority, maybe I was strange to them. After a while the fascination with my hair wore off, and the other children became used to my differences.

During this period I tried desperately to deny that racial prejudice existed—not only because I did not want it to exist but also because all of my teachers endlessly preached equality and togetherness. It only made sense that if, "all men are created equal," then all people should be treated equally. But I soon began to realize that just as my teachers chose not to tell me that, according to the Constitution I was only three-fifths of a man, they were knowingly lying about how wonderfully harmonious the world was.

It was the middle of my second-grade year when Mrs. Hill, the fourth-grade teacher and the most hated teacher in the school, called an assembly to deal with an important problem in the school. The entire second grade dreaded dealing with this woman until it was necessary in her fourth-grade classroom. We all treaded down the long hall to the gymnasium to find out the bad news. I walked down with my good friend Beth, who had been my running buddy throughout the past three years of elementary. We took our seats on the floor and waited for the *lecture* to start. Mrs. Hill walked up to the podium and began an uninterrupted speech:

> As you all know, it is our policy at this school to make all of our students feel as welcome as possible. Unlike the past we have students of many different groups here working harmoniously to learn as much as we can together. As teachers here, we take great pride in our students from different backgrounds, and we feel that all of us can contribute together to the learning process. As teachers, we have witnessed a problem in the way you students are dealing with one another. It seems like the Black students are excluding themselves from the rest of us in the cafeteria and on the playground at recess. We called you students down here to let you know that we are determined to keep the harmony that we have begun here. We want to tell all of you children to sit with people from other groups in the lunchroom and not avoid each other as you have been. Now I would like to let Mr. Becker address the same problem. . . .

She's the teacher, and she must know what she's talking about. Beth and I just looked at each other and shrugged our reluctant approval of what she had said. We did tend to sit together with our own group, so maybe we were excluding ourselves. We looked forward again to listen to Mr. Becker, another student favorite, reiterate what Mrs. Hill had just said.

As we left the assembly, another friend of mine named Steve, a white kid, said, "Yeah, it does seem like the Blacks always sit together. You guys should stop separating yourselves."

"Well, we just sit with our friends when we eat, what's wrong with that?"

"Well, Mrs. Hill said that's excluding yourself."

"Yeah, she did, didn't she?"

This was brilliant. What a way to manipulate a group of kids' minds. Not only were there only a small number of Black kids in the school, now we were made to feel guilty for seeking each other out. Moreover, when the white students didn't see any Blacks around, they had a quick and effective answer: "Black students are excluding themselves again." With a newfound enthusiasm, we Black students tried to sit with whites in the cafeteria, and it seemed like "the problem" was solved. How simple. All we had to do was make a little effort, and we would be accepted by white students. Maybe they were right about this harmony and working-together stuff. Gradually, however, we settled back into our old, more comfortable ways. The cafeteria became "segregated" again.

What about My *History?*

Black history week in my elementary school was what I like to call a "feel-good" affair. It was a time for all of the white teachers and students to show that they were concerned about "Black" issues and to express their pride in how far we had come as a nation from those horrible days of slavery. It seemed that the only Black leaders we talked about were those who had helped to free Blacks from slavery. For Europeans history went far beyond this country; for Blacks, however, it seemed to reach only to slavery. No one mentioned the fact that Africans had built the pyramids or had cultures long before Europeans had moved out of caves. No one mentioned that the Greeks had stolen Egyptian philosophy or that the foundations of science all come from Black Africa. I guess this was just too controversial.

We learned about the slave trade coming from the western coast of Africa. One point that my teachers made sure to emphasize was that Africans interned other Africans and sold them to the white man. This statement served to remove blame from whites and place it on the Africans. It was their way of saying that the blame for slavery doesn't rest only on the white man's shoulders. It wasn't the white man's fault for murdering 100,000,000 Black people and oppressing them; it was their own African brothers who had caused them to face this plight. My teachers denied me an enormous part of my history prior to slavery; they placed much of the blame for slavery on the Black man; and they downplayed my people's contributions in the building of this country.

Words Will Never Hurt Me

Throughout my elementary school years my Black identity was suppressed. That stupid little saying had given free rein to the warped concept that injury only comes from physical and not psychological abuse. Therefore, when I was misled to think that segregation was a

Black problem, I was not harmed. When I was misguided about my history as a Black man, I was not harmed. When my violent response to overt racial hatred and insults caused me to be labeled a "bad guy," I was not harmed.

My experience in elementary school forced me to deny a part of myself. Through lack of education and through misguided information, I lost touch with much of what my family had attempted to teach me about who I was and what it meant to be Black. Instead of learning more about my history, I got a distorted image of my past or no image at all. Education in this school did a great deal to destroy my self-concept and to promote a false belief in harmony and togetherness.

A Continuing Struggle

My teenage years were a time of confusion—a time in which I struggled to find myself. The destruction of my identity during elementary school placed me in a tough position as I grew older. Much of my junior high and high school years were difficult because, on top of the typical problems of this time period, I had the combined struggle of being Black and having my race always looked down upon, expected to fail, expected to cause trouble, and expected to be unproductive. During these years I had to fight to maintain my confidence. I did not know who I was. . . . I was confused.

Confused

My junior high school football team had just defeated its crosstown rival, Walter French. The whole team was extremely excited about the victory, and the energy level caused a roar of voices and activity. Our coach told everyone to be quiet because he had an announcement to make.

"The following players will not be allowed to play next week. These people have E's on their midterm marks." He then began reading names. I was only half-listening because I had never had any academic problems.

" . . . Crenshaw . . . Diamond. . . ."

What? There must have been some mistake. I had never had any academic problems before. I was always a good student. There must have been some mistake. I was humiliated in front of the whole team. I had never received an E. It had to be a mistake!

When I arrived home, I made sure to keep this grade business to myself; my parents would have killed me if I hadn't. I told them I was tired and went to bed early to avoid unneeded conversation.

We received our grades in school the next day. I should have known it was that biology teacher, Smith, who had given me that grade. There was still no way I deserved an E in that class. I went to talk to him following class that day. He insisted that it was the grade I had earned and that he wasn't going to change it. The day dragged on, and I tried to figure out how to tell my parents about it. I decided to explain my situation as honestly as possible and deal with the consequences.

I arrived home at 4:30 following football practice, still somewhat reluctant to show my grades to my parents. When they were both home, I told them that grades were in and that I hadn't done too well.

My mother responded, "Oh, it couldn't be too bad, Johnny. Let us take a look."

"Yes, it could," I mumbled under my breath. This was the last thing I wanted to hear—that it couldn't be that bad. "I got a really bad grade in biology."

"How bad of a grade?" she asked.

"Well, uh, he gave me an E, but I didn't deserve one." I said this with the expectation that my parents would both explode, so I added, "I know it's bad, but I went to talk to Smith, and he wouldn't listen to me."

My father said, "What do you mean you didn't deserve it? I'm sure he wouldn't just fail you for no reason. Why would he give it to you if you didn't deserve it?"

"I don't know," I mumbled. I wanted to say that it was because I was Black, but that stuff had ended in the 1960s. There was no way a teacher could get away with that kind of thing now.

"Well, you should know. It takes a lot of energy to get an E." He looked down at the grade sheet, which my mother had taken from me. "And you got a low citizenship grade, too."

My mother seemed to listen to my side a little more than Dad. She noticed that the rest of my grades seemed normal. I had gotten an A, three B's, and a C from that crazy band teacher, Mrs. Best.

"John, the rest of his grades don't look too bad. Maybe there was a mistake." She hesitated and then added, "I can at least go look into it or call the school in the morning."

I held back my smile so that my excitement wouldn't make them think I was lying about not deserving the grade. Mom had a knack for dealing with teachers because she was one herself, and I knew that if she talked to Smith I could get that grade changed.

The next day my mother called the school to set up an appointment with Smith. She came to school at the end of the day directly from her job in East Lansing. We went into the principal's office to discuss the problem. Smith began the conversation.

Well, Mrs. Diamond, your son has not been doing much work in this class. He tends to sit with a talkative group of students, and they are sometimes disruptive to the rest of the class."

My mother interrupted. "*They* are disruptive? Who are *they*?"

"The group of students who he sits with. He tends to be a part of this disruptive group," he stated.

"OK, without regard to that, what has been wrong with his work?"

"Well, many of his assignments have been incomplete, and others have simply been inadequate." Smith seemed annoyed by my mother's scrutiny of him. He seemed to think her concerns were unimportant.

"Why don't we take a look at his papers and see at least what he has done," Mom said in a serious tone.

Mom was going to get him now, I thought to myself. I had done most of my work, and it wasn't that bad. He was exaggerating about my work. He was just clumping me together with some of those other kids in the class.

"Look, Mrs. Diamond, I'll give him whatever grade you want."

"That is not what I am here for!" She was very upset now. "I want to know what grade he deserves."

Smith was a racist as well as a sexist. He could not deal with my mother questioning him. This meeting did not last very long. Later my mother and father met with Smith and the principal to work out the problem. During this second meeting Smith stated that he could "deal with Mr. Diamond but not with Mrs. Diamond." Smith was simply a racist white sexist who had low expectations for Black students and felt that Black students deserved to fail.

He was eventually forced to review my papers. There were a couple of assignments missing; however, these were few in number. He added up the grades, and the average was a C+. How he got an E from C+ work and a couple of missed assignments made little sense. He never did admit to having made a mistake. As I think about it, maybe he hadn't. Maybe he'd simply clumped me together with the "disruptive" students in the class—my group of friends, mostly Black boys, who were not actually as troublesome as he had made us out to be.

Was my hunch right? Did he give me the bad grade because us Black kids talked too much? It scared me to realize that maybe the 1960s hadn't changed things so much. It seemed like, as much as I wanted to deny it, Mr. Smith had labeled me from the beginning: "another one of those troublesome Black kids." He had given me an E not because I'd earned it, but because he'd expected me to deserve it.

I hated the fact that he had labeled me a troublemaking failure from the beginning, and I felt I had something to prove to myself. I had half of a term to pull my grade up from this C. I came to class with determination. I worked hard to show this white man that he could not get away with treating me like this. I earned a high B for the remainder of the term and wound up with a B in the class.

P.S.

When I began my eleventh-grade year of high school, I was elated. My acne was gone. For me this meant the opening of new doors. I felt that women were attracted to me again, and I was prepared to take full advantage. I started the school year with a new attitude. I believed that I was handsome for the first time in five years.

As I thought back to all of the pain caused by my skin problems, I made a vow to maintain a level of confidence in myself. I remembered the pain I'd felt when one of my peers had told me that I "had a face only a mother could love" or when I would be silenced by any reference to my face. I remember crying at night because I knew my face would be red and irritated in the morning. And I thought about the people who would tell me how to rid myself of the problem with remedies that I had tried countless times. My acne was an important part of my teenage frustrations, and now I was finally free.

It was interesting that during this year everything seemed to be going my way. I had been a good trumpet player the year before, but this year I was first chair. In high school band this attracted a lot of attention. There was a certain status involved with being one of the band's "elite" performers, similar to that afforded a quarterback on the football team. The band represented a subculture of sorts, and I was in a prime position within this group.

Given my new attitude and my advantaged position, I began to be approached by girls. Because for so long I had been withdrawn from many social groups, I was extremely shy. Sure, I tried to give off an air of confidence, but it was only there to fool myself and others.

I had short and relatively meaningless relationships with girls in school (mainly those in the band and their friends). It seemed as if the girls who approached me were those who were aggressive. I found myself in relationships with young white girls during this period (to the disbelief of my parents). At the time it didn't seem intentional; it seemed natural. Lansing had a great deal of intermarriage. I was under the false impression that it didn't matter what the color of the skin was if you loved someone. Now, through experience, I feel differently.

It was a Saturday afternoon in the winter during my junior year. This meant that me and my boys would be going to the mall in the afternoon to walk around, see friends, and find girls. This week we traveled to the Meridian Mall in Okemos for a change of pace. (We usually went to the Lansing Mall closer to home in Waverly.) The Mendez brothers, James, and I got together about two o'clock and headed for the mall. We had been out the night before, and we were still tired.

As we got into the car, I started the conversation. "Mark, man, where did you wind up last night? We couldn't find you anywhere."

"I was with that babe Cindy," Mark responded.

"Who? Was that the blond babe with the short friend?" I asked.

"Yeah, she's from Holt. Fine as hell."

"Why does this ugly ass always get babes? Man, I never will understand that," James chimed in, smiling.

"Yo, why you trippin'? You know they love me."

I was driving, and my mind was focused on the slippery road. I thought the snow was really pretty when it first fell. The trees took on a different appearance as well. I looked around the car and thought to myself, "We make a great team."

I pulled into a parking spot, and we anxiously jumped out of the car. We headed directly to the Burger King to grab something to drink and look around. There was a certain ritual that we followed. We always went to the B.K., then we would walk down to the record store or at least in that direction. The main objective was to scope out women and look cool doing it. Therefore, much of our time was spent standing in a strategic spot and trying to make eye contact.

After the ritual was complete, we decided to walk back to B.K. James spotted this girl he knew and her friend. He called them over and introduced everyone.

"Shawn and Angie, this is Mark, Jesse, and John D. . . . The D is for dangerous."

That last comment seemed to interest Angie. It made me seem mysterious or something, and I could sense her interest. I wasn't comfortable with that silly title, but it worked. I figured I might as well make my approach. She was an attractive girl, so I tried to talk to her.

"Do you want to go get something to eat?"

"Yeah . . . um, let me talk to Shawn for a minute."

She talked to her friend briefly, then we left the rest of them and went to eat. I said the typical things like, Where do you go to school?—but she seemed so receptive. I got her phone number and promised that I would call her soon.

I met back up with my boys, and we prepared to leave. It was about seven o'clock and it was time to go. At least my mission was accomplished, and it was getting late.

Pick me up at Brockton

Angie was my "first love." I prefer to leave it in quotes because I don't know why, or even if, I loved her. There are two possible answers. First, maybe it was genuine love between two young people who were able to separate themselves from society's race issues long enough to truly care for one another. Second, maybe it was just two young people who were too naive to understand where their true feelings were coming from. Maybe we were simply in love because we each represented what was taboo for the other. Maybe we bonded because we wanted to believe that we were different. And maybe then, if the latter is true, we were never actually in love.

Our relationship lasted approximately six months. We seemed to be obsessed with one another for the entire time. We would always want to be together. It got to the point where I would see her during the day, come home about midnight, and sneak back out at 2:00 a.m. to pick her up again.

I hate to remember this period because during the relationship I allowed myself to be treated without full respect. I never met her parents. Once I met her mother, but I was introduced as Angie's friend's cousin and not as her boyfriend. Her father was blatantly racist and hated Black people with a passion. We would talk about it sometimes, and she would be proud because she thought she was different.

My parents hated the situation. Once they'd found out, I could tell they didn't like it. Time passed, and, as they began to realize that the relationship was not going to fizzle, they began to act differently. My father continued to dislike the situation. The only difference was that he acted friendly toward Angie even though he didn't like what was going on. My mother found herself torn between her feelings of discontent with the relationship and her history of teaching my sister and me that everyone should be treated equally. This led her to suggest that I give Black girls at least a fair chance. I took offense at the suggestion. Color did not matter to me. I did not know why she couldn't understand that. Besides, I had dated Black girls, Hispanic girls, and white girls—what was the big deal?

The most humiliating thing about the relationship was that I rarely picked Angie up at her house. Her parents were never forced to question their racial hatred because they had absolutely no idea who I was. Usually, I would pick her up at the Brockton Junior High School near her house.

When I reflect upon the situation, I find it hard to believe that I did not feel humiliated. As I saw it then, it was us against an unjust world that was trying to make us separate. It was the two young lovers who had each other to lean on and did not need anyone else. As I see it now, it was two naive young people who were afraid to face reality, who were afraid to deal with their own confusion about their own identities. If she'd really loved me, she would have been able to face her father. If I'd really loved myself, I wouldn't have allowed her to treat me like I was not worthy to step foot in her house. Racist household or not, we had not come to grips with our own feelings, and we were not prepared to face reality.

Just a Phase

It was very difficult for me when Angie moved away. Whether I loved her or not is an open question; whether I thought I was in love is definitely not. During the August before my senior year, her family moved to Houston. I remember the tearful good-bye as if it were just yesterday. I remember crying when the lyrics of the song on the radio hit so close to home. "Let's Just Kiss and Say Good-Bye" was so difficult to listen to knowing I may never see her again. Something very strong existed between us. It was something that I have trouble understanding to this day, but nonetheless it existed. We talked for a while and promised to stay in touch and never to forget one another. I dropped her off and watched as she walked toward her house and out of my life. The tears streamed down my face. I was once again all alone. My "first love" was gone forever.

As time passed, we wrote letters and talked on the phone. I was still attached to her but was seeing other women. She would always write me, but I neglected her. She was still dear to my heart, but I did not take the time to show her.

I was accustomed to getting her letters frequently and began to expect to hear from her. Therefore, I made a habit of going to the mailbox to look for her letters. I was excited to find one around the end of November. She had planned a trip back to Lansing to visit around Christmastime, and I suspected that the letter from her had something to do with her trip. I opened the letter anxiously and began to read:

Dear John:

I hope you are doing well. I have missed and been thinking about you a great deal and decided to drop you a letter. I am writing this letter to let you know about my trip to Lansing this Christmas. I will be there around the 20th of December and am looking forward to my trip.

This is a very difficult letter for me to write. I always have a difficult time with good-byes as you are well aware. I want to let you know that when I come to Lansing we will not be going together for that time period. I have done a lot of thinking and concluded that we should just be good friends for that period. I also want to tell you that I may be seeing other people while I am there.

John, I know that this may be difficult to understand but it is the decision which I have come to. Please respond and tell me that we can be dear friends.

I know this is a bad time but I want to wish you Happy Birthday. I hope you can understand what I have written and I hope you have a good birthday.

Love,
Angie

Needless to say, I was shocked. I immediately picked up the phone and dialed her number.

"Hello," someone answered.

"Yes, can I speak with Angie please?"

"Hold on."

I waited impatiently.

"Hello," she said with her newly acquired Southern accent.

"Hey, how are you? This is John."

"Hi," she said, as if nothing had happened.

"I got your letter today." I thought about the best way to approach the situation. She had to still love me, and I figured if I told her I were upset she would come around. "I don't know what's gotten into you, Angie. We're perfect for each other. You have somebody else or something?"

"No, I just feel like we shouldn't be together in that way anymore."

"What did I do? I mean, I know I haven't written much, but I'm busy. You know how hard it is for me to write. I still love you."

"It's not that. I just feel different about us now."

"Oh, so now you don't love me anymore. All the love I gave you ... All the time I was faithful to you—and now it was just a waste."

"No, things are just different. They've just changed."

"How? We still love each other, or at least I still love you. What's up? Tell me what's going on."

"It's different here ... I mean, in Lansing people could accept us being together. It was easier to be together. I thought that it was cool for us to be together. Now I just realize that I was wrong. See, here there are no couples like us around."

"But what's that got to do with us? Hell, we had our problems before. . . . We managed."

"It's not that simple. The more I think about us the more I think it was just a phase in my life. You know, maybe it wasn't real love like I thought it was."

This hit deep and hard. I had given my all to this relationship, and now she was telling me that I had wasted my love. That the whole thing was a lie. That our relationship was just a phase. That she had outgrown me!

I don't remember how the conversation ended. I guess I remained cool and tried to be a man about it, whatever that means. But it hurt. The rage in my heart burned uncontrollably until it boiled over. I looked around the room, grabbed a tennis racket, and started pounding it on the ground. I was being destroyed inside, and I needed to hurt something to retaliate. I broke the racket into practically nothing. I left it in the basement and made my way upstairs to my bedroom.

Unconditional Love

A couple of hours later my father came into my room; he was furious. I had destroyed the tennis racket he had had since he was a teenager. I got up and followed him down to the dining room area to talk about what had happened. I was trying my best to hide the reason behind my actions. I apologized to him for having broken his racket, while he tried to explain its significance to me. It was sentimental to him because he had gotten it when he was a young boy. It was one of the few things that he had been able to keep track of over the years. He just couldn't understand how I could have broken that racket.

I looked in my father's eyes, and I could see his desire to understand. He wanted to know why I'd broken it. I couldn't tell him the story. I was just so hurt by what Angie had said. I was so sorry that I had taken something away from my father. I just broke down and started to cry. When he saw this, he didn't care about his pain anymore; he just wanted to help me. He hugged me tight and told me not to worry about it. "It'll be okay, son," he said. "It'll be okay."

Just a Phase

It had just been a phase. Angie was right. We probably should have never been together. This relationship was a symptom of my own self-hatred. With all of the lovely Black women around me I had made a conscious decision to form a relationship with this white girl. I had been conditioned by my social environment and by the media to think that this girl represented what should be desirable. I was still confused. I have matured since that time and now know that I would never date a white woman again. I don't pass judgment on others who do (if I can avoid it), but this relationship was just a phase in my life. It was a phase that taught me that I could never love anyone fully until I truly loved myself.

It was finally time to take my SAT test. I had already completed my ACT; however, my score was not as high as I would have liked, and I was somewhat embarrassed to have those be the only scores sent to Michigan, Notre Dame, and Cornell. I woke up early to prepare myself for the 8:30 a.m. test. When my preparation was complete I traveled the twenty or so minutes to East Lansing High School. I was a bit nervous, not only because of the importance of the test but because I was going to take it in unfamiliar surroundings. I walked into the test room and was glad to see another student from Lansing Sexton. I believe his name was Jim. He was a tall, brown-haired white kid: a typical student in my high school. We were what I considered friends—not close, but we knew each other. I walked over and sat down next to him.

"What's up?" I tried to hide my concern about the test.

"Hey, John, how are you?" he responded.

"Pretty good, just not enough sleep last night." High school students have this desire to present themselves as party animals who never study but somehow manage to get good grades. And for this reason no one in his right mind would admit that he had slept from 11:00–7:00 a.m.

"Yeah, I know . . . seems like I never get enough sleep."

"Well . . . how do you feel about the test?" I said, after a brief hesitation. I was wondering if he was as worked up as I was.

"It shouldn't be too bad," he responded, smiling falsely, as if he were unconcerned. He then gave me a curious look and asked me an ignorant question. "Are you smart?"

I was shocked. Why the hell would I be taking the test if I weren't smart? Who was he to ask me something like that? Who the hell did he think he was, anyway? Any of these responses would have been appropriate, but I chose none of them. Instead, in a sarcastic tone, I simply smiled and said, "No, I'm not."

For that brief instant I thought, Maybe I *don't* belong here. I was able to catch myself and realize that, if anyone belonged, it was me. But at the same time I began to wonder how others would have responded under the same circumstances. Maybe for them it wasn't so easy to overcome that initial doubt? Maybe they really believed they didn't belong? I looked around the room and saw only a few Black faces, and then I thought about my response to his question. I thought about how I had understated my abilities. I started to tell him how I really felt about him having the audacity to ask me something like that, but, as I began to open my mouth, I was given my test and told not to speak.

Trapped

My best friend was getting married. It was not under the best of circumstances, but a celebration was in order nonetheless. We had held a bachelor party at a local hotel the week before, and this was the Friday night just before the Saturday wedding. A group of friends and I were going to spend our final night together. Mark and Jesse Mendez, Marcus, James, Kenny, and I hung out on most Friday nights; however; unlike most other Fridays, there was a cloud of tension this time that dimmed our excitement. It was as if we were trying to hold on to our feelings because this was our last opportunity.

We traveled to the Outer Limits, an East Lansing club, and stayed for about three hours. After we were tired of dancing, we started thinking of other things to do. We had all had a good bit to drink, and we had plenty of energy for another party.

I started in by asking, "What now? It's only 12:30. There's got to be something else to do."

James, the groom-to-be, chimed in, "Yeah, we got to do something tonight. The fun ends tomorrow!"

"Shut up, man, it ain't even like that. You act like marriage is death," I responded hastily, half trying to convince myself. "What we gonna do?"

"There's a party in Holt at Cindy's crib," Mark stated.

"I don't know about that. Who's Cindy, anyway?" I was somewhat reluctant to go to this hick town to a party where I wouldn't know anyone.

"It's cool. I know Cindy and them from school." Mark had attended Holt High School for his senior year, and he thought that he knew these people well.

"Let's stop at B.K. first. I'm hungry as hell," James said, and we all agreed.

We stopped, grabbed some food, and headed out toward Holt. By the time we got there it was about 1:15 in the morning, and I still felt uncomfortable about this location. For some reason, as we drove through the field toward the barn-style house, the grain silo and dirt pathway were not welcome sights to me. I just had the feeling that this was not cool. The first car had arrived before ours, and Kenny,

Mark, and Jesse were already talking to some of their "friends" (all white) up by the house. We pulled up with a carload of people, and the tension seemed to mount.

"What's up?" I said to one of the white guys.

"Hey," he said reluctantly.

I looked toward the house and saw Mark and Jesse arguing with three or four of these Holt locals. As I moved toward the dispute, I began to hear what was being said. "What made you come out here, anyway?" someone said.

"Well, Cindy said to come and check the party out, so we just came out."

Why did he say that? White boys hate when you talk to their sisters. Shit, how could he be so stupid?

"I don't want you here," said one of them.

"Ah, man, we ain't here to cause no problems."

"Well, I don't want you here!"

I turned around and saw some guys coming out of the silo in the backyard, and I knew something was not cool. My boy James nudged me as if to say "let's get the hell out of here." James said, "All right, then, we'll leave. Ain't nothin' out here for us anyway." He couldn't just let this white boy punk him out, so he justified our leaving.

"Yeah, you better leave," one of them said reluctantly.

"Yeah, we're leaving . . . but what are you gonna do about it, anyway?"

What had possessed me to say this? Of the stupid things I had done in my life this had to top the list. Now I knew a fight was inevitable. One of the other guys got in James's face, challenging him, and then he pushed him in the chest. James hesitated for a second and then punched him in the chin, knocking him unconscious. The next thing I knew one of the guys was on me punching me in the chest. Because we were outnumbered three to one, I tried to hold myself back. I didn't want to fight these fifteen guys on their own territory. Finally, however, I began to retaliate. I started pounding the white boy in the face and stomach until he curled over. The scene had turned into a brawl. The fact that we were outnumbered made our situation terrible. I was pounding his face continually until about five of his boys jumped me and threw me against a shed, which was located near the house. The fact that they were beating me in the face to the point that I saw stars was not important. The thing I was concerned about was that I had lost my keys. I was trapped in a place where I didn't want to be, and I was being beaten for being there. All

I wanted to do was escape. Marcus somehow got those guys off of me, and I tried to look for my keys. Luckily, as the conflict died down, one of the white guys gave me my keys, and we were able to make our way to our cars and get out.

We drove back to Lansing and stopped by another one of our friend's house. Russell was outside of the house, visibly upset about something. We talked to him about what had happened to us, and he told us how some white guys from Holt had trashed his party earlier that night. Our anger toward them had reached a level seldom attained. I was ready to kill the next one of those white boys I saw.

"I got a twelve-gauge in the crib. Want me to get it?" Russell said, the effects of alcohol were apparent in the way he slurred his words.

"Yeah, man, the least we should do is shoot up the crib." Jesse stated.

"I'll get it, and then we can go out there and get them white boys!" Russell stated with anger and hatred in his eyes.

"All right, then, get the gun, and we'll go back out there," I said. Now I was not about to go back to this hick town with a gun and wind up in prison somewhere. I figured that, when he went into the house, we could just drive off and avoid having to argue. He went into the house to get his gun, and I told my friends to get into the car. The only one who still wanted to shoot up the crib was Jesse, but, when I threatened to leave him, he jumped right in. I dropped my boys off, and James and I drove to his house, where we both spent the night.

I stood at the altar the next day with bruises on my face and unable to fully understand what had happened the day before. I was ashamed to be the best man in the wedding in my condition, but I tried to make the best of the situation. As I looked across at James's bride, I couldn't help but get a strange feeling. Her white skin made me feel apprehensive. How could James be marrying a white girl after what had happened? Deep down she had to be just like the rest of them. The church was full of her family. When I looked at them, all I could envision were those white boys attacking me for no reason except for the color of my skin. Somehow I smiled my way through the wedding and the reception. I went home afterward, iced my face, and thought about what had happened.

Constant Reminder

My mother returned to her car following a grocery shopping trip. It was mid-August, and, although Michigan is not known for its hot weather, it was sweltering. Looking through her purse, which is commonly disorganized, she did not find her keys. Initially, she was not worried because she was sure that they were somewhere. She conducted another search. Looking into the car she saw her keys, bright with the sun's reflection, on the seat. Upset with herself for having made this mistake, she called a cab to take her home to get the extra car key. She waited in the store for the cab to arrive. Being only a few miles from home made her frustrated, and she was not in the best of spirits. The cab driver, a dark-brown-haired white man, was polite and helped her place her groceries in the cab. Not much conversation occurred during the seemingly short ride to my house. My mother pulled out her extra pair of house keys and told the driver she would be right back. She quickly carried the groceries inside, picked up her keys, and returned. As the driver pulled out of the driveway, he said, "I hope this doesn't offend you, but—." Knowing that this disclaimer generally leads to something offensive, my mother braced herself. "But, you don't talk like a Black person."

"Well, how do Black people talk?" she responded, hoping that he would see the ignorance in his statement.

"Well, you know, I thought you were white. I couldn't tell because you sound very smart."

"How am I supposed to sound?" The anger was becoming apparent in her voice. She was being insulted by a cab driver who was trying to tell her, an English professor, how she should speak.

"Coleman Young doesn't sound intelligent like you, and he's the mayor," he argued, his ignorance becoming more apparent with each word.

"I know plenty of Black people who speak as I do, and, personally, I don't appreciate you trying to dictate how I should speak."

"Oh no, I didn't mean it like that; it's just that I didn't know—."

My mother was incredibly upset by this time; however, she was able to keep her composure.

A welcomed silence was interrupted when the driver started again. "It's nice that you live out here [Farmington Hills, Michigan] because a lot of Black people don't want to work. Just drive down to the unemployment office—you'll see 'em."

"That's not true. No one wants to be unemployed. They just can't find work." The rage in her heart was so strong she could barely restrain herself. What gave this undereducated white man the right to speak to her this way? She hadn't asked for his opinions, and he was lucky she hadn't given him hers.

"I don't buy that," he said, as if he were her intellectual superior. "I started with nothing, and now I have my own business."

Angered by his arrogance but not willing to give him the hostile response he seemed to be aiming for, she told him to just keep driving the cab and not to speak to her any longer. The cab reached the parking lot shortly thereafter. She gave the man his money and, without speaking, walked to her car.

Public Enemy

I am a public enemy.
I am the crime problem.
I am responsible for high taxes.
I am the one who doesn't belong.
I am the problem.

It is my fault that I am imprisoned.
It is my fault that I am poor.
It is my choice to be unemployed.
It is my nature to be undereducated.
It is with me that problems rest.

I am taught to devalue life.
I am trained to be poor.
I am expected to be unemployed.
I am intentionally undereducated.
I am forced to believe that I am a problem.

Trapped

Unlike white people in this country, we, as Black people, are forced to question our role. We must constantly reassure ourselves that we belong. As a group, we were not brought here to participate in society; we were brought here only to be enslaved. As a group, we were not considered human by the Constitution. Our contributions as a race of people in this country, and throughout the world, have been historically understated. We have never been allowed to participate as full members of this society. Thus, we are trapped in a place where we don't necessarily want to be, and we are hated for being here.

White people see us as the enemy—an enemy to the white way of life. We are feared because our current situation as a people represents the result of white oppression. We are feared because white people are afraid of a Black planet. We know the truth in the system, and this gives us the power to destroy it. We don't buy into the myth of individualism, as commonly defined by this society. We know that "liberty and justice for all" means "liberty and justice for all whites." We know that those who choose not to melt into the melting pot are discarded and hated.

We are hated then, because white people are ashamed, as they well should be, of the inhuman ways in which they have treated us. Therefore, whites try to force us to shoulder the responsibility for their actions. They expect us to love a society that has done nothing for us. They expect us to pledge allegiance to a flag that has flown over our ancestors' lynchings. They expect us to be proud of our president's home, which just happens to be called the "White House." They expect us to be proud of a federal government that has practically no Black representation. They expect us to respect police who come into our neighborhoods only to harass us. They expect us to support school systems that consciously refuse to teach Black history. They expect us to love those people who will always hate us. And they make the mistake of thinking that retaliation is not forthcoming. Thirty million Black people will not accept this exploitation forever . . . and the rest of the Black world knows the time.

It Takes a Nation of Millions to Hold Us Back

I have led a good life as an African-American man in this country. The white power structure, through its school system, tried to track me in the wrong direction, but I was lucky. I was able to muster the strength to tell an *entire society* that it was wrong about me. I was able to form my own Black identity. I was able to shake off the white man's guilt and place it back where it belonged. But, for every person like myself who was lucky enough to be born with a supportive family network, an actual opportunity to "get ahead," and the inner strength to define himself, there are millions more who are not so lucky.

Jewish Identity: One Person's Experience

Steven Blonder

I've always known I was Jewish, at least for as long as I can remember. I've grown up hearing the stories about how at my *bris* (ritual circumcision), all I did was cry (I can't imagine any kid not crying); how, as a little kid, I looked so cute in my Haman costume; how I sounded reciting the *mah-nishtanah* (the "four questions" asked at the Passover seder) for the first time; and so on. Instances such as these are my life, my childhood memories. Dad always had synagogue board meetings every month.

I still remember a discussion in Mrs. Ginter's fifth-grade classroom. We were talking about immigration and how those people who came to the United States often dropped their ethnicity in favor of being a part of the melting pot. Those people from Ireland, for example, became known as Irish Americans, Poles were Polish Americans. During lunchtime Mark Miles and I talked about how we would work *Jew* into this pattern.

"... I'm just American," Mark said.

I responded, "I'm an American Jew."

"That's stupid. If you put *Jew* in at all, it would go before American, not after."

"No, I'm Jewish. And I just happen to be living in America."

At this point someone interjected, "What difference does it make anyway? Jewish American, American Jew—it's all the same."

Mark and most of my other friends went to a different Hebrew school than I did. They were Reform Jews, whereas my upbringing had been significantly more traditional. For the life of me I couldn't understand why they only celebrated one day of Rosh Hashanah and not two, or why for them Passover ended a day early. I didn't think of my friends as being real Jews; I saw them more as part-timers.

I remember once we were going to go to a Chicago Bulls game.

My dad said I could invite someone to go with me, and I chose Lenny. The only problem was that he had Hebrew school on Tuesdays (the night of the game). It wasn't a problem for long because his parents just decided he wouldn't go to Hebrew school that week. For the life of me I couldn't understand that type of decision making. Why would you skip a week of Hebrew school just to go to a basketball game? But, then again, it's not like he would have learned anything in Hebrew school anyway since he went to Temple Judea, the Reform temple.

I'd ask Lenny, Mark, Joanne, and the rest of my friends what they had learned at Hebrew school. They didn't remember much. I'd come home ready to talk about something I had learned at Niles Township, the conservative synagogue in the area. I used to laugh at my friends and their ignorance. I used to marginalize my friends in my mind because none of them could understand Hebrew; they didn't have a working knowledge of the holidays and Jewish history, and they didn't practice many of the customs and traditions I had come to respect and enjoy. It was as if I knew what it meant to be Jewish and they didn't. Or maybe I was trying to delegitimize the Reform Judaism they "practiced."

To me, you weren't really Jewish if you belonged to a Reform synagogue. It was like being a part-time Jew. I couldn't fathom someone not enjoying the traditional Judaism I was living.

People used to tell me I was weird because I generally liked going to Hebrew school. Sure, I fell asleep sometimes when Mr. Traube would try to teach Hebrew, or when Mr. Rogalin talked about Jewish history in his sharp Israeli accent. I could even do pretty good imitations of all my teachers. But it never made any sense to me why people threw things and engaged in activities that could harm someone else. Take Rick Burns. Rick was a friend of mine from public school, where he was a good student, a good athlete, and an all-around nice guy. But when it came time for Hebrew school, Rick was a jerk. He used to start fights with people for no apparent reason. He liked to hit people in the back and over the head with books or throw things throughout the room. Rick wasn't the only one.

Once Rick started a fight with me, one of his friends. It was during recess (the five-to-ten-minute break we got during the middle of each day) in the hallway outside Mrs. Citro's room. Rabbi Brusin, the principal, knew I hadn't started it and had tried to walk away. But I still felt extremely awkward having to explain to him what had happened. He just had me go to the bathroom and wipe off my face before going back to class. The worst part was seeing Mrs. Melber, who worked in the synagogue office. She sat in the row in front of our family at Ezra Habonim, the synagogue we belonged to, and had known some of my relatives years back when they all lived in Germany. I felt really embarrassed and couldn't look her in the eye; it was if I had let someone down.

People often tried to start fights with me at Hebrew school. I don't know why, since I never fought back. I would just grit my teeth and keep on going. Maybe it was because I always did well in Hebrew school and genuinely enjoyed the classes. I saw Hebrew school as an extension of public school and carried myself the same in both places. In confirmation class I used to doodle on my legal pad, but for the most part I was a model student.

Confirmation class was really neat; it was one of the more exciting times in my Jewish education. For two of the three years I had Cantor Schuster as one of my teachers. For me, he became more than just a teacher. He was and still is both a role model and a friend. One unique aspect of my confirmation program was that it was parent-child. Twenty or so high school-age students and parents would sit around a seminar table twice a week discussing Jewish-related issues. During the first and last year we studied the Mishnah—a commentary on the Five Books of Moses—and its practical applications for Judaism today. I remember a series of discussions in which we were talking about morality and being a "morally correct" person. We talked about people's obligations to each other, both legally and humanistically. Cantor Schuster would always ask my dad to educate us about our legal obligations (since he is an attorney), and then we would go around the table, parents and kids alike, talking about what the Jewish law had to say. Most of those people who had caused trouble during religious school did not participate in the confirmation program, so the negative dynamics I described earlier were not a factor here.

Cantor Schuster, in particular, has played an important role in my development as a person and, accordingly, as a Jew. He has always impressed upon me the need to be a good person regardless of what I do. But he has always couched that message within the framework of the larger picture, and he and I have had multiple-hour discussions on being a Jew in the modern world—the conflicts that arise, the pressures to "conform" to societal norms, and what Judaism really means. Cantor Schuster never gives me answers to questions I ask, but, rather, he and I just talk. Together we explore how I can come up with my own answers to questions by using a "Jewish imagination," by which I consider issues in the context of my Jewish values.

One particular instance sticks out in my mind. Three years ago, when campus tensions were at an all-time high (or so I then thought), I really didn't know what to do or where to turn. I was a freshman and had never before seen a social movement forming—a large-scale sit-in and blockade of an administrative building—or even such a large group of minorities coming together for a common cause: to stamp out racism. I was naive and didn't understand the issues at hand, having grown up on the North Shore of Chicago where racial issues did not usually command significant amounts of time and energy. I knew what I wanted to do as a person and as a Jew, but somehow I couldn't get myself to act. I was scared. Moreover, I was confused. I really wanted to join the blockade of the University of Michigan Administration Building, and eventually I did. But, even after doing so, I felt extremely uncomfortable.

So I did what my instincts told me. I put in a call to Cantor Schuster in Skokie. He and I talked about the value of individuals and how everyone is a person above everything else. The Torah makes no distinctions based on skin color but, rather, talks about how to treat a neighbor as we ourselves would like or expect to be treated. We talked about how, as Jews, we were once subjected to the same conditions the Blacks and other groups now were, and how various Jewish groups had reacted. After talking to him, I really felt good and more secure with myself. I had come to see the issue as a Jewish issue as well as a human one. Cantor Schuster and I have done this on a lot of issues, ranging from actions of the various foreign governments (as well as our own) to the Steve Cokely affair to Jews moving out of Chicago proper and into suburbs, and so on. Our talks empower me to take action and work to help other people and other groups while helping me feel stronger about my Judaism. I've already decided that Cantor Schuster will officiate at my wedding.

I've only had one experience in which I left a synagogue feeling extremely dejected. I had gone during my senior year of high school to meet with a representative of the Jewish Theological Seminary (JTS) at North Shore Congregation Beth El. I walked into the synagogue with a yarmulke (Jewish head covering) on, but it was obvious that I was not a congregation member because I was not wearing a tallit (Jewish prayer shawl) under my shirt, I was not conversing solely in Hebrew, and the yarmulke was not bobby-pinned to my head in a semi-permanent fashion. Rabbi Frain, the rabbi of that congregation, asked me if maybe I was in the wrong place, and I said no, I had come to see the JTS representative. At that point Rabbi Frain snickered and suggested that I was not fit to become a conservative rabbi. He suggested that I was not "Jewish enough," whatever that phrase means, to listen to the JTS speaker or enter the rabbinate. This rabbi was judging me because I did not live in Highland Park and did not practice Judaism as he did. This experience was frustrating, but it forced me to think about the meanings of Judaism.

One of the first people I turned to for answers was Rabbi Levine, the rabbi of our congregation for the past fifteen years. The Friday night after my experience of listening to the JTS speaker I went to services by myself, since my parents were out of town. I don't know why I went by myself; I do not usually do that. After services I waited until Rabbi Levine had made the perfunctory rounds before sitting down to talk business.

"Rabbi, I went to Beth El Wednesday night to hear the representative from JTS . . ." I filled him in on what had happened.

"He didn't really say that. You must have misunderstood."

"No, I don't think so. His message was very clear."

" . . . how do you feel?"

"Extremely frustrated and confused. How could a rabbi have said what he did? . . . I thought Judaism was supposed to comfort people, not drive them away. Right now I'm not sure what being Jewish really means. Is something wrong with me as a Jew because I don't follow every commandment to the letter? . . ."

The ensuing couple of months were very hard for me. I was struggling with some pretty tough issues. Religion? Judaism? How could a religion that meant so much to me and that had guided me in my everyday life be so divisive? Had I missed the inherent meanings of Judaism? I tried to answer all of these questions by thinking back to what Rabbi Sud would have said. Rabbi Sud, who died while I was in high school, had been our congregational rabbi before Rabbi Levine.

Rabbi Sud was always full of hope—hope for Jews, hope for the world. And everything for him could be related to numbers. He loved to engage in *gematriah*, which is a mystical idea of using numerical values to affirm or endorse particular events. And somehow everything always ended up on the number 18, or *chai* (life) in Hebrew. Rabbi Sud would take the Hebrew word and add up the value of each letter, divide by something or multiply by something else, or just manipulate the numbers so the end result was always 18. If not 18, the number was 36, or *double chai*. This number is significant because legend dictates that the world is held together by thirty-six righteous people. This positive outlook on life and the future rubbed off on me, and I adopted *chai* as my own "trigger," or catchword. Everything to me revolves around this celebration of life.

Rabbi Sud used to get extremely upset if anyone interrupted his sermon—anyone, that is, except for a baby crying. I remember several times when a mother would get up to leave the sanctuary with her crying baby, and Rabbi Sud would stop in mid sentence and ask the child to be kept in. No, the baby probably wasn't understanding the mathematical computations Rabbi Sud had just explained, but that baby represented life and the future.

More than anything, though, Rabbi Sud was preoccupied with life. He always discussed the rabbis he had studied with in Breslau, and how having to leave the rabbinate in Czechoslovakia had impacted on his life. Considering that most of our congregation had at one time been rooted in Germany, this topic coming up was not so unusual. One thing he always emphasized was togetherness. Rabbi Sud always discussed the people he studied with and how they were such good people; he would tell us all about their good names. It all seemed so exciting to me, like another world that I could never know or understand. I still have a set of books Rabbi Sud gave me. I've read the books often; they are a series from the 1950s dealing with the power of Judaism and the meanings behind the traditions—something I hope never to lose.

That power proved particularly important to me during my freshman year at the University of Michigan, when my grandmother unexpectedly died. We had been back from winter vacation for about a week or so. Mom and I talked on Saturday since I was going to the Michigan-Syracuse basketball game on Sunday and then into the *Michigan Daily* to write an article. My roommate called the *Daily* to tell me to call my mom just as she was calling on another line. Something was strange because I had talked to her yesterday. I went about my business, making plane reservations. I felt unphased by the whole thing because what my mom had said had yet to sink in. My parents and sister met me at the airport that night, and I still thought I was dreaming.

The funeral was not until Tuesday morning, so I had nothing to do Monday except think. I kept asking myself, Why did this happen? The chemotherapy had seemed to work, and I had talked to my grandmother on Saturday afternoon. That Monday I had the subject of G-d on my mind a lot. Someone gave me a book to read, Harold Kushner's *When Bad Things Happen to Good People*. One passage in the book particularly struck a chord inside me:

> When David saw the servants whispering, he said to them, Is the child dead? And they said, He is dead. And David rose and washed and changed his clothing and asked that food be set before him, and he ate. The servants said to him, What is this you are doing? You fasted and wept for the child when he was alive, and now that he is dead, you get up and eat! And David said: While the child was yet alive, I fasted and wept, for I said, Who knows whether the Lord will be gracious to me and the child will live? But now that he is dead, why should I fast? Can I bring him back again? I shall go to him; but he will not return to me. (II Samuel 12:19–23)
>
> (Kushner 1981, 133)

I was able to come to grips with the idea of a positive and loving G-d and the fact that someone close to me had died. Something inside of me clicked after the funeral, and I felt like a "complete Jew." The contradictions I had recognized seemed to be explained and had worked themselves out. I felt a certain wholeness or completeness pervading my life. It was as if now I were a part of a people, if I hadn't been before. I felt as if the entire Jewish nation were standing and saying kaddish (a prayer honoring G-d said while mourning a family member) alongside of me.

The day of the funeral I sensed a G-d watching over me, guiding me for the first time in my life. Sure, I had spent countless hours as a kid praying to Him for something—be it to do well on a test, get me out of trouble, or whatever. But I never really believed in His existence. However, now I felt empowered in ways I never had before. Now I wake up every morning possessing a new sense of determination. It's like G-d is my best friend in that He listens to me and helps me sort out my feelings. I turn to Him for guidance, and I know He is always looking out for me. One of my favorite parts of the service is at the end our singing "Adon Olam" (Lord of the World), because it reminds me that my G-d is watching over me.

> Lord of the world, the King supreme,
> Ere aught was formed, He reigned alone.
> When by His will all things were wrought,
> Then was His sovereign name made known.

And when in time all things shall cease,
He still shall reign in majesty.
He was, He is, He shall remain
All-glorious eternally.

Incomparable, unique is He,
No other can His Oneness share.
Without beginning, without end,
Dominion's might is His to bear.

He is my living G-d who saves,
My rock when grief or trials befall,
My Banner and my Refuge strong,
My bounteous Portion when I call.

My soul I give unto His care,
Asleep, awake, for He is near,
And with my soul, my body, too;
G-d is with me, I have no fear.

My mother's aunt passed away on Friday. Her death was not exactly unexpected; she had a terminal cancer, and the doctors had told her there was nothing more they could do. She chose to spend her last days at home in Rochester, New York. My sister and I didn't go to the funeral; it was not really an option. As I write this, my parents and grandmother are standing graveside as Aunt Else is being laid to rest. I called this morning. I reread Kushner's *When Bad Things Happen to Good People*. I've been thinking a lot.

I hadn't seen my aunt for several years now. She used to come to Chicago for a couple of weeks at a time at least once or twice a year. It was a family joke in a way because she snored very loudly. When I was six or seven we took her apple picking with us, and I remember deliberately dropping apples from the tree to her so fast that she could not possibly catch them all. One found a lucky spot right in the middle of Aunt Else's head. At every family occasion she would make her presence felt. For the past few years she had not been feeling up to making the trip, however, and, although we made jokes about it, something was missing. She always loved to visit Chicago, and I never thought I would miss her annual trips.

But today I haven't been thinking about her annual visits. I've been thinking about some family history. Most of my mother's family perished during World War II. My mother's father had a brother and a sister. The brother's name is Martin, and he lives in Miami. The sister was Else. Martin is the only one of the three still alive, and the effects of his being taken by the Nazis remain evident. I've heard the story numerous times of how the Nazis came to his house in Eitorf (Germany) and demanded that either he or his father come with them. The overall effect would be the same, since his parents were eventually taken to a camp, never to be seen or heard from again.

A year ago December we were having dinner with Uncle Martin in Miami. His wife was making it clear that she wanted to go home, but he had some things he wanted to say.

"Fifty years ago today, I escaped from the camp . . ."

None of us was aware of the date. We sat around the table, and tears formed in everyone's eyes, as we intently listened to his story. Uncle Martin told us of his experience, how he had been taken away and escaped, not once but twice. He told us of how he had snuck through a fence at night and remained in hiding during the day, about the underground network that had helped him. . . . Up until this point it had only been stories void of any details. But now everything was coming together.

We sat around discussing history for almost an hour, no one daring to move and nary a waiter coming near our table. Uncle Martin made sure that my sister and I understood everything he was telling us. I found myself in tears. I had just completed Professor Endelman's Holocaust class. My uncle's stories sounded like others I had heard, but something was different. This was my family he was talking about. Our family. The names of the places he mentioned were too painful for me to hear, let alone for him. I found myself crying on the inside at the horror before an angry feeling enveloped me. I don't know who I was angry at, other than the world as a whole. I was just angry that my uncle had had to go through the process of naming the extermination centers where our family members had died. Some of the people he mentioned I had never heard about before, while about others the names and dates were all too familiar. His story is not the only one in my family. My mother's grandfather had thirteen brothers and sisters. The number who survived can be counted on one finger.

I've been ingrained with stories about the Holocaust since I was a little kid. While I could never really comprehend the details or the atrocities that happened, nothing was ever hidden from my sister and me. If we wanted to know something, all we had to do was ask. For most of my life I never really understood. But that night with my uncle all of the pieces finally fell into place.

Initially, my family's experiences in the Holocaust helped in distinguishing me from those living around me. I always knew I was different—Hitler saw to that. But I enjoyed being different. None of my Jewish friends could relate to my feelings about the Holocaust or my pride in living the life of a Jew. Being Jewish was never a burden or a chore, and performing things related to Judaism gave me a sense of inner pride, of joy. Skipping a basketball game or bowling league in seventh grade because I had to go to Hebrew school was no big deal to me. After all, I was doing something more important—being Jewish. I decided that being Jewish would never be a burden; it would be a privilege, an honor.

No matter what anyone else says, I am different; I am Jewish, and no one can tell me otherwise. Hitler answered the question fifty years ago of who is a Jew, and inside I feel a special bond to those people. From these initial experiences that bonded me, if you will, to Judaism, I have grown to try and understand everything about the way Jews lived in the *shtetlach* (a type of traditional Jewish village located in Eastern Europe). I wish I could go back and see the blooming Yiddish culture and distinctly Jewish way of life practiced by those Jews, completely separate from the outside society. But we never can because, once a culture or way of life is destroyed, it cannot be resurrected. The best we can do is read and study how our ancestors lived and try to imagine what it would be like living in an all-Jewish world.

In one sense, I lack a normative sense of being Jewish since I have never lived during a period of organic Jewish life. Today I live in a world in which Jews are more similar to the surrounding populations than they have ever been in history. But the Holocaust continues to keep Jews apart from others and is a rallying point for the expression of a Jewish identity. But still, more and more people do not have a complete notion of how or why they are Jewish, and the Holocaust can serve to answer some of their questions. Any Jew today has a relationship with other Jews because all Jews are tied to the Holocaust. All Jews are victims.

The summer before my freshman year in high school my grandmother took us to Germany and Belgium so we could see where the family had come from. I vividly remember visiting the cemetery in Munster, where I could trace my roots back several hundred years. For the first time in my life I really understood where I had come from and who I was. Rows upon rows of stones comprised the history of my family, and I was able to see it, but only from a distance, because visitors were not allowed inside the cemetery. We stood on the tips of our toes looking in, arms resting on the stone wall surrounding the cemetery. In the same town a synagogue existed bearing a plaque listing the names of whose who had died during the Holocaust. Included on that list were several relatives. The houses my ancestors had lived in still stood, but they were filled with a new generation of Germans who knew nothing firsthand of the pre-Hitler days to which my ancestors belonged. I had never before felt so Jewish than on this trip, and that includes my first trip to Israel during the year preceding the visit to Germany

One town in Germany made me shiver. We were in Eitorf, the town where my mother's father's family had lived. My grandmother stopped a woman on the street and asked in German for directions to the house our family had lived in. My grandmother said it had been many years since she had been to Eitorf, and, while the two women were talking, the German woman said, "We didn't know what had happened to all of you. We assumed you would be coming back..."

We found the house and knocked on the door. No one answered. We walked around to the back and saw a car in the driveway and made several attempts to enter the house. After our unsuccessful attempts we were huddled across the street under an awning, attempting to stay out of the rain. Suddenly we saw someone peek out of an upstairs window from the house we had wanted to visit. Then, with us standing in front of the house, the new owner exited and quickly drove away. An hour later we were having a late lunch at the train station. While we were trying to shield the lentil soup from the flies, we overheard a conversation at the next table. All the townspeople were talking about us.

My grandmother always tells me about my mother's father since I never had the chance to know him personally. She talks about how when they had first arrived in England from Germany, on the first *Shabbat* my grandfather had gone to the synagogue, met people, and immediately felt at home; how, when he got the news that his parents had been taken to a concentration camp and been gassed, he went to the rabbi and talked with him. He came home quiet and relaxed. My grandfather was religious from the inside out, which helped him to survive the many horrors that befell him. He had believed and that was that, which, my grandmother says, seems to have been inherited by my mother and then me. She continually tells me that, in the way I believe in my religion and use it on a daily basis, I am a mirror reflection of my grandfather, whom, by coincidence, I am named after. My grandmother describes this ability to believe as being a gift, and I agree. I wish I could have met my mother's father so I could see firsthand what he was like.

During the summer preceding my junior year at Michigan, I worked for the most extraordinary man, who taught me some important things about being Jewish. His name is Mark E. Talisman, and he currently directs the Washington Action Office of the Council of Jewish Federations, in addition to heading his own foundation, Project Judaica. Mark remains extremely involved with Soviet Jewry and authored the Jackson-Vanik amendment, which links trade status with emigration and the plight of Czechoslovakian citizens. Mark travels the country from coast to coast, speaking at various seminars and meetings. Whenever Mark speaks, he always tells one particular story of a concentration camp where the children planted a tree to celebrate *Tu B'Shevat*. He details the Czechoslovakian woman, then a Gentile teacher, who took the children under her wing and went to the camp with them; the children who would sprinkle a small portion of their water ration onto the tree each day so that it would grow; and the smoke rising in the distance from the furnace at Auschwitz. Then Mark describes the tree, which today stands as a mature, blossoming tree and serves to memorialize the children who died. Every year on *Tu B'Shevat*, according to Mark, this Czechoslovakian woman, who is now up in age, kneels down beside the tree and remembers those children who never saw their tiny twig grow.

Preceding this story, Mark always would talk about the social problems facing America today—poverty, homelessness, and people not having enough food to eat, among others. He would talk about Israel having to spend a substantial part of her revenue on the military. I must have heard Mark give the same speech at least fifty times. And each time I saw people being mesmerized; he had them in the palm of his hand. I, too, was mesmerized, but in a different way. Every time Mark spoke I had different sections of the Torah (the Five Books of Moses) flashing through my head. Things were starting to come together—the texts I had studied so many years earlier in Hebrew school. It was as if the Five Books of Moses and the prophets' writings had come to life. I found myself moved to action, ready to really apply the messages of Judaism to everyday life.

As a lobbyist, I was responsible for many issues, including welfare reform, Soviet and South African Jewry, and medical programs for the elderly. The most common comment I received from my peers was: "Those aren't Jewish issues. You should be worrying about Israel." But I couldn't worry about Israel; something inside of me wouldn't permit it. Every Jew worries about Israel, but I kept asking myself, How many other Jews worry about people? I asked my Jewish friends, and none of them saw anything Jewish about social issues or having a social consciousness, which to me remained at the core of everything I had learned. The meanings of Judaism became much clearer to me, particularly when I would observe the workings of the American-Israel Public Affairs Committee (AIPAC), the pro-Israel lobby. People who worked for AIPAC carried themselves as if they were the only ones doing anything Jewish. Yet they never worked on any issue other than Israel. Their interns laughed at social issues, saying that Israel was all that mattered, that the homeless people can fend for themselves.

I wanted to puke; hearing this made me sick to my stomach. I would go back to my office, asking myself if I was missing the part of Judaism that commands us to blindly support Israel and relegate everything else to a lower role. By the end of the summer I came to the conclusion that I wasn't missing anything.

In December, 1987, a rally was held in Washington, D.C., to support the cause of Soviet Jews. The timing of the Freedom March was such that it took place one day before Mikhail Gorbachev arrived to meet President Reagan. I was part of the media covering the event, reporting for both the *Detroit Jewish News* and the *Michigan Daily*. I had never seen so many people marching together before—nearly 300,000. From the press area I could see the whole crowd. Standing on a scaffold, I turned and looked behind me to see a sea of people blanketing the Mall. I had goose pimples and felt a certain connection. People had brought guitars, and they were singing. People who did not know each other joined hands and danced. I trembled, particularly when Peter, Paul, and Mary sang their song "Light One Candle."

Walking to Yom Kippur services a few years back, one of my friends announced he had a joke to tell, and it went something like this: A Jewish man bought a new Porsche, and he wanted to have it blessed by a rabbi. The man went to the Orthodox rabbi and asked him to recite a *b'racha* (blessing) over the Porsche. The Orthodox rabbi responded by asking what a Porsche was. The man left and went to the conservative rabbi, where the same scenario played itself out. So the man went to the reform rabbi and asked him to bless the Porsche. The reform rabbi asked, "What's a *b'racha*?" I didn't really know what to make of this joke. But I didn't laugh because I didn't find the story to be particularly humorous.

I learned a lot about myself at camp, Olin Sang Ruby Union Institute (OSRUI), which is located in Oconomowoc, Wisconsin. I was a camper for four summers and then went back as a counselor before starting college. As a camper, I lived Judaism every day and night, even though the camp is run by the Reform movement. I kind of expected to be disappointed by the amount of Jewish observance and tradition since the Reform Jews I knew at the time really didn't care about being Jewish. But camp changed those misconceptions. We observed Shabbat as well as other relevant holidays such as Tishah-b'av. We did the usual camp stuff—swimming, sports, drama, and arts and crafts—but we also spent a lot of time on Jewish issues, Hebrew, and singing, after reciting the *Birkat HaMazon* (grace after meals). There is definitely something to be said for learning Hebrew under a tree or having unit-wide *Maccabiah* (Jewish olympics) games.

Shabbat at camp was special. The routine on this day was different than on all other days. Preparations would begin on Friday afternoon, after swimming, when everyone participated in cleaning our unit before changing into their good clothes. We would gather outside of our tents, ready to join the procession when it came by. Everyone was singing, even those people who would not sing at other times, and kisses flew everywhere. All differences were put aside. We would form a circle on the hill. From that circle we proceeded to a dining hall, where we would eat with a different unit. After dinner was a raucous song-and-story session from which we retreated to our own individual units for services and Israeli dancing.

Saturday morning we could sleep late (as compared to the 7 A.M. wake-up on other days). We would have services at ten, followed by a *kiddush* and buffet lunch. The afternoon was open time to go swimming, play basketball or soccer, sit under a tree, or whatever. The day would end with a havdalah service. Shabbat at camp easily became my favorite day of the week, and I have never experienced a Shabbat that compares to the ones in Oconomowoc. There was always a spirit of good feeling in the air.

Going to camp from fifth grade until high school really served to reinforce my Jewish identity. I was able to redefine myself as a Jew while being surrounded with people doing the same thing, both at conscious and subconscious levels. At camp you really didn't have much choice about being Jewish since Judaism was "in the air"—or, rather, it was encompassed in everything we did. I learned at camp, for the first time in my life, what it meant to be living as a Jew, and this resulted in a sense of exhilaration. Sure, I had gone to Hebrew school to learn the *Aleph-Bet* (Hebrew alphabet). But camp provided something more. Through the songs we sang, I grasped a new level of understanding. So much was written into the lyrics we sang and the cheers we chanted. For the first time I experienced Judaism as a way of life.

Songs have always played an important role in my Jewish identity. I have grown up listening to folk music, much of which has been Jewish folk music. My cousin Stu, who doubles as a cantor, sings professionally. No family occasions are complete without him bringing his guitar. A substantial portion of his repertoire is Jewish folk music, which has always been central for me. I enjoy sitting back and listening, not just because Stu sings well but also because the song lyrics and the mix of old and new melodies provide me with a feeling of Jewishness. It's an inner feeling originating in the heart that has, on occasion, helped me feel good about my Jewishness at times when I've been questioning Judaism. I have a copy of Stu's tape, and, whenever I need some inspiration, I listen to it. The usual reaction from my roommates can best be summed up as: "What the hell are you listening to?" But just hearing the Hebrew makes me feel good inside and reaffirms my links to my Jewish past.

Holidays have played an important role in my upbringing because they provided an opportunity for our family to be together. I still remember walking during the afternoon break the mile up Touhy Avenue to my great-grandmother's apartment on Yom Kippur. Those of us fasting—my mother, grandmother, aunt, uncle, and I— would walk together, which always instilled me with a good feeling. That walk provided a sense of community and security. The only year I have been home on Yom Kippur since my great-grandmother died was two years ago, and then we walked to Indian Boundary Park, where a small zoo is kept.

Those people who weren't fasting took the opportunity to go for lunch at Barnaby's, a pizza place about four blocks from the synagogue. Barnaby's is very dark and is a common eating place for those synagogue members who choose to eat. The funny part is that they all try to pretend that they didn't go for lunch. I remember from before I was old enough to fast the amusement at seeing certain synagogue members squirm down in their seats in an effort not to be noticed. What they failed to realize is that, by doing so, they were inadvertently calling greater attention to themselves.

The first memory I have of a religious holiday is Hanukkah. This particular Hanukkah happened while I was in nursery school. My parents laminated the picture of me that appeared in the *Chicago Sun Times,* wearing a crown and lighting the menorah. I keep that picture with me everywhere I go, and it serves to remind me of who I am. In the picture I have a big smile on my face. I probably didn't know much more than the basic story of Judah the Maccabee, if even that much. Lisa Sandlow, who is in the picture with me, probably didn't know much more. One day in high school I brought the picture with me and showed it to Lisa. We both laughed. We had gone to different schools after nursery school, and it took us three years of high school before either of us made the connection. I look at the innocence of what it means to be Jewish inherent in that four-year-old and then think of myself today. I think of how much of an understanding I've gained since then.

For as long as I can remember, my father and I would build a *succah* (traditional: a temporary dwelling or booth) in the backyard. We would take some two-by-fours, build a frame, surround the top and three sides with chicken wire, and then go to a local forest preserve to get materials for the roof. We would make paper chains to run around and hang gourds to make the *succah* more colorful. My sister, Jill (our next-door neighbor), and I would sit in the basement stringing beads and cranberries. All of the New Years' cards we had received would hang around the entrance. We would have a little party, or open *succah,* and all of the family and some friends would come over for some apple cider and cake or other snack. For the week of *Succos,* we would eat every dinner outside in our *succah.* If it was cold, we would simply run inside and bring out jackets to wear. Even though at the time I didn't fully understand the meaning behind the holiday, building and eating in the *succah* made me feel particularly Jewish. It is something I miss today while I am away at school.

Simchas Torah has always been an interesting holiday for me. I remember parading around the synagogue behind the Torahs, collecting candy from all of the congregants standing on the aisle. I always insisted on walking by myself, or with my sister at hand, as opposed to with someone older. My grandparents used to come, and my grandmother recently told me she has not been to synagogue on Simchas Torah since I left for school. To me the holiday was an empowering one because I had a certain sense of power and prestige from joining in the Torah procession.

My father used to get involved, too. He never had a real Jewish upbringing, and he has enjoyed reliving his childhood through me. Particularly memorable will always be Purim, when Dad used to dress up in crazy costumes—blinking glasses, bow ties, and all. Dad enjoyed being one of the kids because he had never really been one. The only adult who had costumes anywhere close to Dad's was the rabbi, who would come in a variety of different attires. Dad and other adults dressing up used to lend a particular innocence to the holiday, an innocence that had seemingly ended by the time I was a teenager. For most of my teenage years, I entered the synagogue wearing a jacket and tie because I was the megillah (the scroll containing the Book of Esther) reader.

One year we celebrated Passover on a beach in Florida with some friends, who always went camping for the holiday so that they didn't have to kosher their kitchen. We flew from Chicago on the third day, immediately following the second seder, to spend the rest of yom-tov (the holiday) in Pensacola. It was a unique experience, and being away from the big city brought the holiday closer to my heart. I spent a lot of time sitting on the beach thinking about the meaning of Passover. Ever since then Passover has been one of my favorite holidays because it brings me closer to the world on a spiritual level. Sitting by the Gulf of Mexico, I saw myself leading the Jews across the Red Sea. I felt like I had lived in the times of the Pharaoh, and that is why the holiday is still special to me.

Preparing for Passover also has played a role in my Jewish identity. It was always a source of pride for me to go Passover shopping with my mom. We would have contests each year to guess what the total amount of the bill would be. But I loved picking the necessary Passover groceries off the shelf. Then we would get home, and it would be time for Mom to make the gefilte fish (yuck), and my sister to make the haroseth (traditional food eaten at Passover seder). She really liked chopping up the apples and mixing in the wine. Deb (my sister) inevitably would scrape a little skin into the apple peelings, and we used to joke that the skin added some taste and/or texture.

This year, for the first time, Debbie did not come home for Passover. Even though we had twenty-four family members around our dining room table (with a few extra tables added on the end), the holiday was not the same. I set the table, went out for the traditional "last lunch," and did all of the other things—except for making the *haroseth*. I found enough other things to do so as to avoid having to fully take over my sister's role. She always enjoyed making the mixture, and something inside me said: Stop. Don't do this.

Sharing Passover with Debbie (my ex-girlfriend) sophomore year was really special. She came to our house for the first seder (ceremonial meal on Passover), and I was with her family on the second night. Her mother sings in their synagogue choir, and just listening to her lead some of the songs sent a tingle up my spine. So what if the melodies were different than what I was used to? Granted, I hadn't gone for the whole seder, but only for desert; I still felt a part of her family. Her cousins, grandparents, . . . and all the rest of the *mispacha* (family) accepted me as one of them. I guess Deb had told them that I wanted to become a rabbi. All of a sudden these people, who I had never met before, starting asking me about my Jewishness. I felt they were making me out to be some kind of "Super Jew."

These people were making me an example, setting me apart because of my strong faith. It really pissed me off. A Jew is a Jew! One group of Jews isn't better than another group of Jews because of the amount of devotion they have or the number of mitzvoth (commandments) they fulfill. Why couldn't other Jews accept me for my choices about religion? It's not like my position on religion is so unusual, or extraordinary, or even a result of some screwball experience. I just don't believe in doing something halfway, and religion is no exception. If you're going to do something, give it 100 percent. While I may not observe things 100 percent to the letter of the Torah, I do what I feel comfortable doing—no more, no less.

Regardless of the intent, this exchange spawned many unpleasant feelings inside of me.

I always wear the same *keepah* (Hebrew for yarmulke). Even at my bar mitzvah, when everyone wore the specially ordered and printed blue *keepot,* I was a renegade in my white one. My *keepah* is not ordinary. My great-grandmother knitted it for me when I was eight years old. At the time it was too big for my head, but I wore it anyway. Wearing the *keepah* gives me a good feeling. When I was ten I thought I had lost my special possession. But my fears subsided several months later when it reappeared in one of my dresser drawers. Various family members express amazement that I still use my yarmulke after all these years and that it still looks so clean. No, it has never been washed. I intend to use my *keepah* at any life-cycle events, including my wedding. My great-grandmother would have loved to be at my wedding, and in my mind she will be. Wearing this *keepah,* I feel a connection with my past, and the people who have died, in addition to Great Omi, are seemingly alive with me.

Since coming to Michigan, I have primarily focused my studies in two areas: Jewish history and sociology. Through my course work I am trying to discover who I am and where I came from. Nothing excites me more than my classes on Jewish identity. I have taken two of them, and each has really forced me to think a lot about what in life is important. My Jewish history classes are running a close second. The readings for these classes are never too much since I enjoy learning about my heritage. I have so much pride in who I am that I want to understand the tradition I uphold in every way, shape, and form. I want to learn what life was like in a shtetl, where Jewish culture flourished. I want to understand the evolution of particular practices and rituals so as to enrich my own experience. I want to be able to use *kabbalah* (Jewish mysticism) to reach a new level of understanding myself.

Since age ten I've wanted to become a rabbi. Other people wanted to be doctors, teachers, and lawyers, but I always wanted to be a rabbi. I never cared that rabbis don't make as much money as some other professions or that rabbis need to have undergone an extensive period of study leading up to ordination. I have always envisioned myself standing up in front of a congregation on Yom Kippur, giving a sermon on a pertinent topic, or helping a troubled teenager determine how he or she could use Judaism in everyday life, or giving a eulogy at the funeral of a congregation member. The positive and negative aspects seemed to come together into a whole I felt I would be comfortable doing for the remainder of my life. I spent many hours talking about this with my rabbi and Cantor Schuster, among others. With my cousin being a cantor, I dreamed of one day sharing a pulpit with him.

I decided against going on to rabbinical school about two years ago. At the Council of Jewish Federations General Assembly in Miami I talked with a rabbi from New York who has had a lot of experience dealing with people like me. I found this rabbi to be quite offensive, but something he said clicked in my mind. I realized I didn't want to take a chance getting stuck with a congregation in Hickville, Kansas. If I were going to be a rabbi, I wanted a congregation in Chicago, Washington, D.C., New York, or some other large city. Being in a large city is important to me because a large part of my identity is cultural, and a small town cannot afford me with the culture on which I am dependent. I realized that I could carry out my mission of furthering Judaism without necessarily being a rabbi.

During the Passover services last week, Rabbi Levine talked about singing "Hatikvah" (Israeli national anthem) in three different places (Auschwitz, Budapest, and Israel) for three different reasons during his recent mission to Eastern Europe and Israel. He related his feeling of connectedness with an entire people at each place. I don't remember if I felt this way when my family was in Israel nine years ago. We went with a tour group from California organized by a rabbi and his wife, who were among my mother's childhood friends—two weeks in Israel after a few days in Cairo. We did all of the "tourist things" in addition to spending a few days on a kibbutz, and so on. On our first day in Israel, we checked into our Tel Aviv hotel and walked three blocks to a falafel stand for lunch. I'm not sure why, but it's something I will never forget.

This summer I will go again—not necessarily to see the sights, since I retain vivid pictures in my mind of what I saw before, but, rather, in an effort to feel that connection with something I can't quite explain. I hope that my travels will take me to Auschwitz, Bergen-Belsen, Dachau, and some of the other death camps. I don't know why I have this intense desire to see these places, and I have no real clue of what it is I'm searching for. But a voice from inside my heart is commanding me to go.

This is my story. I don't know how it ends. But I do know it is only beginning.

Yo Soy Chicana

Anne M. Martínez

España

"I'm not Spanish, de España, 'man or woman of Spanish stock.' Así, don't call me Hispanic."

That's the way I've felt for years. My foremothers, centuries back, are from Mexico. Some spoke Spanish, some spoke English, some spoke languages I don't even know the names of. I'm not religious, but la Virgen de Guadalupe is more my mother than Queen Isabella.

Last Thanksgiving I went to Spain to visit my brother, sister-in-law, and nephew, who are living in Madrid for nine months. I had a lot of anxiety about going to this land that four hundred years ago invaded Mexico and started a system of colonization and racism that persists in and around Mexico today—a reign of oppression that killed, raped, and tortured so many of my foremothers, their brothers, fathers, and husbands. I, unlike many of my peers, have never had the desire to see Europe. I'd rather backpack through Mexico, Belize, and Guatemala than France, Germany, and Switzerland.

I've been to Mexico several times, and I've felt the chills run up my spine, knowing that this nation, these people, are in my blood, that in many ways this is my home. I've felt the confusion of knowing it was home but, somehow, not my only home. I have a home in the United States as well.

Of course, I didn't expect to walk the streets of Madrid and be singled out as a Chicana, imprisoned, and tortured—but then nobody expects the Spanish Inquisition. Something in me knew that there was something not quite right about going to Spain. The major reason I went was to see Michael, my nephew. He was fifteen months old when I went. The eights weeks since he and his family had left had been the longest time we had gone without seeing each other. I was used to being with him several times a week, and, for the last six weeks he was in Ann Arbor, I lived with him and David and Teresa. Michael is very special to me. He's the next generation—the first of the next generation. And I was special to him, too. I was the only family member, other than his parents, that he recognized. From the time we met in the hospital when he was half an hour old till the time I left them at the airport in September, Michael and I were buddies. So the fact that I was going to Spain wasn't as significant to me as going to see Michael.

I expected to do some looking about, going to Toledo and Sevilla, mostly to see the art. I've always been fond of the Spanish surrealists: Miró, Gris, Picasso, and so on. I was looking forward to getting away from Ann Arbor for ten days. The last couple of weeks had been really tough, and really stressful. My last day in Ann Arbor was spent planning for and speaking at the regents' meeting, followed by an "appearance" on "El Mundo Latino" radio show, and the five-hour drive to Chicago, getting me to my parents' house around 1 A.M. Getting on the plane to New York the following morning was a tremendous relief; I was leaving the Midwest and all its problems behind, even if it was just for a few days.

The flight to La Guardia wasn't bad. In fact, we arrived early. Of course I had the standard La Guardia two-hour layover, which was kind of boring. I spent most of my time trying to find a place where I could get comfortable.

The flight to Madrid was delayed—some engine problem or another. Comforting thought for an eight-hour plane ride. Eight hours? That's like an entire working day. Yeah, OK.

With my usual flair, I just went around customs in Madrid. After the several-hour delay, I wasn't in any mood to have it out with Spaniards about the computer accessories, rolls and rolls of films, baby formula, and other oddities I was bringing for my family. David and I spent another hour on the bus and Metro getting back to their apartment on General Pardiñas. By that time I was ready to drop. I don't sleep on planes, and it had been about sixteen hours since I had left my own home in Ann Arbor.

When I saw Michael and we started to play, and talking to Teresa for the first time in eight weeks, I just couldn't sleep. Michael didn't recognize me at first, but once we started playing our old games it was like we had never been apart.

I slept a lot that night. And in the morning Teresa and I went to the bakery where they got bread every morning. When I spoke with the clerk, she knew I wasn't Spanish and asked where I was from. I told her I was Mexican American. Teresa had taken first-year Spanish the previous summer, so she mostly picked up on the Spanish spoken in Madrid and had Spanish affectations. People could tell she was a native speaker of English, and some could even tell she was North American. I, on the other hand, spoke my father's Spanish, the Spanish of a Mexican-turned-American—Chicano Spanish. Everywhere we went, that was the case. I was an oddity. Although the Spaniards had been responsible for the "modern discovery" of the "New World," they seem to have since forgotten that it existed.

My third day in Spain I got very sick, and, like most travelers would, I assumed it had to do with different surroundings, different food, different water, jet lag, etc. But after five or six hours of vomiting and diarrhea, I started to worry. Teresa was trying to find me an American doctor from all the information the Fulbright Commission, the American Women's Club, and the American Church had given them. Most places that advertised American doctors only had one or two, and none were available at 7:00 p.m. We gave up on the house call idea, and David decided to take me to a clinic that had a good reputation in the city. According to his handy *Guide to Madrid for Fulbright Students,* the clinic handled all the severe trauma cases. Interesting that they have that sort of information in a booklet for foreign students.

Out in the street trying to get a cab I would stop every half-block to puke. A woman nearly knocked me over trying to get me to stop to tie my shoelaces.

Eventually, we got a cab and headed for the Ruper Clinic. After the cab ride from hell—swerving across lanes and through yellow-oops!-red lights—we got to the clinic. We spent four hours there, where I continued being sick. They took blood, stuck an IV in me, and attempted to get a medical history out of me. Although I knew Spanish, I had never used the Spanish words for things like "tetanus," "allergic to erythromycin"—you know, those relevant medical things. Who knows what kind of medical atrocities could have been committed in the name of miscommunication? After more blood and X-rays, Dr. España (translates to Dr. Spain) told me I would die that night if I didn't have my appendix removed. However, they didn't have any beds, so he gave us my X-rays and the address of another hospital and pushed us out into the night.

The hospital I ended up at was a Catholic hospital. As a recovering Catholic-turned-atheist, I wasn't pleased. We had to ring a bell and tell what had happened to a custodian who decided to let us in. A nun took me into an operating room, poked me all over, and said, "Sí, la apendicía." And "You're not Spanish, are you?" (In Spanish, of course.) She got me a room, hooked up the IV, and took off.

At both hospitals getting registered was quite a trick. There was a lengthy discussion each time about my name. I had a Spanish surname, but the Spanish tradition is to use the surnames of both parents, and explaining that Martínez was the only one was difficult. Even with my passport in hand, it just didn't make sense to them. I almost came to appreciate the University of Michigan Medical Center check-in. Almost.

The nurse had called a doctor who arrived around 3:00 A.M. Dr. Perez-Anton poked around and said we'd wait till morning, take blood, and see how things were. It took me until 7:30 A.M. to fall asleep, and at 8:00 they came to wake me, take my temperature, blood pressure, more blood, change the linens, and ask where I was from. They wouldn't let me have any water or food (not that I was interested in food after twelve hours of vomiting) and wouldn't give me anything for pain. Every time someone came in, I'd ask what the doctor said, but no one had seen him. Around five o'clock that evening two nurses came and shaved what seemed like most of my body. No one would admit to anything, but I knew something was up. At 7:00 P.M., the doctor came and told me he was going to operate. As if I hadn't guessed. He tried to impress me with his knowledge of English. He knew "hi" and "bye," which was more than anyone else I had met in Spain.

Over the next two weeks I had a lot of time to think. The only people I knew in Spain were David, Teresa, and Michael. Teresa and Michael were at Montessori from 8 A.M. to 4 P.M. every day, and David was trying to finish a grant proposal. They brought me *Time* magazine and the *International Herald Tribune,* when they could find it. Other than that I read Madrid newspapers and Spanish car magazines. I had brought some schoolwork—linguistics and Spanish. At this point I couldn't really deal with *Language in Use* or Bernardo de Sahagún's *General History of New Spain.* The TV in my room was broken, so I just spent a lot of time looking at the telephone and the crucifix and the IV.

During the time I spent in the hospital I learned a lot about myself in a lot of ways. Besides reaching new levels of pain tolerance with the somewhat outdated medical techniques, resulting infections, and various allergies, I discovered more about my identity, but more from without than within. If I said I was American, people asked what country I was from, thinking I was Latin American. In the United States we think we have a trademark on the word *America,* often forgetting or ignoring that the rest of the Western Hemisphere is American, too. I learned to say I was from the United States or North America to tell them what I meant. Some of the nuns would come and talk to me and ask me lots of questions about the United States. They had heard everyone is divorced and that there's lots of crime. They asked why I was traveling without my husband or parents. They loved my nephew. Unlike American hospitals, Spanish ones welcome any members of the family, regardless of age. Talk around the nunnery was that Michael was really my son, not my nephew. When they found out I didn't eat ham, they thought I was Jewish. But when I refused to eat fish as well, they realized I was just picky. They really enjoyed having a foreigner around who they could communicate with 75 percent of the time. There were times, though, when I chose not to understand, feeling more like a carnival sideshow than a patient.

There was something I liked about Spain, difficult as it is to admit. While I was in the hospital, I read a lot of newspapers. Being in the capital city, there was a good deal of political activity by people of all ages. While I was there, the anniversary of Francisco Franco's death was commemorated by supporters and opponents, young and old. In the two days I had in Madrid after I left the hospital, I went to different parts of the city, including the university, where there were political posters and rally announcements everywhere. The political apathy of North Americans in general, and U of M students specifically, has always bothered me. If I hadn't been so caught up in trying to change the university, I would have found out about my appendix before I had left Ann Arbor. I had been under a lot of stress in the week before I left. The times that I did eat, I usually vomited. I assumed it was stress-related.

A lot of attention was attracted to Latino concerns on campus before I left. A lot of eyes and ears had been opened, including those of the administration and the regents. Somehow, I ended up at the forefront of all of this activity. I feared that everything would pretty much die down while I was gone, and, as it ended up, I was right.

When I first got back from Spain, after my somewhat unusual experiences there, I said I never wanted to speak Spanish again, let alone return to Spain. I've since changed my mind. I'd like to return and spend some time getting to know the place and the people. Even so, I now know more than ever: "I'm not Spanish, de España, 'man or woman of Spanish stock.' Así, don't call me Hispanic."

Secret Admirers

I feel like I was raised to believe that we, human beings, should want everyone to like us; we should fear not being liked by people and fear being alone. Well, a lot of people would say I'm a quart low on oil, but I worry when too many people like me or when people like me too much. Most of the time I'd rather be alone.

Fate has thrown me a number of breaking pitches—one being my political ideas, which seem to throw me into the limelight. I've come across some real characters while in the limelight; most of them I'd prefer never to see again.

Take Joe Customer Service, for instance . . .

A couple of months ago I walked into Border's book store, looking for *Occupied America: A History of Chicanos*. They didn't have it. Over the next few days I went around town to other bookstores, and nobody had it. It is *the* book on Chicano history, and no one in Ann Arbor had it. So I went back to Border's to order the book.

I approached the customer service counter where a woman asked, "Can I help you?"

"Yes. I'd like to order a book."

"OK. What book is it?"

"I would like to order *Occupied America* by Rudy Acuña."

Another clerk cut in. "I would love to order that book for you! A history of Chicanos, third edition, 1988, right?"

"That's the one." I have to admit, I was impressed with this guy's knowledge of the book. He pulled out an order form and started to fill it in.

"Are you a student here?"

"Yes, yes, I am."

"Are you involved with the Latino studies program?"

"Yes, as a matter of fact, I am. I'm a Latino studies/anthro major."

"Oh, how exciting."

Yeah, I thought to myself, it's been a thrill a minute.

"So, what's the program like? Are there a lot of courses?"

"Well, it's not much of a program. There's one assistant professor, and her appointment is split between sociology and Latino studies . . ."

"Oh, really?"

"She teaches a course each semester, and usually a prof from another department teaches something, and one or two grad students has a course."

Oh . . . you know, I was in Berkeley a couple of weeks ago, and I almost bought *Occupied America,* but I figured, Why lug it back with me when I can get it here? I was really surprised that we don't carry it."

"Yeah, so was I. In fact, I looked all over town for it, and nobody carries it."

"Do you know anything about him? Acuña, that is."

"Well, I've met him at a couple of conferences and heard him speak a number of times. He teaches at Cal State-Northridge. I also have the second edition, but word is the third edition has a much better organization, and, of course, it's updated, too."

"Uh-huh. So are you interested in Puerto Rican studies, too, or just Chicano studies?"

"Well, both, but Chicano studies, more so."

"Are you Chicano?"

"Chicana, actually."

"Really? You don't look it, but then I'm Jewish, and I don't look it either."

My god, I thought, that strikes me as a racist comment. Am I supposed to be dark, with long black braids, maybe pregnant with a few young kids dangling from my legs, and wearing huaraches in Ann Arbor in December?

At this rate, buddy, it's going to take you an hour to fill the eight blanks on that form there.

By this point most of the employees and patrons at the service desk are listening to this somewhat animated conversation.

"Let me check the ISBN here. . . . Well, from what I read in the papers it seems like this Anne Martínez is trying to single-handedly change the university."

I started to laugh, felt my face turning red, and choked out, "Oh, my goodness." I started to shuffle about there in front of the customer service counter.

"Why are you laughing?"

"Well," I muttered, "I'm Anne Martínez."

"Oh, my god! It's so wonderful to meet you. It's really a great pleasure, and an honor! My name's Joe Customer Service. Let me shake your hand! You don't look a thing like your picture. I just can't believe this! This is such a thrill! I'm so pleased to meet you! . . ."

Well, by this point I think most of the store was watching and listening. So Joe and I talked Latino studies for another ten minutes while he filled in the other four blanks on the order form.

I walked out of Border's feeling more strange than anything. I guess it was gratifying that somebody had taken notice of what I had been doing, but I wasn't quite ready to have my name up in lights.

About a week later Joe called and left a ten-minute message on my answering machine. He had just met somebody whom he thought I should meet, and blah, blah, blah. I was absolutely furious. Certainly he meant well, but, really, the guy has no business digging up my order form, getting my phone number off of it, and calling me. My public life is something that I can't hide from. Publicity is very important in dealing with the university, and, even though I have always hated having my picture taken, I haven't yet gone so far as to use Sean Penn or Mike Tyson methods on photographers. I have never been accurately represented in print by the *Michigan Daily* or the *Ann Arbor News*, but I've felt that the exposure is still necessary and have continued to talk to reporters about whatever projects I've been involved in. But for someone to enter the private domain of my home uninvited was terrifying to me. I felt like I had been robbed. Joe, a stranger, had entered my private life. For all I know, next time he'll show up on my doorstep.

A couple of weeks earlier I had returned from being away from Ann Arbor for about three weeks. I had twenty messages waiting on my machine; twelve were from a woman I had never heard of who "absolutely must speak with [me] urgently."

My immediate response to these two people was to get a new, unpublished number to try to retain my privacy and sanity.

In the months to come the woman on the answering machine would track me down again. People I knew started telling me she was trying to get in touch with me. As it turns out, she, like Joe, thinks I'm the greatest thing since ready-made tortillas in the refrigerator section at Kroger. She finally got my new number from an undisclosed source. I agreed to meet her for lunch. I was there ten or fifteen minutes early and got a head start on some coffee. When she arrived, she recognized me right away (even though I don't look a thing like my picture), came to the table, and hugged and kissed me. I guessed it was her but still felt a little like saying "Excuse me, have we met?" Don't get me wrong, I'm a very affectionate person, but I try to contain myself to hugging and kissing people I know.

Over grilled cheese and roaches at the Southside restaurant, this woman told me how much she admired me—many times. The hour we spent together was consumed by her telling me how wonderful she thought I was. After forty-five minutes she revealed that she was nominating me for two awards, and the reason she wanted to have lunch with me was to find out enough about me to do the nomination forms. I guess *dumbfounded* is the best word to describe my feelings at the time. How in the world did she feel qualified to nominate me for awards before she had even met me? Why in the world would someone do all this "for me," when she didn't even know me? I still don't have the answers to these questions, but I started to think some more about the whole thing.

In November I spoke at a regents' meeting and afterward was greeted, hugged, and kissed by all kinds of people I had never met before, in addition to my friends and other supporters who were there. Off the top of my head I can think of five people who overwhelmed me with their unanticipated and unappreciated affection.

A couple of weeks ago a woman I'd met a couple of years ago and have had in a class this term asked me if I wanted to go out for a couple of beers. I liked the idea. In a crowded bar during Friday happy hour, she proceeded to tell me that she had been in love with me since she saw me in a meeting with University of Michigan president James Duderstadt four months ago.

Sometimes I think I've been unofficially declared the goddess of uplifting *La Raza* and have become everybody's pawn in some crazy game of chess. I don't think people realize that I'm no different from them. I feel like a lot of people think I'm perfect—like I always know what to do and say, like I have it all together, like I'm there for them, like I'm doing what I do for them. I'm a student; I'm struggling; I'm just doing what I can, what I have to do in order to stay sane. I'm not impressed with people who don't know me and think they love me; I'm impressed with people who do know me and still find it within themselves to love me.

I don't want to be considered a leader. Sure, I'm a vocal person, but a leader needs followers. I don't want followers; I want people with whom I can have mutually supportive, mutually caring relationships.

I spent a couple of days thinking about "being a leader" and "being in the public eye" and what I should expect. And maybe it's wrong, but I feel strangers have no business imposing ten-minute messages on me as if we went way back.

I don't know who I am. If and when I find out, I don't think I'll even tell anybody. They just wouldn't appreciate me. They'd be disappointed to see I'm just like them. Not Anne Martínez, uplifter of *La Raza;* or Anne Martínez, sex symbol; or even Anne Martínez, doer of good. Probably something like Anne Martínez, *Homo sapiens sapiens.*

The man of my dreams

I don't dream about men
    as impossible as that may seem

I don't dream of being rescued
    by a (white) knight in shining armor

I don't picture the perfect wedding
    with brides maids, ministers, flowers
and all that

My parents have a man
    intended for my dreams

I imagine he's catholic
    and anglo
      25
                with a promising future
on Chicago's north shore

I have a man now
    if one person can have another

he's not anglo
    not 25
        not catholic
and has an uncertain future

I don't dream about him
    'cause he's here

When he leaves or I leave
    I might miss him
but I don't expect I'll dream about him

I expect I'll move on
    to California most likely
and maybe dream

of happily ever after
                with Molson
    my dog
            and an occasional man
                    so Molson doesn't get bored

A poem for marshall

            (not because i love him
            but because i laugh
            whenever i think of him)

white women
and men of color
think
            if i open my mind
                    and my heart
            i can understand
            what it is
                    to be
            a woman of color

(it's not that easy

            you don't see
                    that because your mind
                            and heart
                    are only ajar
                    it is you
                    that makes
            the woman of color
                            hurt   sad   cry)

you say
            join my struggle
            we want the same things
            we can work together

i say
            join my struggle
            we want the same things
            we can work together

you say
> no   no   you're missing the point
> > (yeah   i guess i am)
>
> we have to work together for the greater cause
> > (which happens to be your cause)
>
> by fighting oppression we can free all of us
> > (all of us   but you first)
>
> once we free the people of color   [women]
> then we can free our women   [people of color]

i say
> so until then
> you'll just keep us in bondage
> —for the greater cause—
> of course

you say
> now you understand

yes now i understand
> either i laugh or i cry
> and i'm tired of crying

so marshall
> i laugh whenever i think of you

Reflections

Sabrina Austin

Looking Back

I don't in any way regret how I grew up. At times, however, I feel out of place with my Black counterparts. I think that this is because I haven't experienced all of the hardships of being Black. In many ways I'm really fortunate, but I did not realize how fortunate I was until I came to college and realized the differences between other Blacks and myself. Since I went to school with all whites, and very rich whites, I felt as though I were just an average student, especially in terms of parental income. Sure, I had a car, plenty of clothes, and spending money, but that was only average in terms of the other students that I went to school with. Audis, BMWs, and Jaguars were common in the high school parking lot, and clothes from Bloomfield and Farmington Hills were the norm. The other students' parents owned Little Caesars, the Red Wings, and clothing stores; they were doctors, lawyers, stockbrokers, and entrepreneurs. My mom did not have a bad job—Internal Revenue Service appeals auditor—but it certainly did not bring in an income of $100,000 a year. It did, however, keep us happy.

Until I went to college I did not realize just how happy it kept us. There has never been anything that I really wanted that I didn't get. But when I got to college I found out that for many others this wasn't the case, especially for Blacks. I found that having a car was a luxury and too many clothes meant that I was spoiled, having more than one Gucci was outrageous, and $400-shopping sprees were unheard of. When I entered college I was no longer average, at least in the eyes of my Black counterparts. And for the longest time this proved to be a real problem for me.

When you first meet me I don't seem any different, but, as you get to know me and talk to me, the differences surface. I am Black no matter what, and when whites see me or have contact with me they treat me like any other Black. And I feel strong ties to the Black community; like most other Blacks, there is nothing that I would not do to help other Blacks in need. But somehow similarities were not always noticed by my peers. My peers, especially my university peers, never seemed to acknowledge the fact that I was the victim of the same things as they were: racism, stereotyping, segregation, etc.,. . . . I experienced the same injustices that they did. And when you get right down to it I'm just the same.

But for the longest time I was always struggling with my Black identity. I really wanted to be like other Blacks, and then I really didn't. During college I was called the "Bouge." I am a member of a predominantly Black sorority, and I was labeled the Bouge of the chapter. To them I was part of the bourgeoisie, the upper crust. The label evolved as a result of two things: (1) my differences from the "norm" and (2) jealousy. I didn't attend the same schools as they did. I didn't live where they did, and I didn't grow up the way they did. I had advantages that my peers did not have and could never have. I don't think that anyone ever meant to make me feel bad or out of place, but I did. I felt weird because I wasn't on financial aid and I didn't work. I never had to make the choice between going to a party or a movie and eating. Don't get me wrong; I enjoyed not having to deal with those things. But, nonetheless, I still felt different. A Black student at the University of Michigan not on financial aid was almost an extinct being.

And now that I look back I realize that I was always trying to make excuses for what I had and how I felt. I was constantly trying to compensate for the differences between Blacks and myself. I am and was Black, and I wanted to be viewed that way and only that way, just like everyone else. But because I was different it was almost a bad thing. I'm not sure if being different was as bad a thing to others as much as it was bad to me in my own mind.

Instead of accepting the differences that existed between myself and others, I tried to be like everyone else, even though I never really could be. I think that is why I put so much into my work with the sorority. No matter what, I was committed to the sorority and its goals, but I think that at times I went beyond what I had to do or what was expected of me. When I was sick I would attend service projects when I shouldn't have, or I would work several shifts in the rain during the bucket drive to collect money for the UNCF (United Negro College Fund) or I would work the door of our parties all night so that people wouldn't sneak in or steal the money we made for our scholarship.

In a way I was trying to make up for the differences that I had with others by filling in the gap or void that had created the differences. I wanted to help everyone, and in some way I must have thought that my helping everyone I was helping another part of me or my own. It was almost like a mother teaching her child: the child has instinct on its own, but Mom's help makes it a little easier. I must have thought that I was superwoman.

At times I feel as though I'm "too analyzing"—that maybe I've taken too many of the wrong courses in college. I never take things at the surface. And I've always wondered if maybe my membership in the sorority had some underlying meaning, that possibly it established or reaffirmed my Black identity.

Black Sisterhood

I have always had contact with Blacks and Black issues, but until college I was never totally put into a Black categorization. Let me explain this. I have always been Black and always will be; however, in a university setting any Black issue affects you as a Black on campus. The sorority provided me with a support system to deal with being Black at a very predominantly white university. So in that sense I did use the sorority to reaffirm my Blackness because, when I needed to, I knew that I had thirty other women going through the same things I was, regardless of our other differences.

The sorority also reaffirmed my Blackness because, through my work in the sorority, I was able to help other Blacks (i.e., with food, clothes, companionship), but those whom I was helping also helped me by the experience.

It means a lot to me to be in a Black sorority. I do not regret my decision to pledge in the least. I pledged as a freshperson, and the sorority is a significant part of my overall college experience. For me it was a long and difficult process, and I had to evaluate and reevaluate myself about what I really wanted from the experience. I didn't want to be popular or in the in-crowd; I believed in the goals and dreams, and I wanted to be a part of them. I never considered pledging a white sorority, and I don't respect those that do. I know that that is a really harsh statement—and probably it's unfair to those that do pledge a white sorority or fraternity—but to me a white fraternal organization does not accomplish the true goals or purpose of an organization of this type. A sorority is supposed to bring about sisterhood or a common bond. Certainly you don't have to share everything with a "soror," but you should share something. As a member of a Black sorority, I share the experiences of attending a predominantly white college. When the times get rough my sorors, who really are my sisters, know what it's like. They know what it's like to be called a "nigger" or have racist slurs put on the door of your dorm room, or even to experience harsher grading by a TA (teaching assistant) or professor. Membership in a white sorority could never give me that support because white women would never experience the same things at the University of Michigan as a Black woman.

Even the purpose of pledging a Black sorority is different. Both systems do have in common the pranks, practical jokes, and the humiliating incidents. But pledging for me was like building a sand castle at the beach. It takes a long time to build one; you have to add to it a section at a time, but it's your first time doing it, and there are quite a few flaws; but then a huge wave comes by, and the castle is destroyed because it couldn't withstand the pressure from the water. Well, the second time you don't build the castle so close to the water, and you remember the mistakes that you made the first time, and you think and you remember, and this time it's a lot stronger, and there are not half as many flaws, and it's not only stronger outside but inside as well. And when a wave comes by this time, the pressure from the water doesn't destroy it; it only affects the edges of the castle, but it's nothing that can't be fixed. I am that castle.

I had a job one summer with the city of Detroit as a play leader. It did not seem all that bad of an idea. Eight hours per day playing with kids—now, how difficult could that be? It was a lot more difficult than I'd expected. At first it seemed as though I just couldn't relate on their level, despite the fact that we were all Black. I'm sure they were just as dumbfounded with me as I was with them. Here I was, a twenty-year-old college student coming into their neighborhood as a play leader. I stuck out like a sore thumb. I never wore jeans, only short sets or color-coordinated outfits. I wore Emanuel Khan sunglasses and drove an Italian sports car.

Being an only child, I never had to take care of brothers and sisters or my sibling's kids. I just took care of myself. I like kids, but I don't have a lot of patience all of the time. I am also very particular when it comes to manners. I was always taught to say thank you, please, and excuse me, and these words were not a part of their everyday lifestyles. There were also a lot of little things that irked me, like calling a nectarine a peach, little kids swearing, believing that bologna was better than ham. I did not understand why they would spend large sums of money on gym shoes or jeans and then eat the free lunches in the park. I didn't see how working in Arby's could be a big deal.

I didn't understand because I wasn't as tuned in as I thought I was. I couldn't relate because I was sheltered from their perspectives of the Black experience. I was on a totally different track from the Blacks in the park. They were caught up in a vicious cycle—a cycle that is virtually impossible to break out of; a track where day-to-day survival is the only priority—whereas I'm on a track where the means to survival is through education, a long but hopefully rewarding process.

Like I said, I heard all of the stories, I've seen the films, but nothing clicked until I worked in that park, and I haven't been the same since.

Vicious Cycle of Poverty

I feel really stupid now. All that time I thought that I was tuned in with my Black identity, and I really wasn't. I was only half tuned in. I am grateful for the way that I grew up, but I now realize that I was sheltered from the most vicious perspectives of the Black experience. I thought that hard work and perseverance could overcome everything, and they don't. Sure I'd heard the stories of the dogs, the bus boycotts, and white men attacking female members of my family during the 1960s. I remember the stories that my mother had told me about how poor my family was; about not being able to afford real shoes, only cardboard ones; about having two skirts and one blouse per daughter; or the fact that they usually ate bread, salt pork, beans, and chicken only on Sunday. I remember all of that, and it still brings tears to my eyes when I think about it. Life wasn't fair to Blacks, and it still isn't. But until recently I still believed that, through a good education and hard work, all obstacles could be dealt with.

After my job in the park I'm beginning to realize that we, as Blacks, really haven't come all that far. Whites have only allowed a few Blacks to succeed so that they can say to Black leaders, "See, those Blacks worked hard and see how far they've come"—and all the time thinking that Blacks are still inferior by nature or that the ones who work hard are not Blacks in the truest sense. That's right—Blacks do work hard. They work *damn hard*! A lot of Blacks work twice as hard as whites to receive the same or half the success of whites. Unfortunately, this is not the case for most Blacks.

The community surrounding the area of the park where I worked has not progressed. Sure its members get more food stamps, and there are free-lunch programs to balance where the parents cannot provide food, but overall the same problems still exist for them. Every unwed sixteen-year-old girl has at least one child; the majority of the community uses crack; almost everyone drops out of high school, or they graduate and end their education there.

I will never forget the picture of seeing those long lines of people waiting to get a free lunch, children and mothers alike. I remember mothers sneaking lunches so that they could eat some of the lunches later or the mothers that would send their children to get food for the whole family while trying to savor what little pride they had. The lunches weren't much—just a sandwich, juice, milk, and cookie or fruit—but when there is nothing else to eat, a sandwich means a whole lot.

It took me a long time to get used to the kids. I wasn't used to playing with a lot of dirty kids with dried snot on their faces and clothes that smell like urine. It took a lot for me to pick them up when they were hurt and help them to tie their shoes. For a while I just saw it as a job. I was getting paid five dollars per hour to play with some kids. But it became more than that. The kids began to symbolize all the injustices that my people have endured.

The people from the park don't realize that there is anything wrong with their lifestyle. For them life is a game, the game of survival. No matter what, you have to do whatever it takes to survive. And really this concept is not new; it is the same ole manifest destiny, just revised by urban Blacks. When you don't have food and no job and the food stamps have run out and another month to go before the welfare check comes, then you steal or you sell drugs to make some money. You have to survive.

But the people in the park have nothing to compare their lifestyle with to see that their way of living is wrong because for them it's not wrong; it's the only way they know. If everyone you ever knew was a teen mother on welfare or sold drugs, then how would you know that it was wrong? You wouldn't, and they don't.

The Black All-American Family

I think that so many people have been suckered into believing that all single-family households are detrimental to Black youths. The white American concept of a stable family is always a nuclear family. The nuclear family consists of dad, mom, and 2.5 kids. Everyone is supposed to feel sorry for single-parent households and almost pity them. I know that there are many situations where a single mother is alone and trying to raise a child alone, and economically and emotionally it is difficult.

But I was raised by my mother, and I think that I am a stronger person because of it. I also grew up in an extended family. I was brought up with three generations of family wisdom. And because of that experience I feel that I am a better person. I am more well-rounded because of the different perspectives that I was exposed to while growing up. I have had plenty of friends who were products of single-family households, and, whether it was a single father or single mother, my friends still managed to turn out all right.

The belief that there is only one way to raise a child is a misconception. It's the equivalent to baking a chocolate cake from scratch or mix. With scratch you need flour, baking soda, sugar, salt, eggs, etc. . . . and with mix you just add water. Although these are two different methods, you still end up with a chocolate cake. Whether there is one parent, two parents, or grandparents, it is still a family.

Role Models

My mother and father were separated right before I was born. So I can't really say that I know my father at all. I don't know what he looks like, and, if I were to see him on the street, I wouldn't know who he was. For the longest time I didn't realize what a father was. I had a mom and a family. I didn't know that I was supposed to have a dad to have a "happy and complete" family. My mom took care of me, she played with me, she helped me with my homework, she disciplined me, and what she didn't do my aunt, uncle, or grandfather did.

My family is a lot older than most, and, by the time I was born, I was the baby of the family—and the baby girl that everyone wanted. If I was ever spoiled, I was spoiled the most by my granddaddy. He would watch me, drive me to school, and take me out to lunch. My granddaddy was the first person to ever buy me a Big Mac (even though I could only eat half). If I ever wanted something that I couldn't buy with my allowance, he would get it for me. Whenever I did something wrong, I knew where to run: granddaddy. It didn't matter what I did, how bad it was, or what damage it caused; I was the baby and everyone had to leave me alone.

Every winter I had to take castor oil, and I hated castor oil more than anything in this world. Castor oil is like fish oil, but milky; just to smell it sends chills through my body. So every winter when the smell reached me I would go running for protection. I still had to take it, but granddaddy always had something extra to ease the pain.

My aunt and uncle ("unk") are my second set of parents. On summer evenings we would drive out to the airport to watch the planes and talk about how huge they were, and my unk would tell me how times had changed. Once a month I used to go with them to pay their bills at Dittrich Furs downtown and Sears & Roebuck in Highland Park. Sears was more fun because my unk would buy me popcorn and pistachio nuts. I've taken road trips with them to Washington and Niagara Falls, and, even though there's a large age gap between us, we had a really good time. We all learned a lot in Washington; we went to all the monuments and took pictures. In Niagara we looked at the falls, of course, shopped, and cruised down the main strip.

When I was growing up my aunt used to fix my lunch, anything I wanted from bologna to my favorite: jelly sandwiches on nice, soft Wonder Bread with all the edges cut off. My unk taught me how to ride a two-wheel bicycle; he took the training wheels off my four-wheeler. He ran all the way down the block with me and told me all the way that I could do it and that he believed in me. Although when he let go I fell, because he had confidence in me I knew that I could do it again.

I had male father figures, and I had a mom and other female mother figures, so I never really missed my natural father. I truly believe that God blessed me with the greatest family in the world.

Like I said, for the longest time I never really knew that I was supposed to have a dad, but when I started to ask questions I found out some things that I didn't really want to know after all. My mom and father went to the same college, and it was hard for both of them, but, when it came down to it, he really didn't want to pursue a career. He wanted to stay at home and take care of me. He wanted my mom to be the provider since she was so good at it. Now, according to today's standards (usually white standards because in most Black families both parents have to have jobs), a man staying at home is not so bad because the option is open for either parent to stay at home with the child. But at the time that I was born Blacks were just beginning to climb the economic ladder. My mom had struggled too long alone to have to add another person to the list to take care of. So in his case he was just lazy. I understand the situation even though I realize that it might be biased. But I don't understand why he would not want to have contact with me because he couldn't have the relationship on his terms. I don't know why he didn't want to see me. It's hard to deal with the fact that you're unwanted by someone that doesn't even know you. My father didn't fit all of the images that I had seen on TV. So I figured that he probably did want to see me, but my family wouldn't let him, just like on TV.

When I was younger and there were times when my mom would make me mad, I would dream of my father rescuing me and saying, "Sabrina, I've missed you, and whatever you want I will give to you." The father that I created was a combination of all of the fathers that I had seen on television. I even made a picture of him in my mind. My mom only told me that he was tall, over six feet, and very dark, so I added wavy hair, dark-brown eyes, and a gorgeous smile—another Billy Dee Williams.

From time to time I would think of him until one day I was riding in the car with my mother and, out of the blue, she said she was thinking of trying to find my father so that we could meet for the first time. I couldn't believe what I was hearing, I was half scared and half excited; finally I would meet my mysterious father, whom I had only dreamt about. But not even thirty seconds later she said that she had rethought the situation and she felt that, if he wanted to really see me, then he would have tried to contact me, that it's best to leave well enough alone. When she told me that, I wanted to cry; I hated feeling unwanted. But the worst part of it was that it was by someone whom I didn't even know and who didn't know me.

At that time I was fourteen, and since then I have thought and thought again about what she said, and it's true. He only helped conceive me; other than that he's not a part of me. He didn't help me; he wasn't there all those times that I needed him or wanted him or needed support; he didn't teach me how to ride a two-wheeler; he didn't take me to McDonalds. I wasn't his baby. He never took me on trips, and he never played with me. So I don't need him now.

It hurts me at times when my friends talk about their fathers and what they do. I even envy them when they argue with their dads because I don't have a dad to argue with. But then I think of the wonderful and irreplaceable family that I do have, and then it doesn't matter. There is nothing in this world that my family would not do, in their power, to help me. I don't even know if he is alive, but, if he's dead, I don't think that it would affect me. I can't feel emotion for someone whom I don't know.

Mommie

I remember when I was little the big question was, Who's your idol? and all of my classmates would say either movie stars or presidents, and I would say my mom. She's my friend, my mom, and my confidant. She is my idol not only because of what she has done for me but also for what type of person she is. She is a strong Black woman. She has accomplished a lot more than most. She has put herself through school while working a full-time job as well as caring for me and her siblings. My mom, or, more precisely, Mommie, manages to balance me, her job, and family, and we have all turned out right. Mommie is strong and independent, but she still places faith in the power of God. And, God willing, I will be just like her. My mom is like a hot fudge sundae with nuts, whip cream, cherries, bananas, three different types of ice cream, and sprinkles—you can't ask for more.

My mom and I are a lot alike, but then we're very different. My mom is only five-foot and two inches, and I am five-foot and seven inches. I am on the thin side, and my mom is on the stubby side. My hair is short, and hers is long. My mom has a much kinder heart than I do, and she's more forgiving and understanding than I am. But, according to my mom, those qualities will come with experience, age, and children.

Growing Up

My mom is the greatest, but, of course, I didn't always feel that way. Like the time when I wanted to wear an ankle bracelet and she told me that only loose women wear ankle bracelets. Or when my mom used to say that I couldn't go over to boys' houses, that they had to come to mine. At the time I thought my mom was living in the 1950s. And I would always say, "Times have changed," and she would say that they may have but mine hadn't.

I never really got a lot of punishments—I guess because she knew that she would have to work and my granddaddy would let me off my punishment. But I had plenty of hand and butt spanks.

I love to shop, but when I was younger I used to go shopping to take the tags off the clothes so that I could take them home and play store. Well, my mom knew this, so she would try to keep up with me in order to prevent me from taking them. So I devised a system where I could go inside the clothes on the racks and, without being seen, feel and pull the tags off the clothing without anyone being the wiser. Now sometimes I would get away with it, but other times she would catch me at the counter with a pocket and handful of tags and then would come the hand smacks and the lecture.

My mom had a way of instilling fear in me, just with her tone of voice. Her looks meant that you better straighten up or she would straighten you up. I never had a lot of whippings, probably because my mom had when she was younger, and they never stopped her. But I got a whipping whenever I lied. There were times as a kid when I didn't want to get in trouble because I would hear her voice and then see her looks, so I would lie. *Big mistake.* A lie meant a serious whipping. If there wasn't a way to avoid the real truth, I just didn't say anything at all.

I used to watch my aunt iron clothes. Well, my aunt irons clothes the old-fashioned way; she sprinkles the clothes with water to make the creases better and then irons the clothes, and I would only watch half the process, when she would sprinkle water on the clothes. So one day my mom asked me to fold the clothes, and excitedly I said okay. So I proceeded to sprinkle the clothes with water, fold them, and put them in the drawer. At the time I didn't make the connection that the clothes had come out of the dryer and only needed folding. So when my mom checked on what I done, she did it in her scary, threatening voice: *"How did these clothes get wet?"* And because that voice meant the fear of God and you're in trouble, I replied, "I don't know, Mommie, they were like that." Those words secured my fate, a whipping.

My mom was never really really strict. She was strict on morals, but never actions. I never had to go to sleep early, but I had to go to bed. I could watch TV as much as I wanted, but I had to read the books that she had picked out for me. And no matter what I did or how late I stayed up, I had to go to school the next morning. The Mom-I'm-sick never worked with her. She would always say, "Here's the castor oil." As long as I did what I was supposed to do, like homework and getting good grades, I could do just about anything.

I loved school. School was fun. I have always loved learning as much as I could. I learned and became a product of the capitalist work ethic in school from a very early age from my mom.

I can remember when I went to middle school, Grosse Pointe Academy, my mom paid me when I got good grades. And in those days there were tons of categories to get grades in, and I would clean up! I would get ten dollars for an A, five dollars for a B, and one dollar for a C. And at every report card marking I would get well over one hundred dollars. And I guess my mom tried to instill in me that the harder I worked the more opportunities I would get. And it always worked because the incentive was always there. I was always taught that if you work hard it would pay off later.

Stories of Life

My mom is psychic. She has a direct connection with God. He tells her everything that I do before I can. My mom always knows what to say to me because she always knows what I'm thinking ahead of time. My mom always always always has a story for ever situation in life. Whenever I had trouble deciding what to do, my mom had a story for the situation. Without me telling her about my particular situation, and without her actually telling me what to do, her story would guide me to do the right thing.

Every story either dealt with her friends or her friends' children. I remember when I was fifteen and a half and I was about to get my driver's license. My mom had stories of how her friends would use her just for a ride, and they would pretend that they never had any money for gas. And every time there was some type of church event they would call her. So my mom said that she had to be careful of who she called her true friends or acquaintances because of what they really wanted out of the relationship.

My mom also told me a story of how her friend's daughter went to college but didn't do well because she got involved in drinking and drugs, and she was suspended from school for a year. So when the year was up and she supposedly went back to school, in actuality she got a job and lied and said that she was in school. So she was living on campus and partying, with her parents not being the wiser.

Not all of the stories had direct lessons for me; some had lessons about life. My mom had a friend that was in love with this man, but the man was doing her wrong. He would cheat on her and try to "get with" her friends, so my mom, being her friend, tried to warn her. But her friend was so into this man that she ended her friendship with my mom because she thought that my mom was trying to break them up. And eventually he left her.

My mom had another friend who had a husband that used to beat her, and then she would come running to our house for protection. But after every incident he would come back and talk to her and tell her that he was sorry. And then the cycle would begin all over again. The woman never wanted to admit that she was a battered wife; according to her, they only had marital spats.

There was one time I was watching TV, and a story about voodoo came on. And of course my mom had a story for that, too. She had a friend who was in love with a man, but he wasn't interested in her. So she went to a woman who dealt in black magic, and the woman bought some kind of love dust to make him love her back. It must have worked because they got married. And then from time to time she would go back to get dolls or mixtures to affect other people.

For the longest time I used to think that my mom made the stories up to teach me things because they were always so perfect but yet so farfetched, but she couldn't have made them up.

The Ultimate Fear

I think the biggest fear in life is disappointing my mother. I have been given so much in life, so many opportunities that not many people have had. My fear is that, with all that my mom has put into me, I will not be able to live up to her expectations. I guess that every child experiences the same thing, but when I think of all the money that has gone into my education, all of the extras—computers, tutors—that my mom has provided me with, I hope that I have been well worth the effort. My mom has placed a great deal of faith in me; she has given me all of the things as well as opportunities that she never had. And my gift to her will be my success.

Only Time Will Tell

I have always wondered, if I ever have children, could I be as good a mother as my mother has been for me? I wonder if I will be able to guide my children the way she has done for me. At a time of so much confusion, with drugs and violence, it's a great accomplishment to have a successful child. I hope that I can do just half as good a job as she has. But my mom has taught me well, and in the end it will all come together for me, too, I hope.

Independence

I'm not sure if it's good or bad, but one effect of growing up in a single-parent household is that I am an extremely independent person. In a way my independence might also be related to the fact that, due to circumstances, being an only child, my independence has evolved out of necessity. The reason I'm not sure if it's good or bad is because, in a male-female relationship, my independence consistently becomes an issue. It becomes an issue whether it is in the form of low tolerance or in the form of a power struggle. I am always aware of the benefits, and I do not like being taken advantage of.

I understand that a relationship is two people together and working together toward a common goal, maintaining the relationship. But after growing up with just my mom I see what one woman can accomplish alone. Granted, life is much happier when it can be shared, and everything can't be done alone, and, in order to conceive a child, a partner is needed. But due to modern technology it is not an absolute necessity. Although people like me are destructive to the concept of the family, the Black family in my case, I do not feel that the issue of independence is something that should be ignored. Relationships, like life in general, are very complex, and I feel that I should always be prepared.

Black Male-Female Relationships

Relationships are wonderful, and there is always good and bad, but overall they should still be wonderful. A relationship should not hinder either party involved, and, if it does, it is not meant to be. And in that case life must go on. And I must go on.

I think that what my mom told me a long time ago keeps coming up in my life: "boys and books don't mix." I've always been able to have relationships, but I have always known where my priorities had to be. I guess my top priority is the fact that I have to "make it" first and foremost. And if it is meant to be, love will come, and the one that I love and that truly loves me will understand.

But I don't think that this is always true. I've learned from past experience that others don't operate on my agenda; they have their own. And coming to terms with that has been quite difficult.

For me, relationships are very satisfying, especially during my college years. I enjoy the companionship, the friendship, and the intimacy. It's all rather wonderful. But, like everything, there are problems. And, like I said, because of the fact that I grew up in a single-parent household, independence is very important. Giving and taking and sharing are very important, but there is always a time when my mind clicks and I have to reevaluate a relationship. Relationships always remind me of the Janet Jackson song "What Have You Done for Me Lately?" The commitment in a relationship has to be equal. Lopsided relationships are not for me. I can't just give and give and give and never get anything back. So many of my friends have been used by guys that they loved and thought loved them but didn't. I don't want and will not have that same fate.

The Black community is in an unfortunate situation—for Black women, that is. A Black male-female relationship not only has to deal with the two individuals involved but with the pressures of society as well. The ratio of college-educated Black men to women is at least one to eleven. The rest of the Black men are either in jail or not really doing much of anything. There is no doubt that Black men experience a large portion of racism in the corporate world, whereas with Black women corporate America can get two minorities for one. And the Black community is suffering due to the friction created by the situation: mobility of Black women vs. Black men.

Unfortunately, the available college men realize it and use it to their advantage. It's a shame that, on college campuses, monogamous, committed relationships are a joke. If the guy is not sleeping with three other women, then some lonely woman is trying to move in on someone else's relationship. It's a catch-22 situation; there's no one to trust. And if you're lucky enough to find someone to trust, you still can't trust others.

I guess that's what always sends me back to "What have you done for me lately?" A relationship has to be committed on both sides. What is mine is mine and not some other woman's. And I'm very selfish. I don't share. And if it's not committed, then I don't have time. There are so many things to do in life, I have so many hopes and dreams to fulfill, and a relationship is supposed to add to those dreams, not deter them.

Religious Reawakening

I come from a very religious family. Everyone except for my mother and me strictly obeys the proponents of the Pentecostal religion, or, more precisely, the fundamentalists. They literally follow everything that is in the Bible from not wearing makeup to the man always being the Official Head of the household. When I was growing up, it seemed as though Blacks were either Pentecostal or Baptist, and other religions were for white people.

I also grew up believing that Blacks were the most spiritual people in the world, and I've gone back and forth on that point; but now I'm certain of it. Blacks aren't more spiritual in the sense that their religion is better than others; Blacks just tend to lean toward the higher being for support. For me this is easy to believe. I relate this to the time of slavery. It makes sense that if you had nowhere to turn or to go to that you would turn to a higher being. But then I can also see the other side in that this could prevent you from trying to accomplish goals on your own. But in the last few years my own spirituality has grown tremendously.

When I was younger my mother and I used to go to church every Sunday. I remember when I used to sit in church and watch people jump up and down and run around the church with the Holy Ghost. A lot of times it would resemble an asylum—the screaming, the convulsions, and all the energy in the calisthenics. But I got used to it, and it became the normal occurrence when I went to church on Sundays. We used to sit close to the back of the church because all of the "crazies" sat in the front.

We used to sit in the front, but I became slightly unnerved, and I used to stare a lot, and to stop me from staring we sat in the back. There was a lady that used to jump up and scream, "Yes, Jesus, thank you, Jesus, yes, Lord, yes, Lord." And this would happen every Sunday, during the last part of the minister's sermon. He would get the spirit, and he would say, "Yes, let me hear it, can you feel it say yeeeeessssss.... Lean on the Lord for your support, there's another world, a better world; a higher being, no, not the president, it is the Lord, let me hear an Aaaaaaaaamen.... Reach out to the Lord, let him touch you," and then the music would come in and out for emphasis. Then that's all it would take; the woman who sat in front of us would get to screaming *"Yes, Lord, ... Take me, Lord,"* and then she would shake her hands and swing back and forth; then the nurses would come.

There was an elderly man, about seventy, that, every time the church got rocking, he would start his marathon around the church, cane and all. And all of the nurses that were there for people when the Holy Ghost touched them started after him. Any other time he would walk really slow with his cane, but, when the Holy Ghost touched him, it would take a couple of laps before the nurses would catch him.

There's nothing like it—when a Black church gets rocking and the music is going, the people are screaming "Yes, Lord, Yes, Lord," and the hands are clapping, and the feet are stomping. And everyone in church has a fan waving them in the air in rhythm with the sermon and music. And people stand up waving their hands like the air traffic controllers to spur the minister on. It's an electrifying feeling when everyone is excited and moving around; it sends chills through my body. It's a wild thing to watch and to experience, but it produces so much energy that after church you're raring to go!

I was also used to hearing that the "Lord spoke to me" by acquaintances and family. Now I never thought that people were lying; I just thought that something was missing. In the schools that I attended no one ever understood the Pentecostal religion, the Holy Ghost, or God speaking to people. So I never really talked a great deal about my religion, especially considering that television evangelists are usually fundamentalist and/or Pentecostal. But now my spirituality has grown, and it really doesn't matter what others think.

I have systemic lupus erythematosus. And having lupus has been the one time in my life when I am completely at the mercy of something. There was nothing that my mother, my family, or I could do to stop the disease from progressing. Any other time in my life I could protect myself or my mother would intervene. But in this instance I couldn't stop the weakness, the fatigue, or the high fevers; I had no control. I couldn't take control of the situation. It's like when you're about to crash into another car and you see it coming and you know it's going to be bad, but it's too late to stop; therefore, you just accept the inevitable. I had all types of medication, and at times they helped to suppress the disease, but never completely. Then there were times when the medication would not do me any good; it would either make me delirious or cause me to hallucinate. But I never really had a choice; I had to try different methods.

It was a life-or-death situation. My alternative to the medication was death. I would go into the hospital, and there is nothing worse than a hospital room: the isolation, the despair of being all alone at night, listening to all of the monitors, being cut off from the rest of the world, and wanting to scream but knowing that I couldn't, wanting freedom but not being able to have it. I hated the hospital, and every time I would have to go to the hospital I would cry and cry and beg my mom and my doctor not to make me go. I couldn't stand it. The whole atmosphere was just too much; I had never been that alone before, and I needed someone. And I turned to God.

There were so many times when I would ask God, "Why me?" What had I done that was so bad that I had to suffer in this way? Why did I have to go through these life-threatening situations? Had I done something so terrible that I deserved to suffer?

But then I stopped questioning, and I learned to accept my situation. It was something that I couldn't change. Everything happens for a reason, and my illness happened for a reason. It taught me a lot. And in the end I have gained a lot from my experience over the last three years.

I asked God for strength to deal with my situation, for help in dealing with each and every day. I asked for ways to deal with the pain and the fatigue. And I prayed every day, every night, and I cried and I prayed, and I never gave up. I kept the faith, I didn't ask why anymore; I asked for help. As the Bible says, ask and you shall be given, knock and it shall be opened. . . . I live by this. To me there is nothing too great to ask God for; there is nothing that God won't give to me. Although it might not happen when I want it to, it will happen when it is supposed to. I used to feel that it was selfish to ask God for a lot or for petty things, but no more; I ask. And if my will is not the best, then I let His will be done. If my mom could give those things to me, she would, and he's my Father, so he will to. But I must believe and have faith in Him. I do.

I have never had an experience with the Holy Ghost, at least not that I am aware of, but I do feel that God communicates with me. God communicates to me with a secure feeling and a feeling of peace whenever I pray for answers. It's hard to explain, but I know that He is always with me.

I have truly come a long way, and part of it is my own initiative, but that initiative comes from my faith—faith in God and then in myself to guide and support me. I pray a lot more often now, and whenever I have a problem I ask God to help me solve it. I place a great deal of faith in the power of God. I love God first, and because of that love for him comes the love that I have for myself and others. And there is nothing that I can't accomplish because I have faith.

I'm Not Really Jewish

Joey M. Goldman

Introduction—Thanksgiving 1988:
Running Away

At one time Thanksgiving was my favorite holiday. It used to be so nice to be with my family and not have to say prayers or go through the formal ceremonies of Passover in order to eat. Of course, that was when I could handle my relatives.

When I was younger I laughed when they yelled at each other and told my mother to stop analyzing them. But this Thanksgiving they sent me into a furious madness, one that won't let me return to family events until the months have rolled away and I can no longer remember the turkey and the babies and my own emotional state. Perhaps one day in the future I'll be able to return and smile without hating it or take orders without wanting to become a revolutionary fighter.

The meal itself was the final moment of my sanity. When my aunt fingered a single pea that had dropped from the edge of my plate onto the festive table linen and insisted that it be removed, I refused. Actually, I smiled at her and nodded until she turned away. Then I plucked it from the tablecloth and tossed it onto the floor. Regardless of how reasonable or polite my aunt's request may have been, I was determined to reject any order given to me. I felt as if I were being treated like my cousins—ages seven, two, and nine months. I was seen as a child, but I didn't want to try to change their minds. All I wanted was to leave.

After the eventful dinner, a cousin who had been at another dinner arrived to introduce us to her new boyfriend.

"Everyone, I want you to meet the man I'm going to marry! This is Stan! He's Jewish! And, Mom's friend is his mom, so they're happy."

At that point the relatives pounced in with their questions:

"So you're the man we hear so much about?"

"And your moms got you two together?"

"What do you do for a living, Saul?"

"I thought it was Stan! It's Stan, not Saul, right?"

"Did you go to college?"

I couldn't help but think about poor Stan going through this ordeal. It was pathetic. How could I be a part of this clan? It seemed like things they found important were hiding behind their questions.

I realized I wasn't a member of this family as it functioned but rather an occasional visitor who seemed to disrupt their ordinary way of life. I was an outcast: a Southern rebel at a top university. I also appeared to be happy, which I think was the hardest thing for them to accept because they had very little to do with my peace of mind (their guilt trips never had been directed at me).

The next day I couldn't be perfect any longer. I couldn't sit passively in a role that wasn't mine to play. I packed my clothes and left. My mom understood why I had to go. My grandmother was in tears when I kissed her good-bye and told her it wasn't her fault I was leaving.

In three hours I made the trip back to Ann Arbor to spend the remaining three days of the holiday alone.

Surrounded by Mountains

I remember when I graduated from Briar Vista Elementary School after the seventh grade. I was only twelve years old, and I felt like I'd gone through a lot in the past couple of years with my parents' separation and my grandfather's death.

Although I had been angry with my religious education at Atlanta's Temple—Peachtree Street's long-standing Reformed synagogue—I was happy to be a Jewish child in the accepting environment of my elementary school. Chanukkah was celebrated as often as Christmas, and nearly a quarter of the children were absent on Rosh Hashanah and Yom Kippur. The teachers and students knew I was Jewish. It didn't matter—half of the student population was Greek, Latino, Lebanese, or Jewish. I gave oral reports on Purim. I complained how boring my religious school was and compared it with ones the other Jewish students attended. We were jealous of how much better Greek school sounded than Hebrew school. Perhaps I agreed to go to Camp Coleman because of my religious security and happiness at Briar Vista.

I had spent two summers several years earlier at a Jewish day camp, which I had hated because the activities were planned for us. My two most recent summers had been good ones at a day camp run by a private Christian school. Although I had enjoyed the lessons and events, the campers were wealthy and snobby, my few friends were Jewish, and I never felt that I truly belonged. Each day I refused to bow my head during the morning prayer when "Jesus" was said.

Although my parents had separated, their divorce was not finalized. My mother said that my father was unwilling to spend any money on us and that she was unable to pay the full cost of an expensive sleep-over camp. But we were granted a scholarship from the Temple so my sister and I could go to UAHC (Union of American Hebrew Congregations) Camp Coleman in Cleveland, Georgia. Most of the Jewish families we knew in Atlanta sent their children to Camp Barney Menditz, the Conservative camp in the north Georgia mountains a few miles from Camp Coleman. I was excited, although a bit apprehensive, to be going somewhere different from everyone else.

Camp Coleman was an exquisite oasis. Glassy Lake Shalom spread between the lean pines and the baseball fields. The soft Blue Ridge Mountains embraced the valley where the activity shelters and wooden cabins stood. The sun rose early over a damp clearing called "the chapel," promptly filled with campers from all over the Southeast, the majority of whom were from Miami. Everything was so perfect in this unlikely setting for wealthy suburban Jews.

In my cabin I made friends like I'd never had before. Jamie slept on the bunk next to mine. He was the first person I had ever spoken with about my parents' ongoing altercation. My friend T. J. thought everyone was mad at him and ran away. I really liked him though. I sometimes wondered what it would be like to run away. I thought he was very cool.

I was very cool. I went steady with Jewish girls who weren't whiny and aggressive like the ones who followed me in elementary school. They helped me devise schemes to get rid of Lana, a crazy girl who picked her nose and was in love with me. I had a difficult time hiding from her; soon after she kissed me (I had no part of it), she was convinced it meant we'd had sex. She followed me everywhere.

Camp Coleman made me a very happy person. Not only did it keep me away from being bandied between my home and my father's apartment for a month, but it showed me how refreshing it was to be around so many other nice Jewish people. For the first time I could recall, prayers actually were meaningful to me; we sang them by the lake, accompanied by a guitar, as the sun set.

I started to talk to God at Camp Coleman. I'm not certain that it was necessarily the Jewish God, but it was a God I could feel because I was there. At night I would walk along the deck of the camp office, which hung as a pier over the lake. Dim lights glowed on the fish resting in the still water. The stars illuminated Lake Shalom, and I really felt the peace that its waters reflected. I talked to God, asking if Papa Morrie was okay in heaven. I asked God if He or She would make my parents stop fighting and my life very happy. I wondered if it was the hum of the mountains or the whisper of the trees, or if, indeed, I was right that God was listening. I was lucky, I thought, to be Jewish and feel what I felt at Camp Coleman.

Walking Alone through the Forest at Camp Coleman

"I could run away into the trees and be very free. I could hike forever. I could live outside. Everyone would wonder what happened to me. They'd call Mom and Dad. They'd be upset. If the camp director found me, he'd punish me. Or a snake would bite me and I'd die. Or the KKK would find me here in the Georgia backwoods and kill me because I'm Jewish.

"Excuses. Maybe I'd better not—right now. Maybe someday."

My New School

"You're Jewish, aren't you?" asked Derrick Cargoni. Everyone around was silent.

I turned away from my lunch to glance at him. I hesitated. "Yeah?"

He put his arm on Curt DeLarose's shoulder, and the two of them laughed and walked away. I looked around in disbelief with my eyebrows raised. The students with whom I was eating shrugged their shoulders and returned to their sandwiches.

I had just begun the eighth grade as a "sub-freshman" at unfriendly, unwelcoming Druid Hills High School, where I knew only five other students in my class. Everyone I had known in the seventh grade had gone to Briarcliff High, but I lived in the Druid Hills neighborhood. While my friends had gone to a more suburban, more

Jewish school, I began classes at the county's oldest high school, in the center of white, upper-class Druid Hills. My friends were at a school with a variety of students from different backgrounds; Druid Hills was Black and white, and very Protestant.

For much of the year each time Derrick Cargoni and Curt DeLarose passed me, they smirked and whispered. I smiled at them with a confused expression. Nobody ever had told me that anything was wrong with being Jewish. It never even seemed like a very important part of me until my summer at camp. For the first time I realized it meant that I was different. Obviously, I wasn't a "chosen person" like the teachers at religious school had proclaimed.

I guess I understood from the first day of classes what an oddity I was. My social studies teacher made me realize it. On the day classes began he called my name from the attendance sheet. We had been instructed to stand when called upon, and, as my short, white body moved upward in the first row before Mr. Hamilton's tall, black body, he peered down at me and smiled. His voice was gentle and musical. "Goldman, eh? So you're Jewish?"

I nodded.

He replied that it was interesting and continued down the list of names. He made a few comments after other names, but none seemed as personal or as unfair as the realization he had made with mine.

In the years to come, I would become very active at Druid Hills, smiling for yearbook pictures as officer in numerous organizations. But my first few months were somewhat lonely while much of my time was spent outside of school, at the Temple, where I prepared for my bar mitzvah in Hebrew classes.

Everything improved gradually. I made many new friends at school, who were excited to receive my bar mitzvah invitations. None of them were Jewish, but the idea of a party was exciting to them. And my parents' divorce was finalized after a bitter trial. But my life at home remained the same: I spent every other weekend with a different parent.

It seemed like my entire life was controlled by the rest of the world, which was always refusing to ask me what I thought of it. If I had been given a choice, I would have made changes. Many Thanksgivings had passed since the first time my entire family gathered in Atlanta for its favorite holiday meal. I had spent Thanksgivings with friends, on vacations, and most recently with my father and grandparents in his new apartment soon after he had moved out. But not until many years later, on Thanksgiving in 1988, did I make sure that the people who I believed wanted to control me knew what I thought about being controlled. Finally, I got to run away.

Part One—Christmas 1988: Receiving Gifts

Christmas follows Thanksgiving, and Chanukkah is forgotten. Soon after he married Sherry, my father put more energy into Christmas than ever before. When I was very young, he took an active part with my mother in lighting the Shabbos candles on Friday nights. But once he moved out, Easter egg hunts and Christmas tree trimming became the more common holiday celebrations I spent with him. I always had enjoyed these Christian activities, but they began to disgust me as I got older. And now my father was making a big deal about *their* holidays and not ours? Was he doing it all so he could impress Sherry? Even if Chanukkah wasn't such an important holiday, I found it more meaningful to light candles on a menorah than plug a wire of multi-colored bubble lights into the wall.

My sister, father, and I sat patiently in the living room, sur-rounded by the aromas of turkey and sweet potatoes. Sherry was busy churning her salad spinner in the kitchen of the house she and my father built seven years earlier (of course, they didn't construct it themselves) in suburban Roswell, Georgia.

Sherry's sons, Joe and Kyle, came downstairs when their mother rang the bell to call us to the table. Everything looked welcoming, with holly wrapped around red candles on the bright Christmas table-cloth. After my father led us in a Christmas Eve prayer, we ate. Our conversation was boring, except when I pushed my plate aside in disgust upon discovering that the broccoli casserole contained beef stock, which I wouldn't eat.

After the meal we went to the living room so my sister and I could open our Chanukkah gifts, which were neatly wrapped under the tree.

"Here's a present for you, Joey. Here's one for Beth." Joe and Kyle sat silently as my father dealt us boxes like cards from a deck. Because Beth and I didn't want to spend the night at our father's house, we were opening our gifts before Sherry's sons received theirs. I thought of it as our belated Chanukkah celebration.

Beth and I hadn't stayed for the night in Roswell for many years—since Kyle had moved in with his mother and my father. Previously, he had lived in Conyers with his father. When he entered the seventh grade, he decided to live with his mother. I guess I always felt a bit jealous that he was able to live with my father, while I couldn't.

After sitting around for a while Beth and I gathered our gifts, and my father drove us home. It had been an uneventful evening, and I was glad. Things had changed over the years, and my sister and I no longer hid in the bathroom to whisper about how much we believed Sherry disliked us, as we had when we were younger. When we arrived home, however, we still mumbled about how much more money Sherry must have spent on her own children than my father had spent on gifts for us. But we were used to it.

25 October 1980

I wanted my bar mitzvah to be over. I was tired of memorizing meaningless Hebrew words with no importance to me. At least the first Spanish dialogue I learned at Druid Hills had made sense: it was a true daily conversation between people living somewhere. It wasn't a mess of archaic prayers. If only I were Mexican, I thought, I would be able to speak Spanish perfectly. Instead, I had to memorize useless Hebrew. Hebrew lessons bored me.

I screamed when I arrived home from the Temple one Wednesday afternoon, "I'm *not* going to do the haftorah in Hebrew." (It was a decision left up to the boy or girl being bar or bat mitzvahed.)

My mother looked blankly at me. "Fine. Do whatever you want."

I don't think it was guilt that led me to do it in Hebrew. I decided that, for a reason I couldn't understand, I would feel better if I did. It certainly wasn't a matter of not wanting to let the congregation down. I was challenging myself to do it. With additional studying I learned it. It became important to me.

Other aspects of my bar mitzvah began to matter to me aside from the gifts and parties. One morning my mother led me to her bedroom. She handed a shimmering blue velour pouch to me. It was soft and brilliant, with a large embroidered Star of David on its face. Inside was the tallis (prayer shawl) that my great-grandfather, Papa Ruben, had worn to synagogue every Shabbos. I felt like my mother was presenting a gift to me in an important, formal ceremony. I believed something was very special about it; I could imagine my great-grandfather wearing it. I put it on and was excited that I possessed something so meaningful.

I met with Rabbi Davidow only twice before my bar mitzvah. I felt like I had been cheated because he replaced Rabbi Lerner, with whom I had become familiar. Rabbi Lerner had been patient and helpful until she told me she wouldn't be at my bar mitzvah because she realized she had to attend a retreat at Camp Coleman. Rabbi Davidow was new to me—tall, with frightening horn-rimmed spectacles. I was nervous practicing with him.

My fears are the emotions I remember most. It didn't feel like a special ceremony was taking place. My mind wasn't on the meaning of my bar mitzvah but rather on what was happening because everybody had gathered for it. The only part of the morning that had given me a sense of some of the intensity a bar mitzvah represented wasn't when I read from the Torah in front of the congregation, nor when I was presented with a prayer book, Bible, and certificate. It was at home before we left for the Temple. I stood alone in my room and wrapped myself in Papa Ruben's tallis. I smiled and thought of myself as a rabbi. I pulled the tallis tightly around my shoulders and left to join my family, who were waiting for me to leave.

Strength

Many months after my bar mitzvah I stood in front of the mirror in my bedroom. It was a bright day with birds singing in the tree next to my window. I studied my reflection in the odd, dim light of my room, staring at my eyes. Suddenly, I felt firm, warm hands moving gently over my ribs, below my chest. I glanced at the mirror to see who stood behind me. Nobody was there. I felt the hands continue to move with a friendly, supportive strength as I stood attentively still. I was surprised but not horrified.

I didn't know what it was, but I thought that perhaps it was my grandfather assuring me that everything would be okay. Nothing exactly like it ever occurred again.

Two More Years

I decided to go to religious school until confirmation. I figured that, although I hated it, I would be able to deal with it for two more years. But I also thought that, if I were confirmed, maybe I would receive a lot of gifts, as I had at my bar mitzvah. I later discovered that wouldn't occur.

My final years in school at the Temple were the most miserable ones. The other students seemed to become even greater snobs than they had been before my bar mitzvah. I never was able to figure out how the Jews at Camp Coleman were so friendly, while the ones at the Temple seemed so cold. Perhaps, I thought, it simply was the difference between an Atlanta attitude of "Southern sophistication" and the broad subculture of Miami Jews.

I made a few friends in religious school, but I didn't like most of the others, including Mark Rosenstein. His father and my father had been friends in medical school, but Mark and I never even said hello. His family was wealthy, so I guessed he felt he was a lot better than I. When our families were together, none of us children ever did things with each other. Since my friends weren't Jewish, I figured Mark was probably typical of most Jewish children. Besides, my other classmates were descendants of wealthy Atlanta Jewish families, including one member of a department store clan; one student who was related to Leo Frank, the Atlantan lynched by an angry mob, about whom a television docudrama was made; and one whose family's stationery company is among the nation's largest.

Religious school was so boring. Because my bar mitzvah was over, I no longer went to Hebrew class, for which I was grateful. Instead, the other students and I attended Jewish literature classes and history classes and speeches by the rabbi on Jewish morality. We sat in our desks arranged in a circle and listened to the rabbi discuss birth control and marrying non-Jews as well as point out things to us that were not what good Jews did: conversion to other religions, stealing, being prejudiced against any group of people (though he managed to slip in a couple of antigay jokes), or turning away from Israel.

In a different class our teacher, Mr. Levy, told us we had to kiss prayer books when we dropped them. Because the other students laughed, people were always dropping prayer books so they would have to kiss them. Since I disliked his class and therefore never participated in any aspect of it, Mr. Levy scheduled a conference with my mother. He had been my teacher once before, when I was in the first grade, and he was concerned because I no longer was interested in learning Jewish history, as I had when I was six. Indeed, I wasn't fascinated, and, because he no longer rewarded us with M & Ms each time we answered a question correctly, I saw no need to respond. In the first grade I had collected handfuls of M & Ms from him.

I resolved myself to believing that my religious school was a building full of foolish housewives who enjoyed listening to their own words. Once they heard them, they smiled like gas pains had ended. I decided Judaism wasn't important to me because I didn't like what my temple represented.

Camp Coleman had been a Jewish utopian dream. The Temple was a nightmare. I decided I preferred my own God.

Camp Balagan

As the years continued, Druid Hills High School became more and more important in my life. Being Jewish was nothing other than going to temple on Rosh Hashanah and Yom Kippur. It meant lighting the Chanukkah candles and saying an occasional prayer on Friday night. The rest of my life had nothing to do with being Jewish, which didn't bother me at all. I was quite happy spending time with my non-Jewish friends, doing nonreligious things, and participating in numerous high school organizations, unrelated to any church or temple.

After my confirmation I forgot about my religion when it was convenient. Only during the summer after I completed the tenth grade did I have any contact with a large group of Jewish people; I worked as an arts and crafts specialist at an Atlanta Jewish day camp. The other counselors and activity specialists lived in suburban Atlanta, and, although not as pretentious as students at the Temple had been, they were well acquainted with each other before I began working on the staff. Once again I was surrounded by a crowd of suburban Jews, many of whom had been to Israel and were very active in religious organizations.

Even if I wasn't a part of their clique, I enjoyed being around some of the other staff members. Occasionally, we would go out to eat or assist each other in our activities. I discovered that I still had a positive attitude toward Jews who didn't go to the Temple. I also realized that people who hadn't gone to the Temple knew a lot more about Judaism than I did. But even if they accepted me without reservations, I felt sometimes like I couldn't even relate to the Orthodox Jews, leading me to feel somewhat inadequate as a staff member at a Jewish camp.

I enjoyed working with the children at the camp. I realized, however, that I rarely led them in any activities that dealt with Jewish heritage. In fact, everything at the camp seemed like any other day camp, except for the fact that all of the campers were Jewish. Perhaps in their other activities, religious teachings played a more important role. I preferred to leave being Jewish out of art projects because I didn't feel that I had a strong enough religious background to teach both religion and art.

I'm Not Really Jewish

The following years in high school I was very happy not to be involved in anything related to religion. Instead, I was active in every other type of high school organization that existed. My identity wasn't at all an ethnic one but, rather, an activity-related one. I was the president of the Spanish Club for three years. I was in the Science Club to go on trips to the Okeefenokee, Savannah Beach, and the South Carolina mountains. I was on four Student Council committees. I was a member of the President's Council and the National Honor Society. I was active in the French Club, treasurer of the Beta Club, and a participant on the debate team.

Human rights fascinated me. As president of the Human Relations Committee, I accepted the School Service Award for everything the group had done. Odd as it was, I was responsible for several of the school's Black History Month events. I was active in feeding the hungry in Atlanta, raising money for people starving in Ethiopia, and promoting community volunteer projects.

This was my identity. I was a busy, school-oriented, creative Atlanta activist with divorced parents and a fascination with cities. Being Jewish was only a label, which I chose to set aside; it only complicated things. No longer required to attend religious school, I found Judaism was unimportant to me and I was happy with my freedom from it.

Graduating

I didn't cry when I graduated from Druid Hills. I couldn't understand why people were crying. Didn't they realize it was good to come to the end of five years of shallow friendships, hopeless administrators, and mandatory physical education? Wasn't anyone else excited to leave everything behind and go to college where things would change?

Indeed, I had enjoyed many of my experiences at Druid Hills. My best friend, Anita, and I had been to the prom two exciting years in a row. I had taken trips with friends, done well in my classes, and been active in organizations. But I knew that things would only improve at the University of Michigan. I vowed I would never return to visit my high school teachers. I would be cool and a complete success at college in the Residential College program, a haven for anti-preps, creative thought, and down-to-earth Jews. Even throughout the rest of the university there were a lot of Jews, but few of the pretentious ones I'd known in Atlanta. Everyone looked friendly; being Jewish was apparently welcomed. In fact, it seemed like I would be welcomed regardless of who I was, how I dressed, or how I felt. The summer after I graduated from high school I sent myself to France. It was a way of adjusting to the freedom I soon would have. I spent the rest of the summer "hanging out" and getting ready to go to college.

Graduation changed a lot of things in my life, including the amount of time I spent with my father. I saw him only a few times during each of my brief vacations from classes, and I no longer spent the night at his house. Our relationship while I was away at college became very monetary. Fortunately, he paid my tuition and board. I knew some students who weren't able to go away to college because they didn't have enough money. If it weren't for my father, I might have remained in Georgia, studying at a state school. I hoped my good luck would continue at the University of Michigan.

Part Two—1989's New Year: My Own Agenda

Each year I assumed that everyone else in the world was having much more fun than I on the night between 31 December and 1 January. On television people went to extravagant balls in glamorous hotels and toasted with champagne. I had spent a wonderful night bringing in the year before with my friend Anita, going to an outrageous Indian restaurant featuring a belly dancer and then to a reggae concert at a punk club. In fact, whatever I did with Anita, I had a good time. Regardless of the situation, she always shined.

"So what do *you* want to do tonight?" she asked me.

It was our fifth telephone conversation of the day. My answer was a common one in our discussions: "I don't care. What do you want to do?"

"I don't know," said Anita.

"Let's get wasted and go dancing," I shouted, borrowing the idea from Dave, my housemate at school. "In fact, let's ask Naomi if she wants to go. She's such a joy to be with."

"She's such a potato."

I cleared my throat. "Well, actually, I hope you don't mind. I told Ken that I would join him and that he could join us."

"Yeah, that's fine." Anita hesitated for a second before continuing. "Okay, I'll invite the potato. Maybe the two of them can get to know each other. By the way, do you feel like Thai?"

"That would be great! Why not make it three nights in a row that I eat Thai food!"

"We don't have to eat Thai," Anita added.

"No. Let's do it."

A decision had been made. I wouldn't have relatives to contend with or tablecloths to worry about. *This* was the way a holiday was meant to be celebrated.

An hour later a terrible thunderstorm began. In our next few telephone conversations Anita and I changed our plans to adapt to the new weather situation. The meteorologists said it would rain all night and people shouldn't go out. It was fine with me because the evening seemed very strange to me; I was certain ghosts were dancing on the sidewalks.

We decided to rent videos: *Hairspray,* one of my favorite films, and *How to Salsa,* the rental of which was free of charge at the video store. Anita, Naomi, and I went to a Thai restaurant and then returned to the television for our rained-out evening. Ken joined us as Anita and I were trying to dance along with Alejandro and Lolita in *How to Salsa.* (Let's go dancing.) Naomi remained pasted to the sofa in her usual potato position.

While we sipped very cheap champagne (let's get wasted), Ken handed out red and green condoms he'd been giving out to patients all week at the health center.

By three o'clock I was ready to go to a disco. My legs were bouncing, and my arms were flinging themselves in different directions. Since the rain had stopped, I was insisting that we go out. Of course, Naomi was tired and decided to return home, but Anita, Ken, and I were determined to go out. I was willing to do anything as long as I could move.

Just then a bash of thunder rocked the building while we dodged lightning and rain pellets. We decided to call it a year. I couldn't believe another one was going to start.

Moving In

"Please come this way. My name's Kristen. I'll show you where your room is."

I felt so small inside the dark residence hall. I couldn't believe I was in college; the people around me didn't look very old.

I had gotten used to what college would be like by spending the week before I left for Michigan on the Emory University campus with Anita and her new friends. I saw what a good time she was having, and I was looking forward to the fun I would have once I moved into East Quad at the University of Michigan.

Kristen led me up the stairs and through the endless winding halls.

"402 Cooley. Here it is," she said.

I tapped on the door, and a tall, pale guy opened it. I felt so silly as we shook hands and grinned at each other. My mind absorbed his features and processed the idea that I would be spending the next year in 402 Cooley with him. I only knew him from the letter, covered with purple and pink polka dots, that he had sent to me over the summer.

"Hel-lo. I'm Eric," he said loudly.

"Hi. Nice to meet you. I'm Joey." It seemed so superficial to be talking this way to the guy I figured was supposed to be my best friend by the end of the year.

Then I remembered this room was a triple. From behind the desks in the back I heard another voice. "I'm Lawrence. Are you a Jew, too?"

Lawrence was a name Oon Chye had invented for himself when he arrived in the United States. It was only one facet of a hopeless attempt to shed his Malaysian skin and become as American as Velveeta.

Unlike most students going to college for the first time, I went alone. I had taken a cab from Detroit Metro after spending a couple of hours on a Delta flight, wishing it would never land. An hour later I was in a room with a Malaysian with no sheets and a New Jerseyan in faded purple clothes.

My mother had been at the airport when I left Atlanta. The moment before I got on the plane she told me the six most dreadful words I had ever heard: "You were a good son, Joey." I spent the flight wondering why she said that to me. It wasn't like I'd no longer be her son. I was going away to college. I'd still see her. She was still going to be my mother.

You were a good son. You were a good son. The words raced through my mind, zipping in and out of my ears. When they finally slowed down, I realized they were correct. For what a mother was supposed to be, she was no longer going to be a mother to me. I was my own self, who would have to make my own decisions. I was responsible for creating my future. I was finally a "man," something I hadn't felt after my bar mitzvah.

I called my mother my first day at the University of Michigan. She felt terrible because I was so unhappy. I arrived two days after all of the activities had begun, so I didn't know anybody yet. I missed Anita. I missed my father. I didn't like my roommates. I felt so alone. *You were a good son.*

My stomach hurt the second day. I knew my past life was over. All of my friends, my environment: everything had changed. I couldn't return to high school or the safety of my own bedroom.

Certainly I wasn't a social buffoon. I was meeting new people in my orientation group and having conversations with people I passed in the hall. I appeared completely self-confident. But I felt like a temporary member of the limbo club.

I walked around campus at noon on my second day. Realizing I hadn't eaten since I arrived, I went to Burger King for a Whopper. After only a couple of bites, I felt like I'd eaten too much. I never had felt so sad. I knew that everything was going to improve, but I needed something to happen soon.

I asked God to help me. I remember laughing at the idea of asking for a "Godsend." But if one were to come, I was determined to believe in God. Praying as I walked up and down the paths between ivy-covered buildings, I pleaded, "I need a Godsend, now."

Over the bridge came two other students from my orientation group.

"It's Joey, right?" asked the taller one.

"Yeah, you're Ken, and you're Dave," I told them.

Ken peered down at me. "We were just going to get something to eat. Care to come?"

Yes.

I had a hard time eating my McDLT, not only because of my depression-induced lack of hunger, but my unsuccessful nibbles on the Whopper had taken place only minutes before.

Ken, Dave, and I spoke very little to each other while we ate, but I felt at last like I knew some other people. I spent the rest of the day making new friends. It became one of the best days of my life. Twenty-four hours after I arrived, I began the future that I planned to enjoy—my own life. I thanked God a lot because I think He or She had a role in changing my day. My faith in a God that helped me out of difficult situations was strengthened. Being Jewish, however, wasn't an important part of God helping me. In fact, now that I no longer lived at home, I was determined that being Jewish wouldn't be a part of my life. How could I be free and independent if I still went to temple and did Jewish things? It was time to become wild and throw away everything I had been taught.

It's Conservative, Though

After a month at college the high holy days arrived. Rosh Hashanah, as it so painfully had done in the past, occurred on a weekday. But because I was in control of my life, I couldn't be bothered with temple. I was determined and excited to go to class for the first time on a Jewish holiday.

Val lived in my corridor, two doors down. She often passed Eric and me sitting in the hall and laughed at our freshman-like attitudes. A few days before Rosh Hashanah she asked us if we wanted to go to religious services with her. Eric didn't seem too enthusiastic about the idea; I was even more certain I didn't want to go. By the end of the day I had been convinced to go with Eric and Val.

On the morning of Rosh Hashanah, Val, nicely dressed in blue, knocked on our door. I looked spiffy, wearing a navy suit. Eric looked ridiculous, sporting an oversized one-dollar yellow-and-black-striped Salvation Army jacket and purple-turquoise tennis shoes.

As we passed students on their way to class, Val told us we were going to Conservative services.

"I hope you don't mind," she said, "but Reformed services just don't seem Jewish enough for me."

I shrugged. "I guess it's OK. I've never been to Conservative services." I was afraid my sardonic tone was obvious to her, so I politely tried to sound enthusiastic. "It will be a new experience!"

It was a nightmare. I realized that I still felt self-conscious, as I had when I was younger, walking around in a suit on a weekday. Because he looked so ridiculous, I was embarrassed to be with Eric. Somebody passed out in the middle of the service. It was hot. It was in Hebrew. It was long. After the first two hours, Val left. But I couldn't leave. I had been taught that one simply doesn't walk out in the middle of a religious service. What was the point of coming if one was just going to present himself or herself to the other Jews and dash away? Once again, I felt like I saw the absurdity of the practice of Judaism.

Eric and I left fifteen minutes after Val disappeared. I gave up on my convictions, conceding there was no reason to remain. I decided to rush back to my room so I could change clothes before going to my astronomy class, where we were to see a film on evolution. The explanations the professor gave in astronomy were so rational, so scientific. How could people possibly believe so blindly in the religion they were babbling about in a foreign tongue in synagogue that morning? It seemed to me a matter of guilt being passed on by parents and religious schools that drove people to synagogues. Students had to be more intelligent than to truly believe what rabbis said. Certainly I was bright enough to think for myself. The last thing I needed was somebody telling me what to believe.

Dead Jewish Kids

My family and my friends at other schools were so impressed with the classes I took during my first semester. The one that created the greatest level of curiosity among them was my seminar: Jewish Children in Nazi-occupied Europe. Even I had to admit that it was rather unusual.

We studied the Genocide (my professor made certain that we didn't call it the Holocaust since, in fact, it wasn't one). We read diaries of children destined to be made into soap for German boys and girls. We saw movies of thousands of pasty, bony Jewish bodies being heaved into ditches, arms crushed under the weight of the machinery as the Germans were scolded. We looked at photographs of Jews in the Lodz ghetto who hauled feces through the dark streets of their pathetic cage in the city. We listened to fat "Aryan" women complain about the Jews, their spitting German language a suitable expression for their inane comments. I was angry.

And still the other students outside of the tiny class saw my frustration as irrational. I explained that I never wanted to visit Germany and that I would never buy a Volkswagen. They asked me if I had something against the German people. I told them yes. They told me my reasons were ridiculous, that I couldn't blame all Germans for what had happened. I explained that I could, just as I could dislike Afrikaners or the Moral Majority. I argued with them. They didn't listen to my arguments. I felt alone with my "irrational" arguments.

And maybe mine were emotional. Perhaps something about religion made it very difficult for me to listen to reason. I was caught between the chatter of the rabbis and the quantitative data of the computers, which said I couldn't blame all of the German people.

But did Blacks not blame all white people for enslaving them? I did. I assumed some responsibility for what "my people" had done. The other students told me my feelings were ridiculous—that my relatives were in Russia the entire time. They said that one person couldn't bear the burden of others.

I examined my feelings about religion again. I saw that it might be important to me, depending on how it was practiced. I couldn't believe I was clinging to religion and irrational morality.

Two years later I decided to return to Rosh Hashanah services. I went again with Eric, but this time to the Reformed service, and listened to the rabbi explain how I should feel, in the language I spoke. I became angry that he was telling me what to believe and how God was going to treat me. But then he added the most important line to the sermon, one that made me return to services the following year. He said that, as Jews, we should question what we are told. He explained that we should think about what the Torah has told us and have our own opinions.

I wasn't sure if the rabbi intended to give us the freedom to doubt everything he preached, but, if he did, I was convinced he was one of the most intelligent Jewish scholars I had ever heard speak. By being given the opportunity by my religion to question and complain about the manner in which things were taught and learned, as well as what the true meaning of Judaism was, I felt that I could find a comfortable place for myself within the religion. I was tired of being told "Jews don't do this," when they did, or "God feels this way," when I knew He or She really did not. I learned that I could call myself Jewish, creating my own idea of what it meant to be a Jew. I was excited that my own special religion was Judaism, even if other people didn't think it was. I was more comfortable as a Jew.

I Wish I Were Indian

In high school I often wished that I were Black. I really couldn't explain why because I didn't understand the reason. Once I became proficient in Spanish, I decided I wished I were Mexican or South American. I never really cared at all about Spain, and I never had any respect for students who opted to study Spanish in Spain instead of Latin America.

I loved to speak Spanish. I had a wonderful accent—good

enough that other students told me I should make language tapes. But by the end of my college sophomore year I was tired of Spanish. I decided I wanted to try something new.

My father wasn't surprised when I informed him that I wished to study Hindi. Nothing I said surprised him since the time I told him I planned to major in African studies. He replied, "Hindi? Why not Serbo-Croatian?" His idea wasn't bad, but Hindi was where I was determined to express my unique identity. My grandparents asked me why I didn't want to study Hebrew instead. I told them that it didn't interest me because I hated studying it in Hebrew school. My interests had turned to India.

I loved to study and speak Hindi. *Merii naam Joey Hai. Aap y'haá se sidhee jahiyee, oor phiir bhaii taraf.* (My name is Joey. From here you go straight and then to the left.) I was excited to know a different script. The more I studied the more excited I was about the language, and the more my friends thought I was crazy.

After my first semester I decided to concentrate my primary studies in industrial design (an idea that lasted only one semester), and, because my schedule presented me with a time conflict, I was unable to continue studying Hindi. I was, however, determined to return to it someday.

Near the end of my semester of Hindi, I began to want to study Hebrew. I realized that the reason I was one of only three non-Indians in the course was because students were there to learn more about their own culture and family life. Although we didn't speak Hebrew at home in my family and the other students heard their parents speaking Hindi, I saw a connection between the languages and the reasons for studying them. I wanted to be a part of a culture like the other students in my class. I wanted to be Indian because I didn't think I would have the same feelings of closeness with other Jews as people from Indian families had with each other.

The following summer, in an effort to strengthen my command of Spanish, I went to Colombia to study and live with a family. I had never had such a great experience, and my desire to study Hindi became very distant. Now I wanted to be Colombian.

Colombian Thoughts

"They can yell at me and want me to die. And steal my belt. They're wearing military uniforms, and they have machine guns. And I'm an American, even if I don't like what America does to them and even if they think I'm Colombian when I'm walking alone and speaking like them. I want this to be my language.

"I can ride the *buseta* and listen to Eddie Santiago music and like what I hear. I can walk down the Septima at night and hand the guards my papers, and they might kill me or put me in prison or smile at me and say go on.

"This little town can stare at me and think they don't want me, but what would a small town in the United States do if a busload of Colombian people stopped in the center and walked around speaking to each other in their language?

"I can walk through the woods and pick tangerines and coffee. But all of us have to scream and laugh when the giant ants crawl up our legs and make them burn. And I feel like I should vomit when I see little worms in the other half of the guava I've been eating.

"I can pretend I don't care that we're in guerrilla invasion territory and that all of the little kids who are standing around us are nice little kids and wish we could all be friends, but their parents kill the people who support their government because my government runs their government. One day they'll also kill.

"That person can lie dead on the road with blood rushing toward the grass, and I will cover my eyes because I don't like to look at dead people. I am so glad that I don't live in a place where everyone is always afraid that they are going to be the next person in the road, even if it's just because they were struck by a bus that was trying to avoid hitting a cow that had gone to the bathroom on a twisting mountain road . . .

"You can get very thirsty when you walk around an island in the middle of the Caribbean, thirsty enough to look at the ground and think about drinking the mud. But I am lucky because I found a soft, fleshy mango—fluorescent orange—that lay in that mud near the shack. I peel it and let my teeth slide into its warm sweetness.

"You think that everyone should be as nice as you folks are, but I don't know if it's such a good idea for a Jewish American to hitchhike in Colombia. I'd really rather not. Really, I want to take the bus. I'm sorry, Carlos, that you're upset, but I'm relieved that nobody picked us up."

Spending the summer in Colombia created a new, refreshed person out of me. It made me think a great deal about who I was and who I wanted to be. I decided that everybody should go to Colombia at one time or another. I also stepped away from myself. I learned that I really wasn't who I was but, rather, what other people perceived me to be, depending upon where I was.

When I walked down a busy road wearing a dark suit in the middle of the afternoon on a Jewish holiday, I was Jewish. I was as Jewish as everybody else around me, the others who were wearing their dresses and sports jackets. Even if I didn't really know why I was going to services, everyone else thought they knew why I was going. The others were probably going because of tradition saying they needed to attend services or because it was a Jewish holiday and that was what Jewish people were supposed to do on important holidays.

I went to services when I was young because I had no choice. I was taught that I had to attend services. I was required to miss school each day for one or two days in September or October. When I went to services in college, however, I went for two reasons, only one of which the other Jews in the room knew. Indeed, they thought I showed up for the same reason they were there, and I did. I was a computer, programmed for guilt and remembering what I had been taught, particularly on Rosh Hashanah. But I was also there to prove to myself that I didn't need to be there, that I was wasting my time. I was going to demonstrate to myself the ridiculousness of a bunch of people who didn't know each other and didn't speak to each other, wearing nice clothes and sitting in the same room, missing work to sit and stand and listen and speak, wasting two hours thinking about what they had to accomplish when they returned to work or school. I was there to show myself that I never needed to enter a temple again.

I failed. I was certain that I was the only person listening to the words the rabbi said. I thought about everything. As I had done the previous year, I didn't treat the service as if it were a service but, rather, an individual session with a therapist and a bunch of observers in a thought trance. Unlike the year before, this time I decided that I needed to be Jewish for myself, to feel as if I were part of a culture that believed that something, religion, could be meaningful in a society where money and sex seemed more important than anything else.

During the service everyone else sat around me and stared straight ahead. I turned around and stared at them to see if I would ever be able to fit in. Could I ever just sit around and chat in Hebrew with my "brothers" and "sisters"? I decided it was hopeless to expect as much but that, nonetheless, I wanted to be a part of their culture. I wanted to be Jewish. If I searched, I thought, I might be able to find the Jews I wanted to be with. I could find a Jewish subculture I was seeking. As white as everyone staring at the rabbi looked, I wasn't "plain old American" but something that could be a bit more unique, with special customs and religious beliefs.

I still couldn't forgive the foolish religious school instructors I had had at the Temple for telling me what I knew were lies. And I wasn't sure I would ever go to a synagogue again. But I actually began to light candles on Friday nights and cook Jewish foods. I started to tell other people I was Jewish without feeling the uneasiness I always had because I had felt like there was something bad about being Jewish and because I never liked other Jews. But even though I accepted my religion and culture as my own, I refused to be only Jewish.

At the University of Michigan I felt a greater bond with other Southerners than with other Jews. When I was in Colombia I pretended—and often successfully—to be Colombian, even though I was nothing but a gringo to everyone around me. When I took aerobics I was a man—because often nobody else was.

There had been a number of different influences on my identity. Religious school was one of them. My friends and experiences with them played key parts. But many of my values are those of my parents. Although they divorced, an event that had a powerful impact on me when I was younger, I'm not hurt by what happened. It might not have been traditional at the time, but I was raised in a good Jewish family.

Sometimes I feel that I'm not really Jewish since I'm not a part of what Jewish-American society is (something that I still haven't defined for myself very clearly). I've had a lot of Jewish experiences, some positive and some negative. I can look back on my feelings about them and continue to explore in the directions I want to go.

Certainly not all of my experiences will revolve around being Jewish. It can give me an interesting perspective from which to look at our society, but I'm not going to be doing only Jewish things.

I'm an intelligent, creative, Southern, short, curly-haired obnoxiousfunnyquietactiveconfusedinterested American who studied at the University of Michigan. And, yes, I'm definitely Jewish, too. Perhaps in the future I'll write autobiographies about each of my identities— *My Life as a Southerner, Living with Weird Hair, Being Creative: A Manual for the Unexciting.* While some of them may be longer than this, I think the fact that I'm Jewish will come up in them often. Until that day arrives, I'll continue with my own agenda, spending each new year keenly exploring different cultures as well as my own Jewish one. Maybe I'll go to Israel. Or perhaps I'll opt for India. Whatever I do, I'll probably be Jewish while I'm doing it.

Contributors

Sabrina Austin is attending law school in the city of Detroit. She hopes to become a federal judge for the Eastern District Court of Michigan. She received her B.A. from the University of Michigan in April, 1989. While at Michigan she served as president of her sorority and chairperson of the Martin Luther King, Jr., Day religious service, participated in the Business Intern Program, and was for two years a member of the Honors Program.

Steven Blonder received his B.A. with distinction in 1990 from the University of Michigan Honors Program, majoring in history and sociology. His sociology interests centered around issues of aging and ethnic identity, while his history curriculum revolved around a series of modern Jewish history courses. Blonder wrote for the *Michigan Daily* in addition to making contributions to the Associated Press, the *New York Times,* and the *Ann Arbor News.* After graduating from U of M, the Chicago native returned home in the fall of 1990 to enter The Law School of the University of Chicago. He hopes eventually to work as a constitutional scholar and litigator.

Sherri Lynn Campbell received her B.A. from the University of Michigan in April, 1990, with a major in sociology. She chose to take a year away from school after graduation and moved to Chicago where she began work in a north suburban bank. She has been admitted to law school in Chicago and intends to settle there.

John B. Diamond received his B.A. in political science and sociology from the University of Michigan in 1990. He plans to pursue graduate studies in law and/or sociology with a career goal of university teaching. As an undergraduate, John facilitated campuswide dialogue groups involving students from Black, Latino, and Jewish backgrounds. He was inducted into Alpha Kappa Delta International Sociology Honor Society, was nominated for the Student Recognition Award for Leadership, served as president of Alpha Phi Alpha Fraternity, Inc., Epsilon Chapter, and was named an outstanding member of the Black Student Union.

Leslie Riette Fair is a senior at the University of Michigan. After graduating, she plans to join the Peace Corps to do work in Africa before pursuing a Ph.D. in African and African-American urban politics. While at Michigan she has been a co-facilitator of Black-Jewish dialogue groups and classes and has worked as a student advisor, resident advisor, and minority peer advisor in the residence halls. She has also conducted research on Chicago politics as part of the Summer Research Opportunity Program.

Raised in Georgia, Joey M. Goldman now lives in Ann Arbor, Michigan, where he is an admissions counselor at the University of Michigan. After graduating from college, he continued to investigate his Jewish identity by spending several months in Israel doing volunteer work on an army base and studying Hebrew on a kibbutz. He plans to continue writing and to seek new adventures in his job and in graduate school.

Max Gordon is a junior at the University of Michigan. He is a pro-feminist creative writing major and a recipient of the Hopwood creative writing award, the Roy Cowden fellowship for creative writing, and the Arts of Michigan Award. Max plans to make writing his profession.

Nicole Hall, who prefers to be called Nikki, was born in Detroit, Michigan. Her graduations from Detroit Renaissance High School and the University of Michigan are a source of pride for her. As a single child, she got to have her wonderful and magnificent mother all to herself. She enjoys swimming, reading, talking about social issues, smiling, laughing, eating, and working for social change. She hopes to get a job in the field of domestic violence/sexual assault prevention because the toll that sexism is taking on women's lives, and especially the lives of women of color, is something that she refuses to sit by and accept.

Carlos Arturo Manjarréz graduated from the University of Michigan in 1990 with a double major in sociology and Latino studies. He is presently working at the Universidad Popular/Centro Latino, a

Latino community-based adult literacy program. By the fall of 1992 he hopes to enter graduate school to the end of someday teaching at the college level. He and Sandy remain very much in love and are currently living in Chicago.

Anne M. Martínez is currently employed by the University of Michigan. She is continuing her efforts to make the university a place that is more accepting of the needs, issues, and concerns of Latino students and other students of color. When she receives her degree and leaves the University of Michigan, she intends to continue to work as an advocate for Latinos and other people of color.

Andre Reynolds is currently working at the Federal Reserve Bank of Chicago as a financial analyst in the Operations Administration department. He plans to further his education beyond his B.A. from the University of Michigan through an M.B.A. program in the Chicago area. He is hopeful that the experience will allow him to reach higher plateaus within the Federal Reserve system.

Lauren B. Shapiro graduated from the University of Michigan in 1989 with a B.A. in English. She is now working for a political media consulting firm that specializes in electing Democrats to office. She is presently living in Washington, D.C., trying to decide what she should do in upcoming years . . . perhaps graduate school, perhaps a career in media, but hopefully lots of fun and happiness.

Amelia Valdez graduated from the University of Michigan with a degree in Latino Studies/sociology and a minor in physical education. One of her many goals is to be a prime motivator and leader in her community. The first step she has made toward reaching this goal was to accept a position with the Boys and Girls Clubs of San Antonio as project coordinator and drug prevention leader. Working with the inner-city children of San Antonio and being a positive role model for them are a dream come true. She hopes to be an asset to her barrio (community) and to continue to "survive in the barrio" as an educator.

Matthew H. Wexley graduated from the University of Michigan with a B.A. degree in 1991. His degree focused on psychology with additional studies in sociology, Afro-American studies, and intergroup relations. Matthew plans on pursuing a Ph.D. in some area of psychology, preferably industrial organizational psychology. Before going on to get his doctorate, Matthew hopes to either teach in a public school or live in Israel for a short time.